Junior Cycle
Science
Revision and Exam Guide

Declan Kennedy
Sean Finn
Rose Lawlor

Authors of:

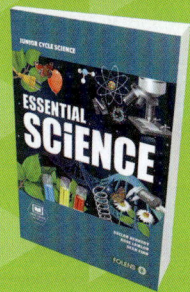

First published in 2019 by Folens Publishers
Hibernian Industrial Estate, Greenhills Road, Tallaght, Dublin 24

© Declan Kennedy, Sean Finn and Rose Lawlor 2019

Illustrations: Oxford Designers and Illustrators
Photography: John Sexton

ISBN 978-1-7892-7007-5

All rights reserved. No part of this publication may be reproduced, stored in a retrieval system or transmitted in any form or by any means, electronic, mechanical, photocopying, recording or otherwise, for whatever purpose, without the prior written permission of the publisher, or a licence permitting restricted copying in Ireland issued by the Irish Copyright Licensing Agency, 63 Patrick Street, Dún Laoghaire, Co. Dublin.

To the best of the publisher's knowledge, information in this book was correct at the time of going to press. No responsibility can be taken for any errors.

The FOLENS company name and associated logos are trademarks of Folens Publishers, registered in Ireland and other countries.

Photograph Acknowledgements
The authors and publisher are grateful to the following copyright holders for permission to include photographic material: Alamy, Getty, iStock, NASA, Shutterstock and Science Photo Library.

The publisher has made every effort to contact all copyright holders but if any have been overlooked, we will be pleased to make any necessary arrangements.

Any links or references to external websites should not be construed as an endorsement by Folens of the content or views of these websites.

Contents

Introduction viii

Steps to success in your study of science ix

Unit 1: The Nature of Science

1 The nature of science 1
1.1 How scientists work – the scientific method 1
1.2 Carrying out investigations in science 3
1.3 Communicating in science 4
1.4 Science in society 4

2 Drawing and interpreting graphs in science 6
2.1 Introduction 6
2.2 Before you get started 7
2.3 The process of drawing a graph 7
2.4 Interpreting graphs 10
2.5 Using the graph as a source of data 11

Unit 2: The Biological World

3 The cell 13
3.1 Cells 13
3.2 The animal cell 14
3.3 The plant cell 14
3.4 The microscope 15

4 The digestive system 17
4.1 Why do we need a digestive system? 17
4.2 The teeth and their functions 19
4.3 Enzymes 19
4.4 How the organs of the digestive system interact with each other and with the circulatory system 20

5 The circulatory system 21
5.1 Why do we need a circulatory system? . 21
5.2 Composition of blood 21
5.3 Blood vessels 22
5.4 The heart 23
5.5 Blood circulation 23
5.6 Interactions of the circulatory system organs with other systems of the body 24

6 The respiratory system 26
6.1 Why do we need a respiratory system? 26
6.2 Gaseous exchange in the lungs 27
6.3 Breathing 27
6.4 Interactions of the respiratory system organs with each other 28
6.5 Interactions of the respiratory system organs with other systems of the body 28

7 Respiration 30
7.1 How organisms depend on respiration 30
7.2 Respiration as a chemical and a biological process 31
7.3 Factors affecting respiration 31

8 Photosynthesis 33
8.1 How Earth is dependent on photosynthesis 33
8.2 What is photosynthesis? 33
8.3 Factors affecting photosynthesis 34

| 8.4 | Crop yields and photosynthesis | 36 |

9 Human reproduction ... 37

9.1	Reproduction	37
9.2	The human male reproductive system	38
9.3	The human female reproductive system	38
9.4	The menstrual cycle	38
9.5	The fertile period	39
9.6	Sexual intercourse and fertilisation	39
9.7	Implantation and the development of the baby	39
9.8	Birth	41
9.9	Breastfeeding	41
9.10	Contraception	41
9.11	Medical, ethical and societal issues in human reproduction	42

10 Inheritance and variation ... 44

10.1	Sexual and asexual reproduction	44
10.2	Variation	45
10.3	Deoxyribonucleic acid (DNA)	45
10.4	Chromosomes and genes	46
10.5	Mendelian inheritance	47
10.6	Mendelian crosses	47

11 Evolution ... 51

11.1	Evolution	51
11.2	Charles Darwin	53
11.3	Variation and diversity	54

12 Human health ... 57

12.1	What is meant by human health?	57
12.2	Human health and inherited factors	57
12.3	Human health and environmental factors	58
12.4	Food tests	61
12.5	Labelling on food	62

13 Microorganisms ... 64

13.1	Microorganisms	64
13.2	Viruses	64
13.3	Bacteria	65
13.4	Fungi	66
13.5	Food spoilage and avoiding it	66

14 Habitat study ... 69

14.1	What is ecology?	69
14.2	Habitat	69
14.3	Community	70
14.4	Steps in a habitat study	70

15 Conservation of biodiversity ... 76

15.1	What is an ecosystem?	76
15.2	Energy flow in an ecosystem	77
15.3	Flow of matter in an ecosystem	77
15.4	Benefits people get from ecosystems	78
15.5	Ecological biodiversity	78
15.6	Conserving ecological biodiversity	79
15.7	Global food production	80

Unit 3: The Chemical World

16 Materials 82
- 16.1 States of matter 82
- 16.2 The particle theory 83
- 16.3 Change of state... 84

17 Elements, compounds and mixtures.. 87
- 17.1 Elements – simple substances............... 87
- 17.2 Compounds... 88
- 17.3 Mixtures.. 89

18 Solutions and formation of crystals 93
- 18.1 Water as a solvent 93
- 18.2 Dilute and concentrated solutions........ 94
- 18.3 Crystal formation..................................... 94
- 18.4 Solubility and solubility curves 95

19 Separating mixtures 98
- 19.1 Filtration 98
- 19.2 Evaporation... 99
- 19.3 Separating mixtures using both filtration and evaporation 99
- 19.4 Separating mixtures using distillation 100
- 19.5 Separating mixtures using paper chromatography................................... 100

20 Acids and bases, pH 102
- 20.1 Acids in our everyday lives 102
- 20.2 Acid-base indicators.............................. 103
- 20.3 The pH scale.. 104

21 Chemical reactions and rates of chemical reactions........ 106
- 21.1 What is a chemical reaction?................ 106
- 21.2 Writing balanced chemical equations. 107
- 21.3 Law of conservation of mass 108
- 21.4 Rate of reaction 110
- 21.5 Factors affecting rates of reaction 111
- 21.6 Rates of biochemical reactions............ 118

22 Reactions between acids and bases 119
- 22.1 Common laboratory acids and bases. 119
- 22.2 Reaction of an acid with a base – neutralisation.......................... 120
- 22.3 Acid rain... 121

23 Energy in chemical reactions 123
- 23.1 Heat changes in chemical reactions.... 123
- 23.2 Activation Energy.................................. 124
- 23.3 Energy profile diagrams 125

24 Structure of the atom................. 127
- 24.1 The atom 127
- 24.2 Particles inside atoms........................... 127
- 24.3 Atomic structure of some elements.... 128

25 The Periodic Table 131
- 25.1 What is the Periodic Table? 131
- 25.2 Drawing Bohr structures of atoms...... 133
- 25.3 Using the Periodic Table to predict ratios of atoms in compounds............. 135

26 Metals and non-metals...............141
- 26.1 Introduction 141
- 26.2 Properties of metals.............................. 142
- 26.3 Properties of non-metals...................... 143

26.4 A metal or a non-metal? 143	30.2 Displacement 159
26.5 Alloys 144	30.3 Velocity 159
26.6 Corrosion of metals 144	30.4 Distance–time graph can be used to calculate speed 159

27 Sustainability 146

- 27.1 What is sustainability? 146
- 27.2 The three pillars of sustainability 147
- 27.3 Sustainability and population growth. 147
- 27.4 Sustainability and fossil fuels 147
- 27.5 Extraction and use of materials – implications for sustainability 148
- 27.6 Disposal and recycling of materials – implications for sustainability 149
- 27.7 How can we as individuals contribute to sustainability? 150

Unit 4: The Physical World

28 Measuring length, area, volume, time, mass and temperature 151

- 28.1 Measuring 151
- 28.2 Length 151
- 28.3 Area 152
- 28.4 Volume 152
- 28.5 Other measuring instruments 153

29 Density 155

- 29.1 Density – definition and calculations . 155
- 29.2 Measuring the density of an object 156
- 29.3 Why a knowledge of density is useful 157

30 Speed, displacement, velocity and acceleration 158

- 30.1 Speed 158
- 30.5 Measuring speed in the laboratory 161
- 30.6 Acceleration 161
- 30.7 Measuring acceleration in the laboratory 162

31 Forces 164

- 31.1 What is a force? 164
- 31.2 Balanced and unbalanced forces 164
- 31.3 Friction 166
- 31.4 Weight and gravity 167
- 31.5 Forces on elastic objects 168

32 Energy – sources of energy 171

- 32.1 Different forms of energy 171
- 32.2 Energy conversions 172
- 32.3 Non-renewable and renewable sources of energy 172
- 32.4 Energy efficiency and sustainability 174
- 32.5 Sustainable and ethical electricity generation 175
- 32.6 Calculating energy usage 176
- 32.7 Calculating power 176

33 Heat, energy and energy transfer 179

- 33.1 What is heat? 179
- 33.2 Effects of adding heat energy 179
- 33.3 Movement of heat energy 181

34 Current electricity: constructing some simple circuits 186

34.1 What is current electricity? 186

34.2 Circuit symbols 187

34.3 Series and parallel circuits 188

34.4 Conductors and insulators 188

34.5 Measuring the size of an electric current 189

34.6 Measuring voltage (potential difference) 189

34.7 Measuring resistance 190

34.8 How voltage, current and resistance are related 190

34.9 To investigate how the voltage across a conductor affects the current flowing in the conductor 191

34.10 Some electronic components 193

34.11 Electrical power 196

35 A technological application of physics 198

Case Study: Nuclear fission 198

Unit 5: Earth and Space

36 Space, celestial objects and the origin of the universe 202

36.1 What is astronomy? 202

36.2 Celestial bodies 202

36.3 Our solar system 204

36.4 The Big Bang and the formation of the universe 206

37 The Earth, Sun and Moon 213

37.1 Gravity 213

37.2 The Sun, the Earth and the Moon 215

37.3 Seasons 215

37.4 The phases of the Moon 216

37.5 Eclipses 217

37.6 Benefits of space exploration 218

37.7 Some hazards of space exploration ... 218

37.8 The future of space exploration 219

38 The water cycle and the carbon cycle 226

38.1 The water cycle 226

38.2 The carbon cycle 227

38.3 What is the problem with the carbon cycle today? 228

38.4 Global warming 228

38.5 What is being done to prevent further global warming? 229

38.6 What has worked so far in the battle against climate change? 230

Suggested Answers to the SEC sample Exam paper 231

Introduction

This book is written to help you to revise the entire Junior Cycle Science syllabus (specification) in a comprehensive manner. Since the written exam is worth 90 per cent of the overall grade awarded by the State Examinations Commission, we have placed a particular focus on the key points in each chapter that may be tested on the exam paper.

The book is written in a concise and clear style that addresses all the learning outcomes in the *Nature of Science*, *Biological World*, *Chemical World*, *Physical World* and *Earth and Space* strands. The exam paper will examine the learning outcomes in each of these strands. Throughout the book, we highlight the key points in each chapter to remind you what you have studied over the past three years. This revision book is not meant as a replacement for the textbook, as it is not possible to give the same explanatory detail in a revision book as one finds in a textbook. However, this revision book will be of great help to you in summarising the key points that you must understand in each chapter of your textbook.

When using this revision book, it is very important that you pay careful attention to the diagrams and tables. As well as studying the diagrams and tables, also read carefully their captions, as these contain important information presented in summary form.

Note that the final section of this book contains suggested answers to all the questions on the sample exam paper published by the State Examinations Commission. Study these answers carefully, as they will help you to understand the standard of answer that you must give when answering questions of this type.

As the *Earth and Space* strand is a completely new section at the Junior Cycle Science level, some additional worked examples have been included to help you prepare to answer questions relevant to this section of the exam paper.

As you revise for the exam, study carefully the 'Steps to success' in the following pages to help you perform to the best of your ability.

We wish to thank the staff at Folens, particularly Conor Walker, Tess Tattersall and Karen Hoey, for all their great help and support. A special word of thanks to Emma Farrell at Dog's-ear for all her hard work.

We hope that you will find this revision book of enormous help when preparing for your exam. *Go n-éirí an t-ádh leat sa scrúdú!*

Steps to success in your study of science

Since the Junior Cycle Science exam paper is worth 90 per cent of the marks awarded by the State Examinations Commission (SEC), it is important that you are well prepared for this exam. It is hoped that the following points will help you to perform to the best of your ability.

1. Be familiar with the layout of the exam paper

The Junior Cycle Science exam paper is very important in the overall assessment of the syllabus (specification) by the State Examinations Commission (SEC). The exam paper is worth 90 per cent of the overall marks awarded by the SEC, i.e. 360 marks out of 400 marks. The remaining 10 per cent (40 marks) is allocated for the Science in Society 'Assessment Task' that is completed in Third Year. This Assessment Task will be marked by an SEC examiner and the marks will be added to the marks obtained by you on the exam paper.

The layout of the exam paper and distribution of marks are summarised in the table below.

Section	Type of question	Number of marks	Percentage
A (Questions 1–10)	10 short filler-in questions; includes graph questions and multiple-choice questions	10 x 15 = 150 marks	37.5%
B (Questions 11–16)	6 short filler-in questions; includes graph questions and lab practical work	4 x 30 = 120 marks 2 x 45 = 90 marks	52.5%
		Total = 360 marks	90%
Assessment Task (Science in Society investigation)	Account of your assessment task written in the SEC booklet	40 marks	10%
	OVERALL TOTAL	**400 marks**	**100%**

Summary of distribution of marks on the exam paper and the Assessment Task

It is recommended by the SEC that you spend about 50 minutes on Section A and about 70 minutes on Section B of the exam paper. The exam paper booklet will be scanned and marked on-screen by the SEC examiner. It is very important that you write your answers in the spaces provided in the booklet. Anything that you write outside of the answer areas may not be seen by the examiner.

You must only use blue or black pen when writing your answers. Do not use pencil.

If you need extra space for writing the answers, there is an extra page at the end of Section A and another extra page at the end of the booklet. Make sure that any writing on these pages is labelled with the number and part of the question.

Note that there is no choice of questions on the exam paper, i.e. you must attempt every question. Therefore, in your revision you must ensure that you cover all five strands of the syllabus: *The Nature of Science*, *The Biological World*, *The Chemical World*, *The Physical World* and *Earth and Space*.

In the final part of this book, we have provided suggested answers to the SEC sample exam paper. Study these answers carefully. In some cases, we have provided alternative answers to help you understand that there may be a number of answers that will be awarded full marks. However, please note that you only have to give one answer if the question only asks for one item of information.

2. Make sure that you can interpret the words used in exam questions

It is very important that you pay close attention to the words or terms used on the exam paper. Study carefully the examples of questions and answers given in this section. All the questions in this section are taken from past exam papers of the SEC. The answers provided are those required by the SEC marking schemes.

The types of questions asked in science exams may be categorised as follows:

(i) Questions that require a short answer

Questions that use words such as *name*, *identify*, *state*, *what* and *list* simply require a brief answer.

Question: State a function of the red blood cells and a function of the plasma in the blood.

Answer: Red blood cells carry oxygen. Plasma carries blood cells.

Question: Identify the state of matter (solid, liquid or gas) that has no shape of its own and cannot be compressed.

Answer: Liquid.

Question: Name the form of energy stored in a battery.

Answer: Chemical energy.

Question: A basketball falls straight through a hoop. What energy change occurs as the ball falls towards the ground?

Answer: Potential energy changes to kinetic energy.

(ii) Questions that require a more detailed answer

Questions that use words such as *explain*, *describe*, *outline* and *calculate* are used to test your understanding. These questions usually require a more detailed answer than given in part (i). A number of points are usually required in marking schemes. Some examples are:

Question: Starch is produced as a result of photosynthesis in a plant. The diagram shows one of the steps involved in testing a leaf for the presence of starch. The purpose of this step is to remove chlorophyll from the leaf.

x

Give a detailed description of the next steps that the student would take when testing the leaf for the presence of starch. Include in your description an account of how the student would know that there was starch present in the leaf.

Answer: The following points were required in the marking scheme:
- The leaf is removed from liquid X (alcohol).
- The leaf is put back in the hot water.
- The leaf is placed on a white tile.
- Iodine is dropped onto the leaf.
- The iodine changes to a blue/black colour.

[Full marks were awarded for any 3 of the 5 points.]

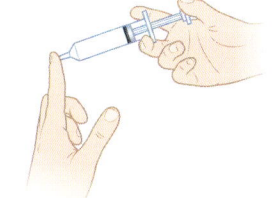

Question: 20 cm³ of air is drawn into a syringe. The tip is covered, as in the diagram, and the piston is pushed in to the 10 cm³ mark.
What property of gases is being demonstrated here?

Answer: Gases can be compressed (squashed).

Question: Explain why the piston could not be pushed in if the syringe had been filled with water instead of air.

Answer: Because the volume of water cannot be changed by the pressure of the piston in the syringe. (Gases can easily be compressed but liquids are very difficult to compress.)

Question: Describe, with the aid of a labelled diagram, an experiment to measure the density of a stone.

Answer:

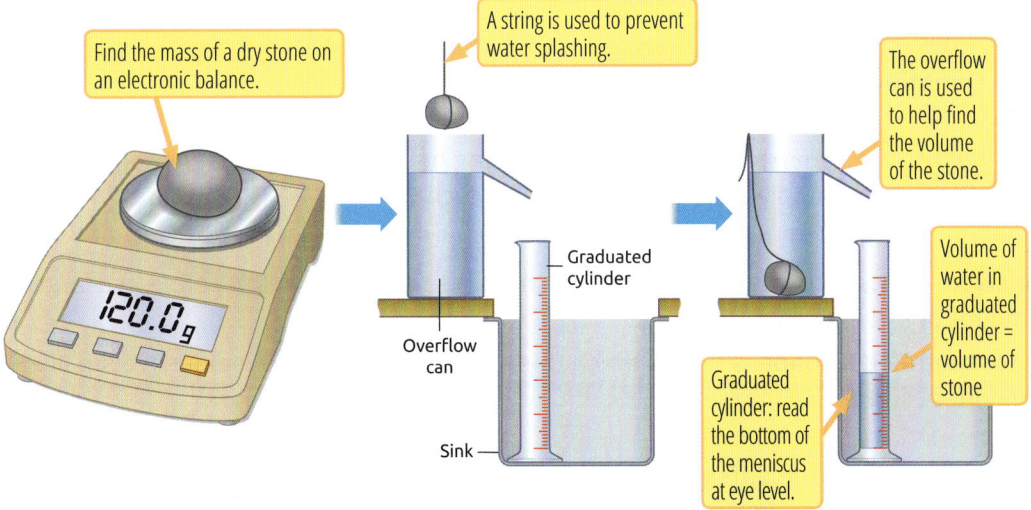

Exam Tip!
Always try to put as much detail as possible in a labelled diagram. If you forget to include a step in your description of an experiment, you will receive marks if this step is shown in your diagram.

When answering this question, the marking scheme required you to draw a diagram with at least one label. If you did not draw a labelled diagram, you lost 3 marks. Remember: no labels means no marks! In addition to drawing a labelled diagram, you also had to show or state the following:

- Find the mass of the stone using an (electronic) balance.
- Fill the overflow can with water.
- Submerge the stone.
- Measure the volume collected from the overflow can.
- Calculate the density using the formula $\text{Density} = \dfrac{\text{Mass}}{\text{Volume}}$

Make sure that you show all steps when carrying out calculations, as shown in the following example.

Question: A motorbike accelerates from 12 m s⁻¹ to 36 m s⁻¹ in 5 seconds. Calculate the acceleration of the motorbike.

Answer:

$$\text{Acceleration} = \dfrac{\text{Final velocity} - \text{Initial velocity}}{\text{Time}}$$

$$= \dfrac{36 \text{ m/s} - 12 \text{ m/s}}{5 \text{ s}}$$

$$= \dfrac{24 \text{ m/s}}{5 \text{ s}}$$

$$= 4.8 \text{ m/s/s}$$

Do not forget to always include the correct units! In this case, the units are metres per second per second.

(iii) Questions that test your understanding of key terms

Questions that contain phrases such as *distinguish between* or *what is the difference between* require you to show your understanding of key terms. When answering this type of question, simply state the definition of each term.

Question: Distinguish between a concentrated and a dilute solution.

Answer: A dilute solution is one in which there is a small amount of solute in a large amount of solvent.

A concentrated solution is one in which there is a large amount of solute in a small amount of solvent.

Question: What is the difference between speed and velocity?

Answer:

$$\text{Speed} = \dfrac{\text{Distance travelled}}{\text{Time taken}}$$

$$\text{Velocity} = \dfrac{\text{Change in displacement}}{\text{Time taken}}$$

3. Answering questions involving graphs

It is very important that you can use data to draw a graph. It is also important that you can use graphs to deduce certain information.

Question: A student carried out an experiment to investigate how the solubility of copper sulfate changes with temperature. The results are shown in the table.

(a) Using the data in the table, draw a solubility curve for copper sulfate.

(b) Use the solubility curve to find the mass of copper sulfate that dissolves at 65 °C.

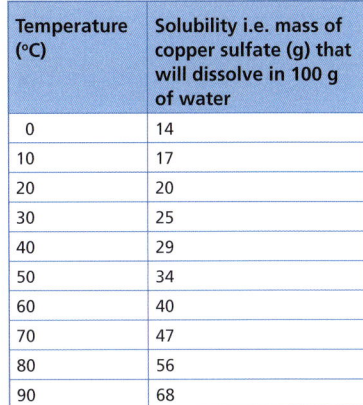

Temperature (°C)	Solubility i.e. mass of copper sulfate (g) that will dissolve in 100 g of water
0	14
10	17
20	20
30	25
40	29
50	34
60	40
70	47
80	56
90	68

Answer:

(a) The solubility curve is shown in the diagram.

When drawing graphs, marks are usually awarded for the following points:

- Correct scaling, i.e. the numbers on each axis are equally spaced to fill up most of the space available.
- Both axes must be labelled with the correct name and the correct unit.
- All points on the graph should be clearly shown.
- The points should be connected correctly. In the case of a straight line graph, the best fit line should be drawn.

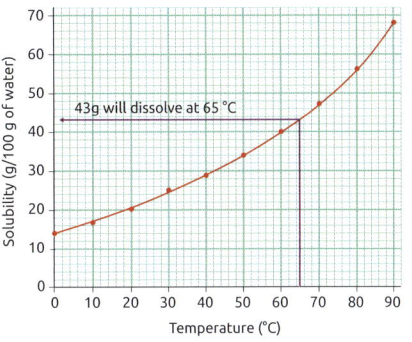

(b) To find the mass of copper sulfate that dissolves at 65 °C, proceed as follows:

- Locate the 65 °C mark on the X-axis.
- Draw a line vertically upwards until it meets the curve.
- Draw a line horizontally across until it meets the Y-axis.
- Note the point at which the horizontal line meets the Y-axis. In this case, it is at the 43 mark.

Therefore, 43 g of copper sulfate dissolves at 65 °C.

4. Answering multiple-choice questions

Multiple-choice questions are commonly used in many countries for examining science. The reason for this is because they test your higher-order thinking skills of analysis and evaluation. These types of questions force you to think hard in order to make the correct choice.

The following strategies will help you to answer multiple choice questions:

- Read the instructions carefully. In the SEC sample exam paper, you are asked to choose one of four options.

- Answer the questions in the order in which they are given. Do not answer the questions in a haphazard order, as skipping around the paper wastes time.
- Whenever possible, use a blank sheet of paper to cover the answers to the questions. This will help you to focus on the question and analyse it without being distracted by wrong answers. Take your time and read the question a number of times to ensure that you understand it. The wrong answers are commonly called 'distractors' because they are designed to divert your attention away from the correct answer. Leave the blank page covering the answers until you decide what is the correct answer. For example, one of the multiple-choice questions on the sample SEC exam paper was: *What is the human female sex cell called*? In this case, it is best to try to think about the correct word from what you have studied in class, before looking at the choice of answers. Having decided the correct answer, remove the blank page to see if your answer is listed in the choice of answers. In some cases, you may have to study all the answers at the very beginning in order to pick out the correct one.
- Verify for yourself that the other answers are incorrect.
- When reading multiple-choice questions, pay particular attention to negative statements, e.g. *Which of the following is not correct?* The word **not** is very important! Similarly, pay close attention to words such as **always** or **never**.
- If you are having difficulty in picking out the correct answer, try to eliminate some of the incorrect answers to narrow down your choice. Then choose your best educated guess. Guessing should only be used as a last resort!
- Get plenty of practice in answering multiple-choice questions!

5. Plan your revision

- Make sure that you start your revision in plenty of time.
- It can be very helpful to make out a revision grid for the weeks before the exam.
- Be realistic when setting the targets to be covered, and tick each section when you have completed the revision. This will help to give you a sense of achievement. A sample revision grid is shown in the table.

Revision Grid

Date	Time allocated	Section	Completed
			✓

6. Last-minute reminders

- The exam paper is of 2 hours' duration.
- Since there is no choice on the exam paper, you must revise the entire course.
- Make sure you get plenty of practice answering the questions in your textbook, workbook and online resources.
- When drawing diagrams, include as many labels as possible.
- When drawing graphs, pay attention to scaling, units on each axis, showing each point clearly and correctly connecting the points.
- If you are having difficulty answering a question, make some attempt at an answer as some marks may be awarded for a reasonable attempt. If you do not make any attempt at the answer, you are certain to get no marks.
- Be familiar with the useful information available in the *Formulae and Tables* booklet of the State Examinations Commission.
- Get organised the night before the exam. Ensure that you have have a black or blue pen, a ruler, an eraser and a calculator available for the exam.
- Get a good night's sleep before the exam.

We hope that this book will help you to succeed in obtaining a high mark on the exam paper and we wish you every success in your studies.

01 The nature of science

The Nature of Science strand

Main topics in this chapter:
- The scientific method
- Carrying out investigations in science
- Communicating in science
- Science in society

1.1 How scientists work – the scientific method

Physics is mainly concerned with the **physical properties** of substances. Physical properties are those properties that may be observed without changing the substance into another substance. Examples of the physical properties of an object are its weight and its volume.

Chemistry describes the substances found in nature. It seeks to discover what these substances are made of, how they react with one another, and how new substances are produced.

Biology is the study of living things. This includes both plants and animals. We study biology in order to learn more about our bodies and the living world of which they are a part.

- We accept scientific ideas because they are supported by evidence, i.e. they are reliable and trustworthy.
- Science may be described as knowledge obtained and tested through the scientific method.

The scientific method may be summarised in the six steps shown in Figure 1.1.

The word *hypothesis* is often used when discussing the scientific method.

> A **hypothesis** is a proposed explanation of why certain events take place.

▶ Figure 1.1 The main steps involved in the scientific method

- A hypothesis is an 'educated guess' or a proposition or a suggestion to explain what is happening when you are carrying out a scientific investigation.
- When it is supported by a considerable body of evidence and is found to have good value for explaining observations, it may be called a **theory**.

1.2 Carrying out investigations in science

When studying this science course, you will be carrying out two types of laboratory practical work. In the first type, you will be following instructions to perform various tasks such as using a microscope, making new substances and setting up electrical circuits. These experiments will help you to develop important laboratory skills such as measuring, observing and drawing conclusions.

In addition to the above types of experiments, you will also carry out experiments where you will not have a set of instructions. You yourself will have to plan how to carry out the experiment. Also, you will not know the 'right answer' before you begin the experiment. This type of experiment is called an investigation.

> An **investigation** is a task for which the student cannot immediately see an answer or recall a routine method for finding it.

There are two types of investigation:
- **Exploration-type investigation**: This type of investigation involves an exploratory type of activity. A scientific study of a particular situation is carried out and then a report is written, based on the study's findings. An example of an exploration-type investigation is a survey of the plant species in a local habitat. In this investigation, you would be expected to study a local habitat and write an account of the work under various headings.
- **Variable-type investigation**: The word *variable* means something that can be changed. An example of a variable-type investigation could involve studying how well sound is absorbed by different types of materials.

When carrying out variable-type investigations, we often use certain terms:
- The variable that you change is called the **independent variable**.
- The variable on which you focus your attention to see how it responds to change is called the **dependent variable**.
- The other variables are called the **controlled variables** or **control variables**, i.e. they are not changed but kept constant.

When carrying out this investigation, you must ensure that it is a **fair test**.

> A **fair test** is one in which only one variable at a time is changed while keeping all other conditions the same.

For example, if you wished to investigate the speed of various runners, carrying out this investigation under the conditions shown in Figure 1.2 would not be a fair test.

▶ Figure 1.2 This is not a fair test of the speed of the runners, since the conditions are not the same for all runners.

1.3 Communicating in science

Scientists must be able to:
- Carry out research that is relevant to a scientific topic.
- Evaluate different sources of information. The original sources of information are often called **primary sources** and these give primary data. In some cases, scientists study papers already published by other scientists on the particular topic. These are called **secondary sources** of information and they contain secondary data.
- Recognise that sources of information may lack detail or show bias, e.g. the researcher reports only the positive aspects of the research findings.
- Communicate their research to other scientists and to the general public

Scientists must also be able to evaluate information about science and technology in the media.

1.4 Science in society

There are many examples of the important role that science plays in society:
- Michael Faraday invented the electric motor and also invented the first generator to produce an electric current.
- Louis Pasteur discovered that many diseases are caused by microorganisms. He found that bacteria could be killed by heat and by disinfectant. Washing our hands prevents the spread of disease.
- Alexander Fleming discovered penicillin, the first antibiotic. Without antibiotics, simple infections could be very harmful to our health.
- Wilhelm Röntgen discovered X-rays. They are used for many purposes, e.g. to identify broken bones or to check for explosives inside suitcases.

Some of the important roles that science plays in society are shown in Figure 1.3. You will meet many other examples of the important role that science plays in society as you study more about science. Society also influences scientific research, e.g. research to develop new drugs to cure cancer and other diseases.

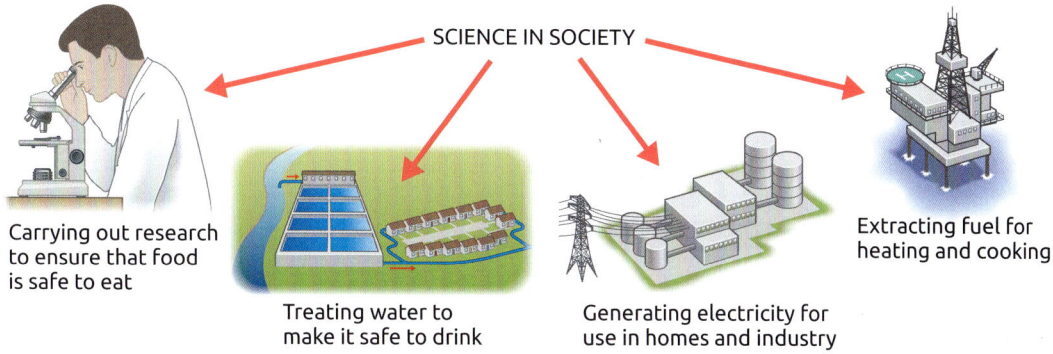

▶ Figure 1.3 Some examples of the important role that science plays in our lives

▶▶ Science Self-Assessment

Now I am able to:	🟢	🟠	🔴
Explain how scientists make use of the scientific method			
Design, plan and conduct investigations in science			
Carry out research on a scientific issue and communicate the results of this research			
Discuss the role of science in society			

02
Drawing and interpreting graphs in science

The Nature of Science strand

Main topics in this chapter:
- How to draw a graph when given a table of data
- How to interpret the relationship between data from the shape of the graph
- How to use a graph to obtain data

2.1 Introduction

- A graph is a visual method to communicate data and the relationship between variables.
- Before you draw a graph, you will first need to look at the data and plan how you are going to draw your graph. First, we will look at a simple graph and some terms needed to draw a graph.

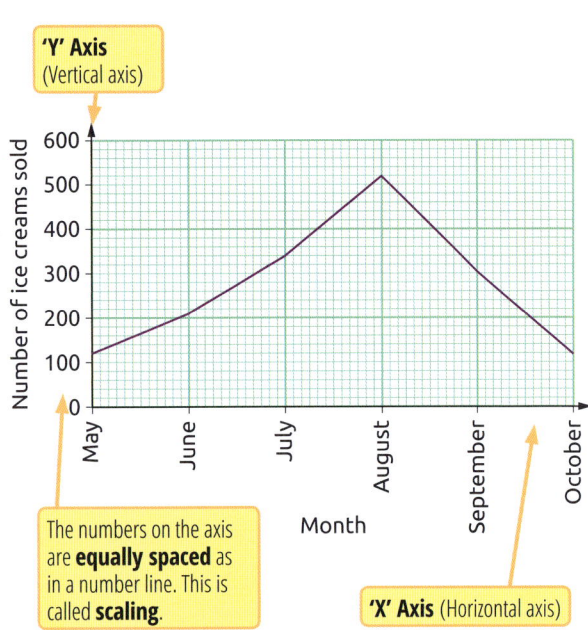

▶ Figure 2.1 Some terms used in the drawing of a graph

2.2 Before you get started

- **Graph paper** is necessary to ensure accurate scaling of the axis, precision in plotting the points, and accurate reading of the data from the graph.
- Usually, all **axes should start at 0**. This allows you to work out the relationship between the data when the graph has been drawn.
- Look at your data and find out what are the **largest values** that you will need to place on each axis.
- Plan for what variable will be placed on each axis.
- The variable that you change (**independent variable**) is put on the **x-axis**.
- The variable that **you measure** during the experiment (**dependent variable**) is placed on the **y-axis**.

2.3 The process of drawing a graph

▶▶ Worked Example 2.1

The height of the bounce of a squash ball was measured when dropped from a height of 50 cm. The temperature of the ball was changed and a table of temperature versus height of bounce was completed, Table 2.1. Draw a graph to illustrate the data.

Temperature (°C)	Bounce height (cm)
25	4
35	9
45	14
55	17
65	21
75	25

The temperature is changed before dropping the ball. This is the independent variable and will be placed on the x-axis.

The bounce height is being measured during the experiment. This is the dependent variable and will be placed on the y-axis.

The maxmimum value for temperature is 75 °C. This helps to plan for the scaling of the axis.

The maximum value for bounce height is 25 cm. This helps in choosing the scaling for this axis.

▶ Table 2.1 This is the information you will need before planning your graph.

1. **Draw the x-axis.** The temperature will be placed on the x-axis. The axis will start at 0 and finish at least at 75 °C. Using the boxes in the graph paper, the numbers will be spaced out evenly (**scaling**). In this graph, each large box represents an additional 10 °C. **Label the axis** with the unit: Temperature (°C).
2. **Draw the y-axis.** The bounce height will be placed on this axis. The axis will start at 0 and finish at least at 25 cm. Using the boxes in the graph paper, the numbers will be spaced out evenly (**scaling**). In Figure 2.2(a), each large box represents 2 cm. **Label the axis** with the name and unit: Bounce height (cm). Note that the scaling on the x-axis can be different from the scaling on the y-axis.

3. **Plot the points** as shown in Figure 2.2(a).

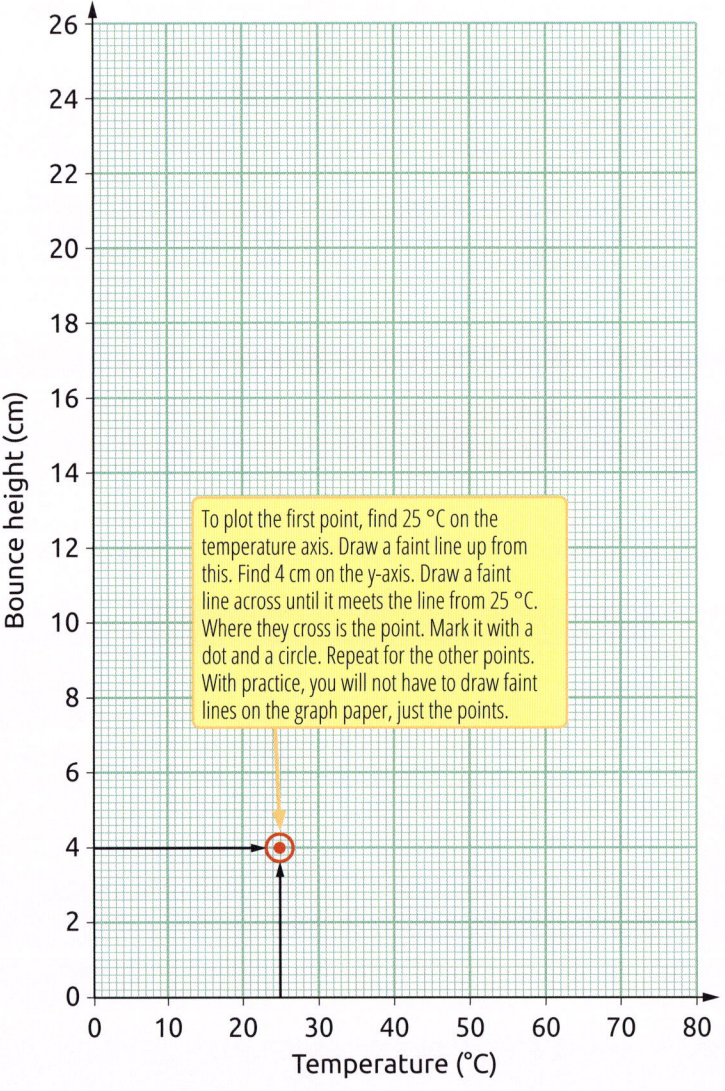

▶ Figure 2.2 (a) Plotting the points on a graph

Exam Tip!

When choosing the scaling for the axis, your graph will be much easier to read if you let each large box stand for a number that is a divisor of 10 (e.g. 1, 2, 5, or 10).

4. **Join the points**. Sometimes the points may be connected with a line, as in Figure 2.2 (b). Sometimes you may need to connect the points with a curve, which you will have to draw freehand.

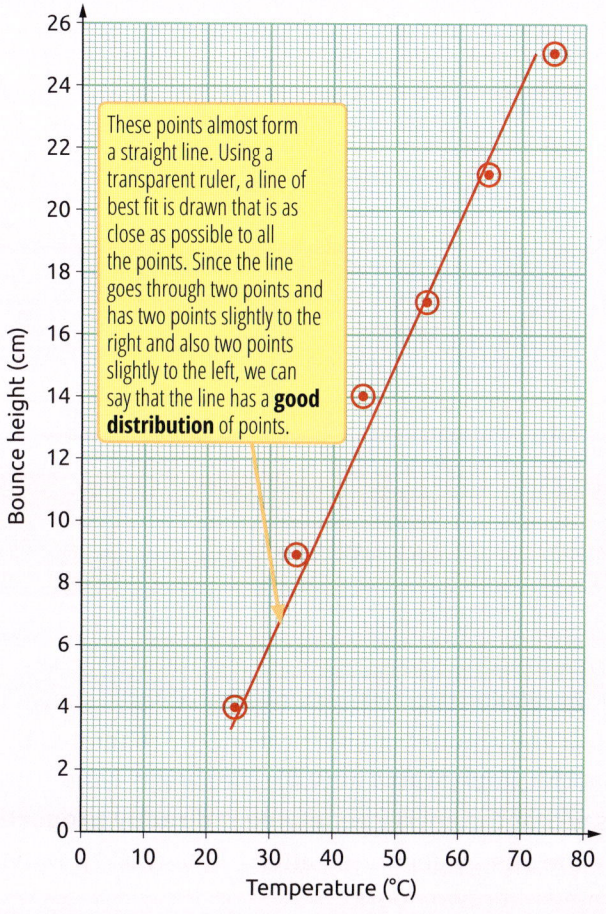

▶ Figure 2.2 (b) Drawing a best fit line

Exam Tip!

When your graph is being examined, the following points will be taken into consideration.
- Are the axes labelled?
- Is scaling of the graph accurate?
- Are the points plotted correctly?
- Are the points in the graph joined together in an appropriate way?

2.4 Interpreting graphs

- Now that you can draw a graph, it is important to be able to interpret the relationship between the variables on the graph. Figure 2.3 gives some examples.

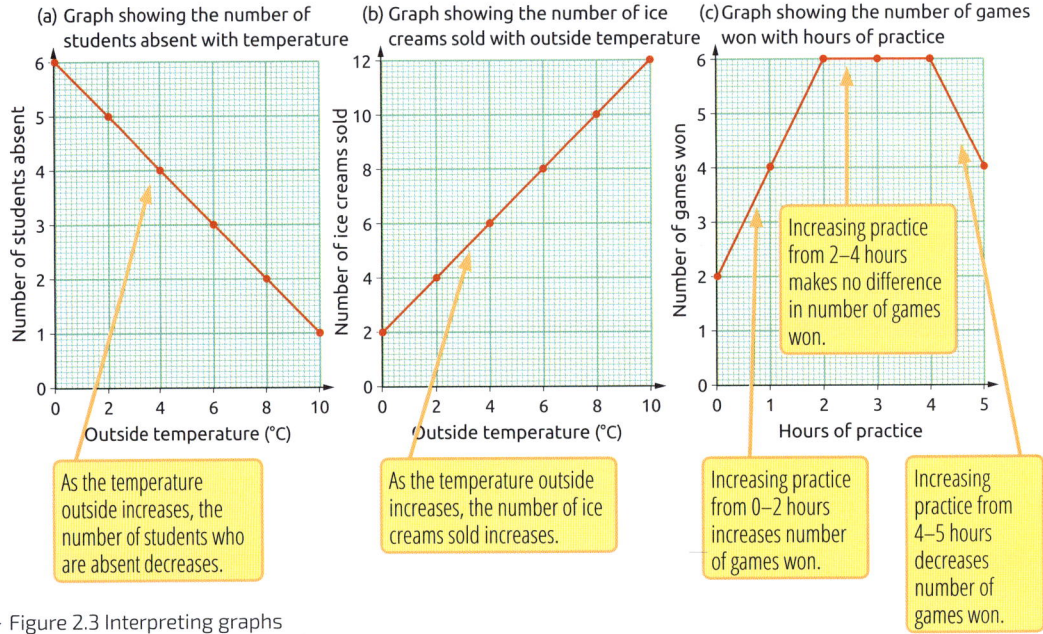

▶ Figure 2.3 Interpreting graphs

- A very important relationship between two variables is shown in Figure 2.4.
- The graph shows the amount of electrical energy generated by a solar panel over time. Note that the graph **starts at (0,0)** – the origin – and it is a **straight line**.
- We can now say that the energy generated is **directly proportional** to the time.
- If we compare the energy generated after 1 hour (2000 J) with the amount of energy generated after two hours (4000 J) we notice that, as the time is doubled, the energy generated is also doubled. If you treble the time (3 hours), the amount of energy generated is also trebled.
- You will need to be able to recognise this relationship if it arises in any graph. You will especially need to be able to recognise it in Hooke's law (Chapter 31) and Ohm's law (Chapter 34).

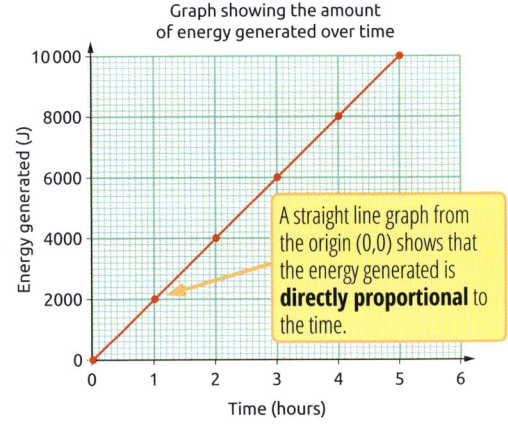

▶ Figure 2.4 A graph of energy generated by a solar panel against time

> A graph that has a straight line from the origin shows that the two variables are **directly proportional** to each other.

2.5 Using the graph as a source of data

- Graphs can be used to show trends in data. They can also be used as a source of data.
- We will use the graph in Figure 2.5 as a source of data. The graph shows the depth of the sea over a period of time. The depth of the sea is changing because of the tide.
- Figure 2.5 (a) shows how to work out the **maximum and minimum** depths.
- Figure 2.5 (b) shows how to work out the depth at a time of 1.5 hours. A line is drawn straight up from 1.5 m until it hits the graph. Then a line is drawn horizontally from this point until it hits the y-axis. This gives a value for the depth (5.6 m). In an exam, **do not rub out these lines** as they are evidence that you know what to do if any error was made, and you will get some marks for these.
- Figure 2.5 (c) shows how to calculate the length of time that the depth was greater than or equal to 8 m. A line is drawn from 8 m horizontally until it hits the graph. Note that it hits the graph at two points. Vertical lines are drawn from these points until they hit the x-axis. These values are read (2.3 hours and 3.7 hours). Between these times the height of the water was at or above 8 m. The height of the sea was equal to or greater than 8 m for 3.7 − 2.3 = **1.4 hours**. Again, **do not rub out these lines**.

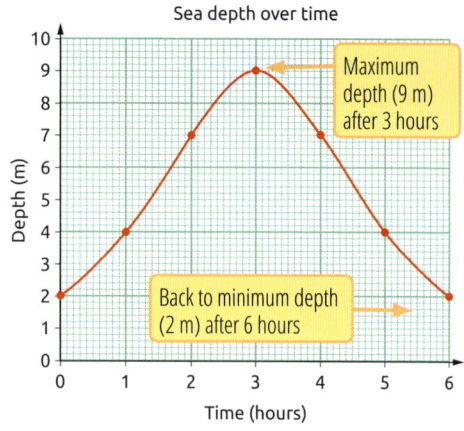

▶ Figure 2.5 (a) Working out the maximum and minimum depths

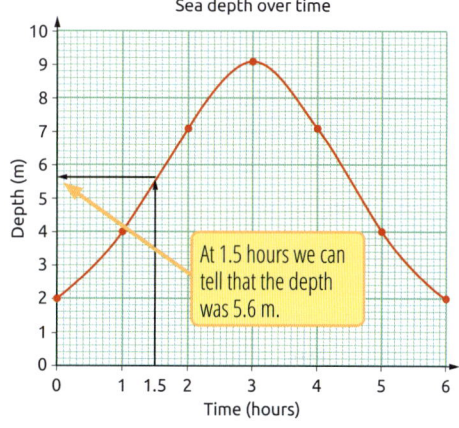

▶ Figure 2.5 (b) Working out the depth at 1.5 hours

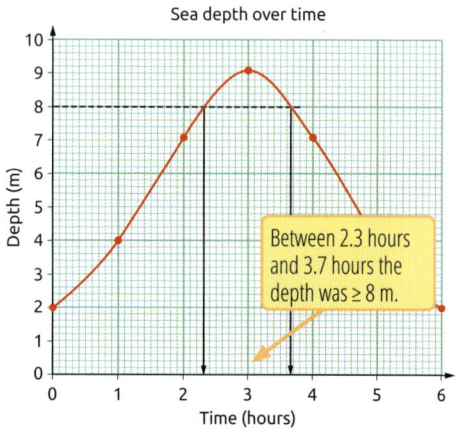

▶ Figure 2.5 (c) Working out how long the depth was 8 m or greater

▶▶ Science Self-Assessment

Now I am able to:	🟢	🟠	🔴
Draw a graph when given a table of data			
Work out the relationship between the variables on the graph			
Use a graph as a source of data			
Interpret data shown in the form of a graph			

03 The cell

The Biological World strand

Main topics in this chapter:
- The structure of animal and plant cells
- How the parts of cells are related to their functions
- The names and functions of the parts of the microscope
- How to prepare a glass slide to observe cells under the microscope

3.1 Cells

A **cell** is the smallest working unit of a living organism.

An **organelle** is a part of a cell, e.g. the nucleus or the chloroplast.

Red blood cell (human – no nucleus)

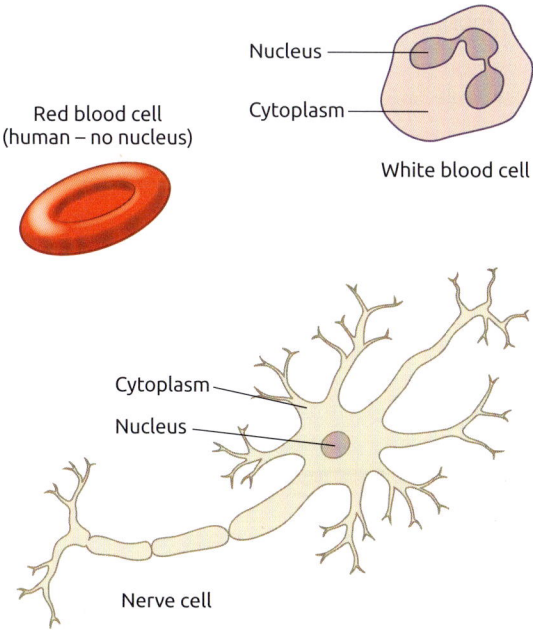

White blood cell

Nerve cell

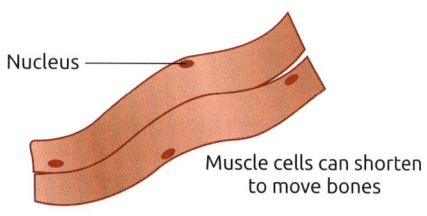

Muscle cells can shorten to move bones

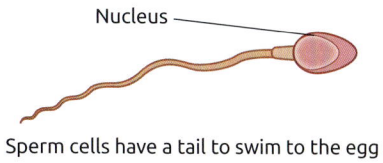

Sperm cells have a tail to swim to the egg

▶ Figure 3.1 Various types of cells

13

3.2 The animal cell

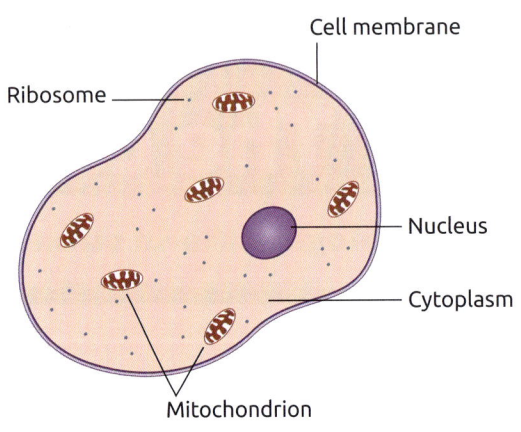

▶ Figure 3.2 An animal cell

Structure	Function
Cell membrane	Allows substances in and out of the cell; it also protects the cell
Cytoplasm	Watery fluid in which organelles float
Nucleus	Contains genes that control the cell
Mitochondrion	Where energy is released in respiration
Ribosome	Where proteins are made

▶ Table 3.1 Animal cell parts and their functions

3.3 The plant cell

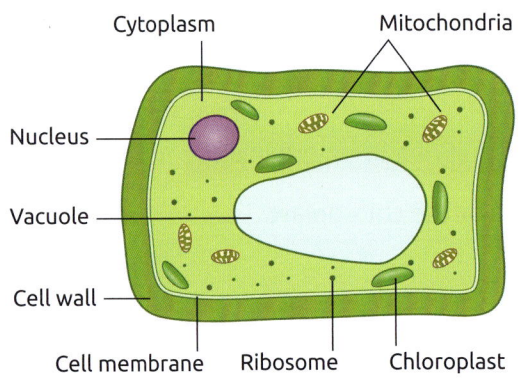

▶ Figure 3.3 A plant cell

Structure	Function
Cell wall	Support and protection
Vacuole	Storage of food and water
Chloroplast	Photosynthesis
Mitochondrion	Where energy is released in respiration
Ribosome	Where proteins are made

▶ Table 3.2 Plant cell parts and their functions

Table 3.3 shows the differences between plant cells and animal cells.

Plant cell	Animal cell
Cell wall made of cellulose present	Cell wall absent
Vacuole present	Vacuole absent (or very small)
Chloroplasts present	Chloroplasts absent

▶ Table 3.3 Differences between plant and animal cells

3.4 The microscope

Why do scientists use microscopes?

Microscopes are used to magnify very small structures in order to be able to see them more clearly and to study them.

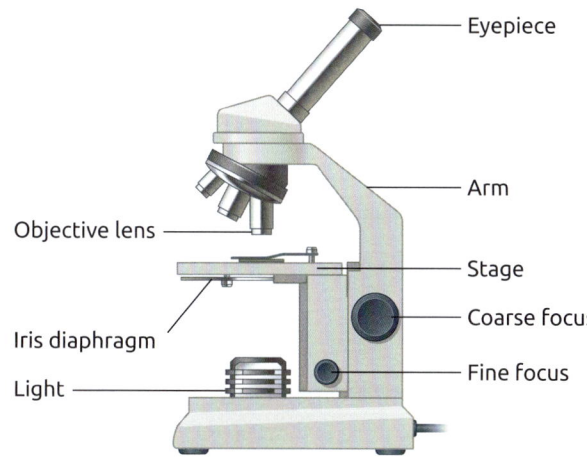

▶ Figure 3.4 The light microscope

Microscope part	Function
Eyepiece	To look through To magnify
Objective lens	To magnify
Stage	Where to place the slide
Coarse focus	To adjust focus – roughly
Fine focus	To adjust focus – accurately
Light	Light needs to shine through the specimen being observed
Iris diaphragm	To adjust the amount of light coming through the stage

▶ Table 3.4 The functions of the parts of the microscope

▶▶ Experiment 3.1

To use a light microscope

- The microscope is plugged in and the light is turned on.
- The low power objective lens is fixed in place.
- The iris diaphragm is turned to adjust the light coming through to the eyepiece.
- A slide with the specimen is placed on the stage.
- The stage is raised to its highest position.
- Looking through the eyepiece and using the coarse focus wheel, the specimen is brought into view, Figure 3.5.
- Adjusting the fine focus wheel, the specimen is brought into clear focus.
- To view under high power, only the fine focus wheel is used.

 www.folensonline.ie/for-students

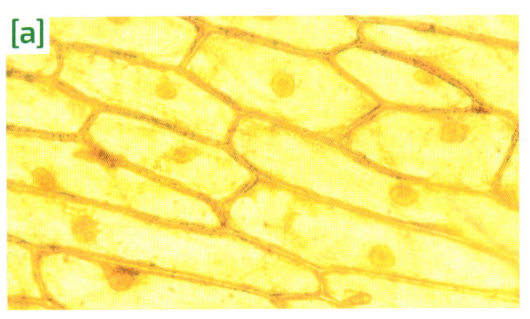
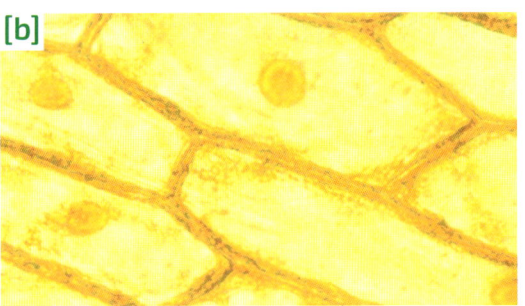

▶ Figure 3.5 (a) Cells under low power (b) Cells under high power

Exam Tip!

Always write descriptions of experiments using bullets (as above) or numbers. Never write descriptions of experiments in the form of an essay.

▶▶ Experiment 3.2

To obtain a good specimen of plant tissue for viewing under the microscope

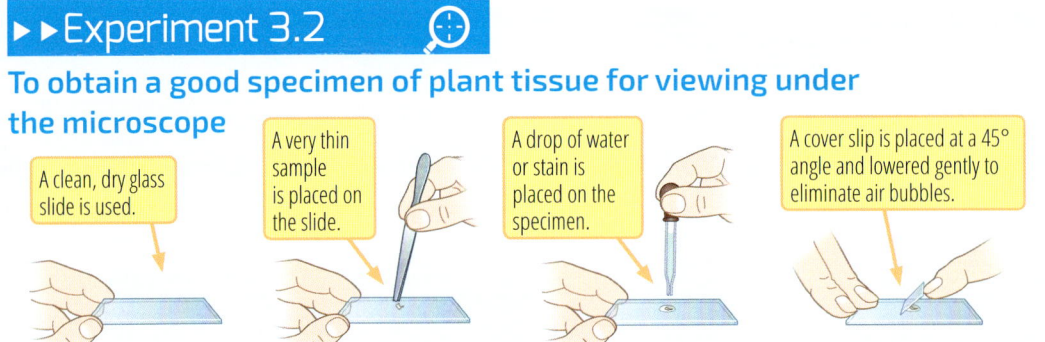

- A clean, dry glass slide is used.
- A very thin sample is placed on the slide.
- A drop of water or stain is placed on the specimen.
- A cover slip is placed at a 45° angle and lowered gently to eliminate air bubbles.

▶ Figure 3.6 A slide being prepared

www.folensonline.ie/for-students

▶▶ Science Self-Assessment

Now I am able to:	🟢	🟠	🔴
Describe the structure of animal and plant cells			
Give the functions of the parts of the cell			
Name the parts of the microscope and give the function of each part			
Describe how to use a microscope			
Describe how to prepare a specimen on a glass slide to observe under the microscope			

04 The digestive system

The Biological World strand

▶▶ **Main topics in this chapter:**
- The structure of the digestive system
- The functions of the organs of the digestive system
- Enzymes and digestion
- Experiment to investigate the breakdown of starch by the enzyme amylase
- How the organs of the digestive system interact with each other and with the circulatory system

4.1 Why do we need a digestive system?

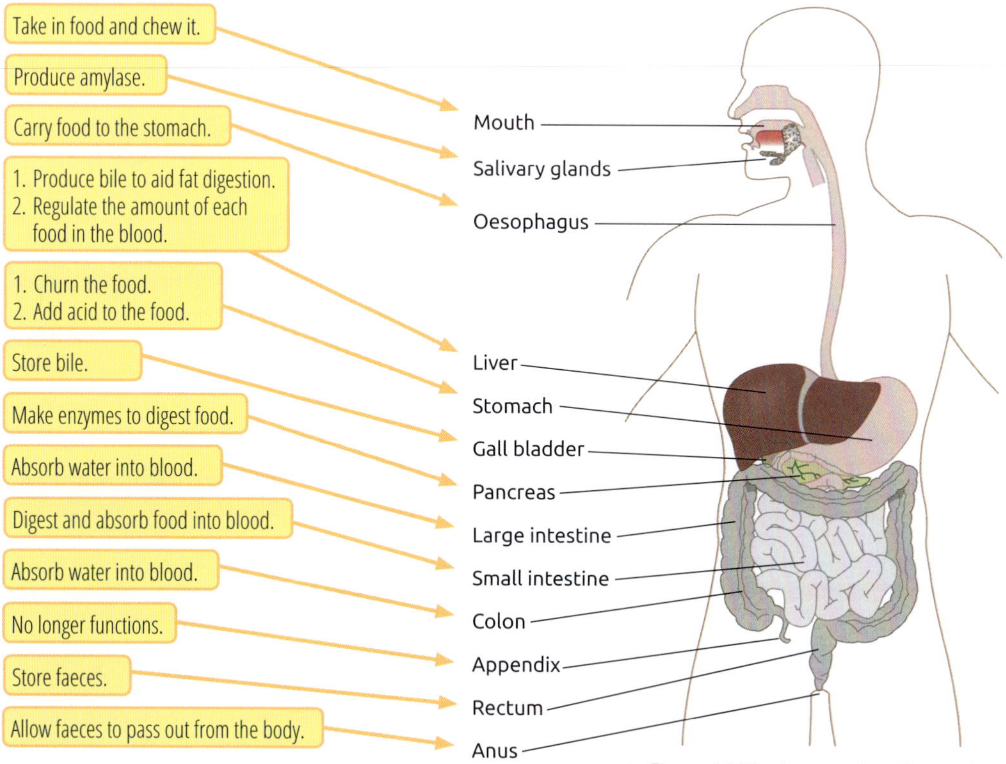

- Take in food and chew it.
- Produce amylase.
- Carry food to the stomach.
- 1. Produce bile to aid fat digestion.
  2. Regulate the amount of each food in the blood.
- 1. Churn the food.
  2. Add acid to the food.
- Store bile.
- Make enzymes to digest food.
- Absorb water into blood.
- Digest and absorb food into blood.
- Absorb water into blood.
- No longer functions.
- Store faeces.
- Allow faeces to pass out from the body.

Labels: Mouth, Salivary glands, Oesophagus, Liver, Stomach, Gall bladder, Pancreas, Large intestine, Small intestine, Colon, Appendix, Rectum, Anus

▶ Figure 4.1 The human digestive system

A **system** is a group of organs working together.

Digestion is the breaking down of larger food particles into smaller particles.

- Every cell in the body needs food to live.
- The blood (circulatory) system carries food to the cells.
- The particles of food eaten are too large to get into the blood.
- The large particles are broken down by the digestive system so that they are small enough to be carried in the blood and small enough to pass into the cells of the body.

Exam Tip!
When defining a word, do not use the word itself in your definition.

Organ	Function
Mouth (with teeth)	• Take in food. • Crush food with the teeth. • Amylase is added to the food.
Oesophagus	• Carry food down to the stomach.
Stomach	• Churn the food. • Add acid to the food.
Small intestine	• Further digestion by enzymes. • Absorption of digested food into the blood.
Large intestine/colon	• Water is absorbed into the blood. • The waste left is prepared for egestion.
Salivary glands	• Make saliva, which contains an enzyme, amylase, to break starch down to smaller sugars.
Liver	• Produce liquid bile, which helps digest fat. • Regulate the amount of each food in the blood.
Gall bladder	• Store bile from the liver until it is needed.
Pancreas	• Make enzymes to break down food.

▶ Table 4.1 The organs of the digestive system and their functions

Table 4.2 shows the steps (stages) of nutrition.

Step in nutrition	What happens
1. Ingestion	Food is taken in (eaten).
2. Digestion	Food is broken down (digested).
3. Absorption	Food is taken into the blood.
4. Assimilation	The body uses the food.
5. Egestion	Waste (faeces) is passed out of the body.

▶ Table 4.2 The five steps in providing nutrition for the body

4.2 The teeth and their functions

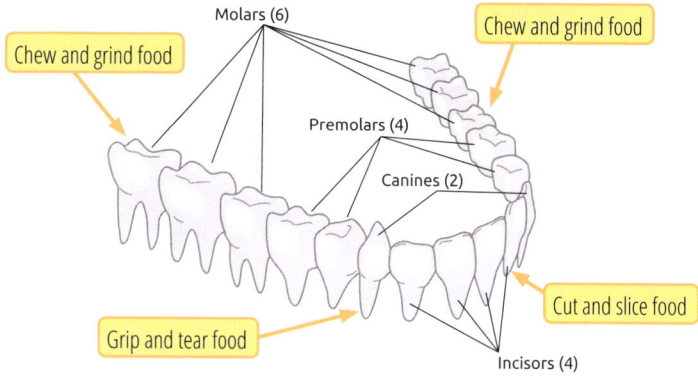

▶ Figure 4.2 Human teeth and their functions

4.3 Enzymes

An **enzyme** is a chemical, found in living organisms. Enzymes speed up chemical reactions, e.g. the digestion of food.

Amylase is an example of an enzyme found in the digestive system. Amylase breaks down starch (a type of carbohydrate) to a sugar called maltose.

Substrate is the name of the substance on which an enzyme acts.

Product is the name of the substance that is formed when an enzyme reacts with a substrate.

Enzyme	Substrate	Product
Amylase	Starch	Maltose

▶ Table 4.3 The enzyme amylase, its substrate and its product

▶▶Experiment 4.1

To investigate the digestion of starch by amylase

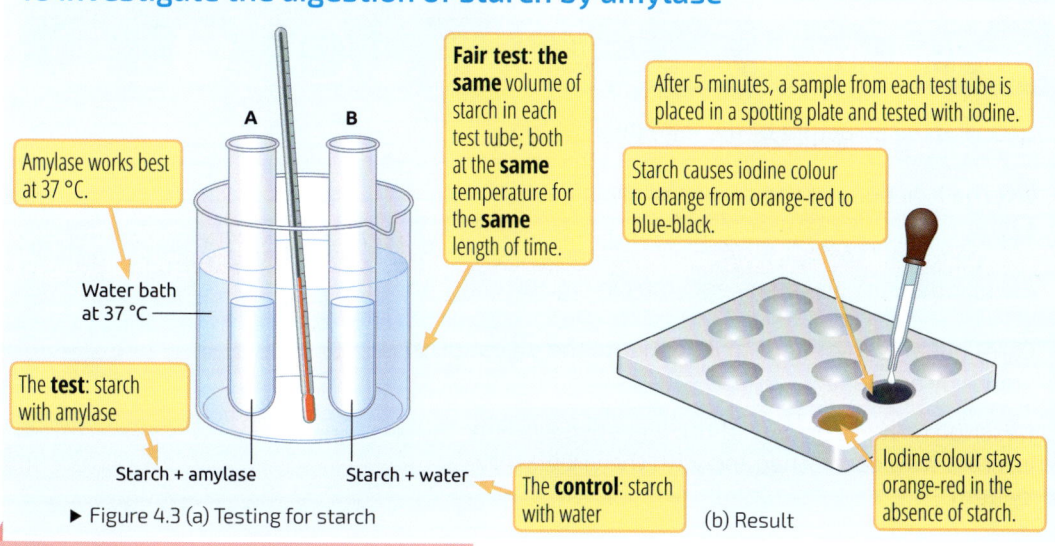

▶ Figure 4.3 (a) Testing for starch   (b) Result

www.folensonline.ie/for-students

19

4.4 How the organs of the digestive system interact with each other and with the circulatory system

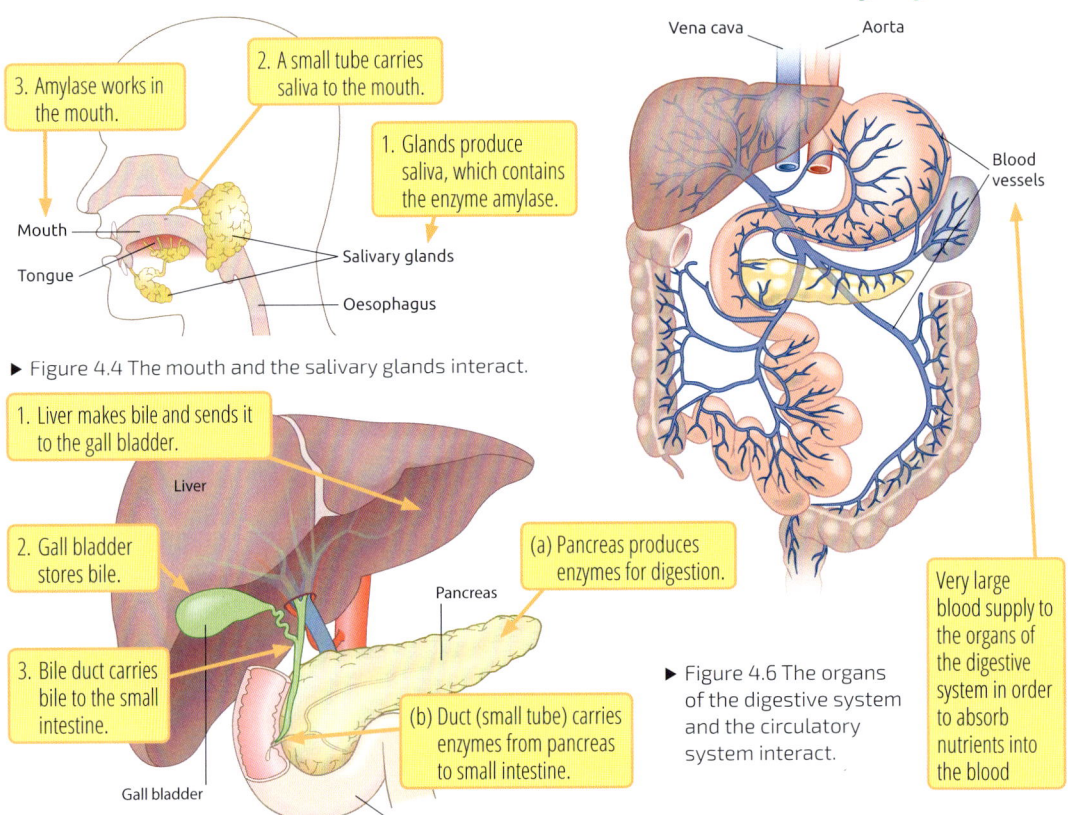

1. Glands produce saliva, which contains the enzyme amylase.
2. A small tube carries saliva to the mouth.
3. Amylase works in the mouth.

Mouth — Tongue — Salivary glands — Oesophagus

▶ Figure 4.4 The mouth and the salivary glands interact.

1. Liver makes bile and sends it to the gall bladder.
2. Gall bladder stores bile.
3. Bile duct carries bile to the small intestine.

Liver — Pancreas — Gall bladder — Small intestine

(a) Pancreas produces enzymes for digestion.
(b) Duct (small tube) carries enzymes from pancreas to small intestine.

▶ Figure 4.5 The small intestine, liver, gall bladder and pancreas interact.

Vena cava — Aorta — Blood vessels

▶ Figure 4.6 The organs of the digestive system and the circulatory system interact.

Very large blood supply to the organs of the digestive system in order to absorb nutrients into the blood

▶▶ Science Self-Assessment

Now I am able to:	🟢	🟠	🔴
Describe the structure of the digestive system			
List the functions of the organs of the digestive system			
Explain the part played by enzymes in digestion			
Carry out an experiment to investigate the digestion of starch by amylase			
Describe how the organs of the digestive system interact with each other and with the circulatory system			

05
The circulatory system

The Biological World strand

Main topics in this chapter:
- The composition of blood and its functions
- The organs of the circulatory system and their functions
- How the organs of the circulatory system interact with each other and with the digestive system and the respiratory system
- The effect of exercise on heart rate

5.1 Why do we need a circulatory system?
- To transport oxygen to the cells
- To transport food to the cells
- To transport waste materials away from cells
- To help fight infection
- To transport heat from organs (e.g. the liver) and muscles to the rest of the body

5.2 Composition of blood

A **tissue** is a group of cells with a similar structure and function.

Blood is a type of tissue because it is made up of similar cells with a similar function.

Blood is made up of straw-coloured liquid called **plasma** with cells floating in it.

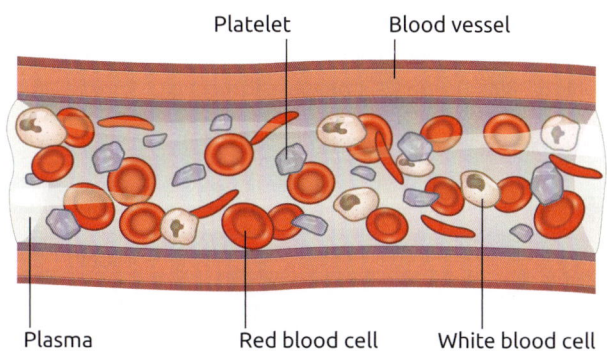

▶ Figure 5.1 The different types of blood cells in plasma

21

Blood cells	Function	Diagram
Red blood cells	Carry oxygen to the body cells	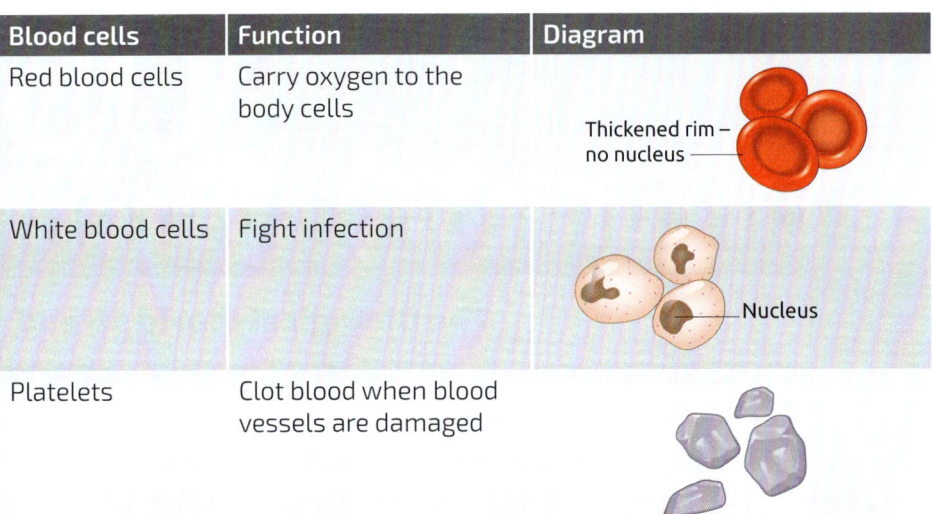
White blood cells	Fight infection	
Platelets	Clot blood when blood vessels are damaged	

▶ Table 5.1 Blood cells and their functions

Plasma carries the blood cells and also carries food substances such as glucose, amino acids, vitamins and minerals.

Heat is also transferred by means of the plasma of the blood.

5.3 Blood vessels

There are three types of blood vessels:

- Arteries
- Veins
- Capillaries

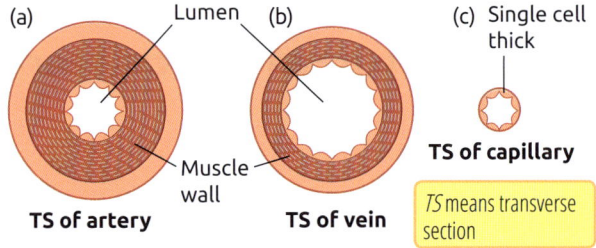

▶ Figure 5.2 A section through each type of blood vessel

Type of blood vessel	Wall of vessel	Function of vessel
Artery	Thick muscle wall	Carry blood away from heart
Vein	Thin muscle wall	Carry blood towards heart
Capillary	One cell thick	Allow substances to pass in and out of the blood

Exam Tip!
A for **a**rtery;
A for **a**way.

▶ Table 5.2 Blood vessels – structure and function

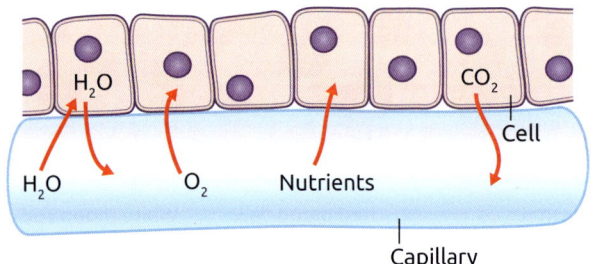

▶ Figure 5.3 Capillaries and cells

5.4 The heart

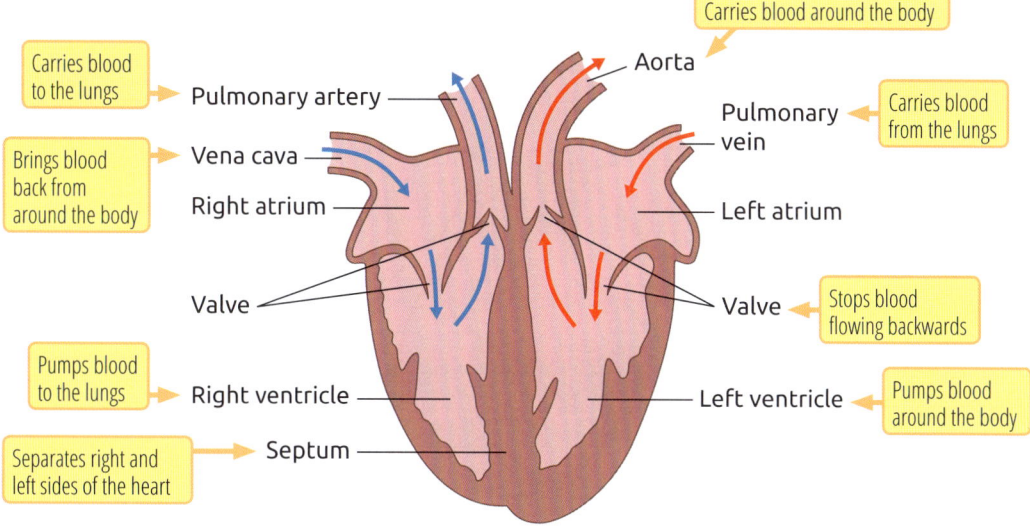

▶ Figure 5.4 The human heart

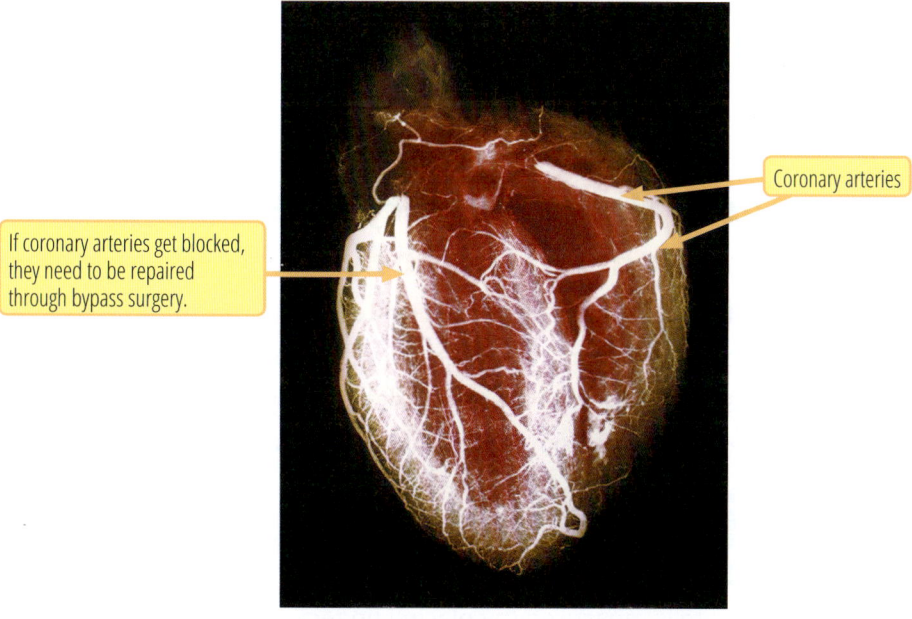

▶ Figure 5.5 Coronary arteries bring nutrients and oxygen to the heart

5.5 Blood circulation

- **Arteries** carry blood **away** from the heart.
- **Veins** carry blood **towards** the heart.
- **The heart** pumps the blood into the **arteries**.
- **Arteries** break up into capillaries.
- **Capillaries** join together into **veins**.

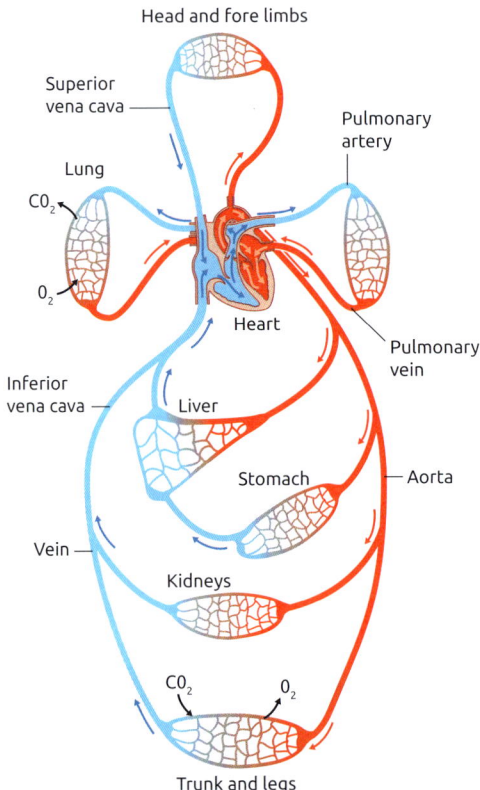

▶ Figure 5.6 Interactions of the circulatory system organs with each other

5.6 Interactions of the circulatory system organs with other systems of the body

Food is absorbed by the **blood** from the **digestive system**.

Oxygen is absorbed by the **blood** from the **respiratory system**.

All the cells of all the systems in the body receive food and oxygen **from the blood**.

Carbon dioxide and water are taken from the **blood** by the **respiratory system**.

▶▶ Experiment 5.1

To investigate the effect of exercise on heart rate

1. The resting heart rate is measured (by placing fingers on the wrist or neck) and recorded.
2. Step 1 is repeated twice, and the average beats per minute (bpm) is recorded.
3. Some light exercise (walking slowly) is carried out and the bpm is recorded.
4. The heart rate is allowed to return to resting rate.
5. Steps 3 and 4 are repeated four times, increasing the level of exercise each time. When the results are analysed, they show that an increase in exercise causes an increase in heart rate.

www.folensonline.ie/for-students

Why does exercise increase heart rate?

- Exercise involves **movement** of muscles.
- Movement in muscles requires the release of **energy** from glucose.
- When more energy is needed, the heart rate increases in order to send more blood with **glucose and oxygen** to the muscle cells.
- Exercise also causes **more carbon dioxide** to be produced by the cells and this must be removed because it is poisonous.

Increase in movement —**needs**→ increase in energy —**needs**→ increase in the rate of respiration —**needs**→ increase in glucose and oxygen to cells —**needs**→ increase in blood supply to cells —**needs**→ increase in heart rate.

▶▶ Science Self-Assessment

Now I am able to:	🟢	🟠	🔴
Describe the structure of blood and give the functions of each type of blood cell			
Describe the structure and functions of the parts of the circulatory system			
Explain how the organs of the circulatory system interact with each other			
Explain how the circulatory system interacts with the digestive and respiratory systems			
Investigate the effect of exercise on heart rate			

06
The respiratory system

The Biological World strand

Main topics in this chapter:
- The organs of the respiratory system and their functions
- Gaseous exchange in the lungs
- How breathing occurs
- How the organs of the respiratory system interact with each other and with the circulatory system and digestive system
- Investigating carbon dioxide in inhaled air and exhaled air

6.1 Why do we need a respiratory system?
- To take in oxygen for respiration in cells
- To excrete carbon dioxide and water vapour, which are waste products of respiration in cells
- To allow gaseous exchange to occur between the blood and the lungs

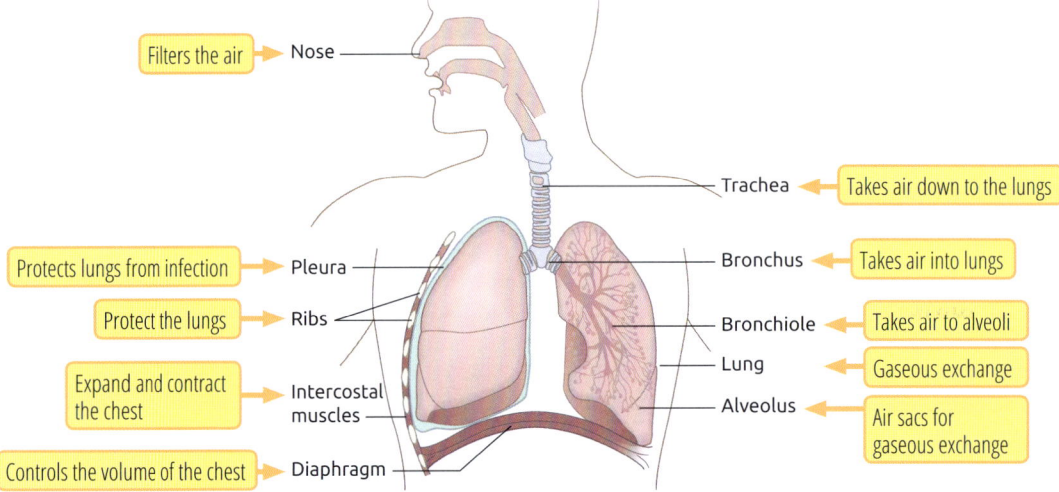

▶ Figure 6.1 The human respiratory system

6.2 Gaseous exchange in the lungs

Each alveolus has very thin walls. Alveoli are surrounded by capillaries with equally thin walls. This allows for a very efficient exchange of gases between the lungs and the blood.

- The oxygen in the alveoli moves (diffuses) through the walls of the alveoli and through the walls of the capillaries into the blood.
- The carbon dioxide in the blood of the capillaries moves through the walls of the capillaries and through the walls of the alveoli into the inside of the alveoli.

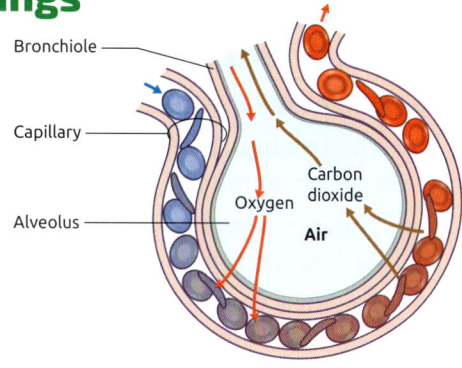

▶ Figure 6.2 Gaseous exchange between alveoli and capillaries

You will learn more about diffusion and movement of particles in Chapter 16.

6.3 Breathing

[a]

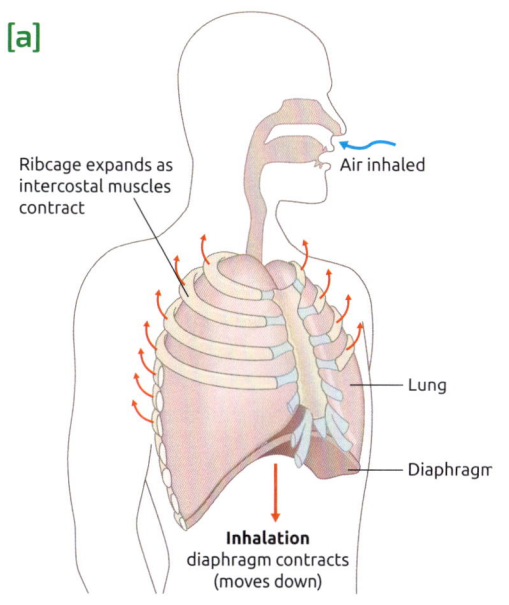

▶ Figure 6.3 (a) Breathing in

[b]

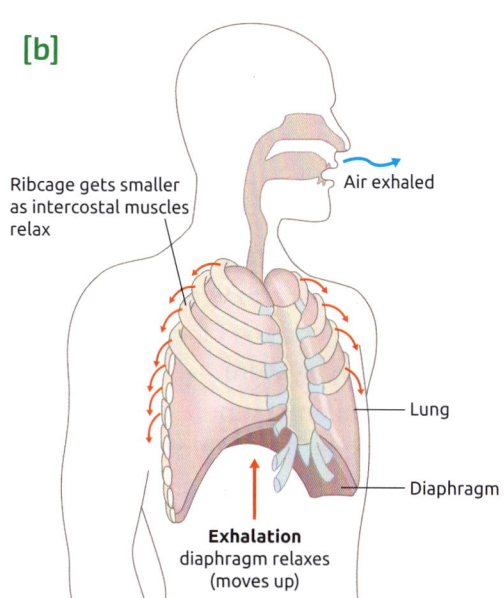

▶ Figure 6.3 (b) Breathing out

To breathe in (inhale):
1. The intercostal muscles contract. This causes the ribs to move out and up.
2. The diaphragm contracts. This causes it to move down.
3. The volume of the chest increases.
4. The pressure on the lungs decreases.
5. Air is sucked in.

To breathe out (exhale):
1. The intercostal muscles relax. This causes the ribs to move in and down.
2. The diaphragm relaxes. This causes it to arch up.
3. The volume of the chest decreases.
4. This causes the pressure on the lungs to increase.
5. Air is forced out.

6.4 Interactions of the respiratory system organs with each other

- The **nose** helps filter and moisten the air before it reaches the **lungs**.
- The **trachea, bronchi and bronchioles** are a system of tubes that carry air into and out of the **lungs**.
- The **intercostal muscles** and the **diaphragm** contract at the same time to draw air into the **lungs**.
- The **intercostal muscles** and the **diaphragm** relax at the same time to push air out of the **lungs**.

6.5 Interactions of the respiratory system organs with other systems of the body

- The **heart** pumps deoxygenated blood through the pulmonary artery to the **lungs** to get rid of carbon dioxide and take in oxygen.
- The capillaries that surround the alveoli join up to form the pulmonary vein, which carries oxygenated blood from the **lungs** to the **heart**.
- **All the cells of all the systems** in the body receive **oxygen** that has been taken into the blood by the **respiratory system**.
- When food enters the **oesophagus**, the **epiglottis** covers the **trachea** to prevent food passing into it.

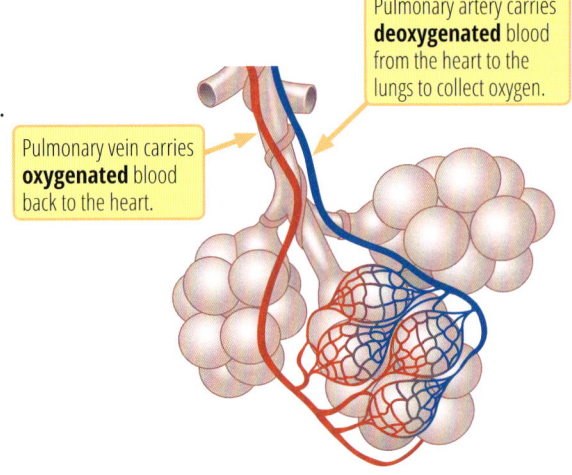

▶ Figure 6.4 Capillaries surrounding alveoli

Exam Tip!

The **pulmonary artery** is the only artery carrying deoxygenated blood and the **pulmonary vein** is the only vein carrying oxygenated blood.

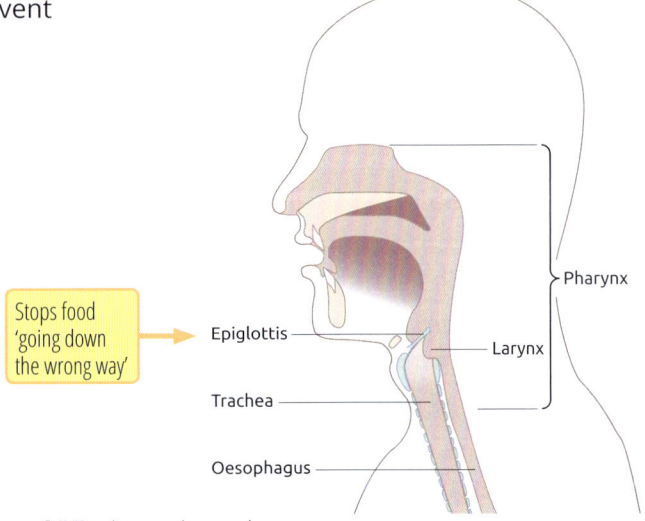

▶ Figure 6.5 Trachea and oesophagus

▶▶ Experiment 6.1

To investigate carbon dioxide in inhaled air and exhaled air

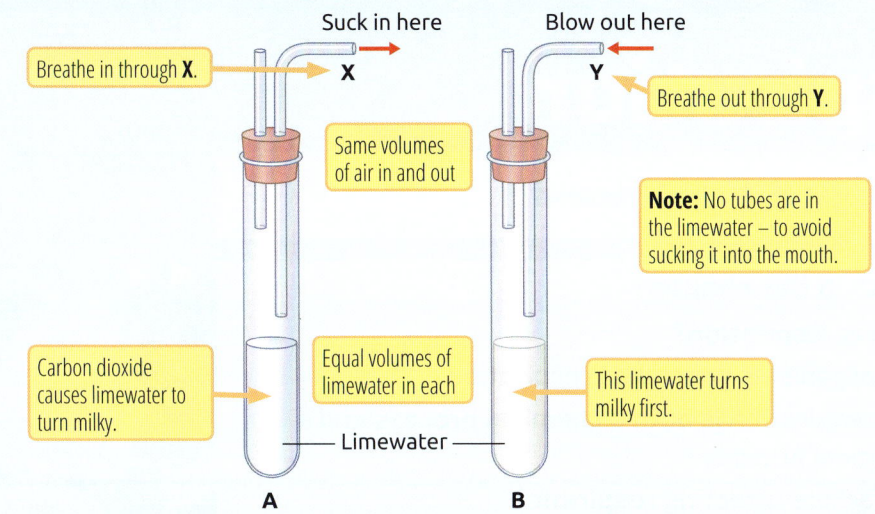

▶ Figure 6.6 To show there is more carbon dioxide in exhaled air than in inhaled air

 www.folensonline.ie/for-students

▶▶ Science Self-Assessment

Now I am able to:	🟢	🟠	🔴
Name the organs of the respiratory system and state their functions			
Describe how gaseous exchange occurs			
Describe how breathing occurs			
Describe how the organs of the respiratory system interact with each other			
Describe how the respiratory system interacts with the circulatory system and the digestive system			
Show that exhaled air has more carbon dioxide than inhaled air			

07 Respiration

The Biological World strand

Main topics in this chapter:
- What is respiration?
- How organisms depend on respiration
- Why respiration is both a chemical process and a biological process
- The factors affecting respiration
- Investigating how temperature affects respiration

7.1 How organisms depend on respiration

Respiration is the release of energy from food.

Remember: Respiration occurs in **all the cells** of the body.

Energy is the ability to do work.

Work is done when a force moves an object.

Glucose + oxygen ⟶ energy + carbon dioxide + water

$C_6H_{12}O_6 + 6O_2 \longrightarrow$ energy $+ 6CO_2 + 6H_2O$

Exam Tip!
Question: Where is energy released from food?
Answer: Energy is released from food in the cells of the body.

You will learn more about energy in Chapter 32.

Organisms depend on the energy released in respiration for all life processes:
- Movement
- Reproduction
- Responsiveness
- Nutrition
- Excretion

Any movement – whether that is waving or digging – requires energy!

▶ Figure 7.1

7.2 Respiration as a chemical and a biological process

Respiration is a *chemical process* because:
It involves a *number of steps* where *new substances* are formed.

Respiration is a *biological process* because:
It takes place in *living cells* and involves *enzymes*.

7.3 Factors affecting respiration

The following factors affect respiration:
- Glucose availability
- Oxygen availability
- Temperature

Why does temperature affect respiration?

Respiration is controlled by enzymes which are very sensitive to temperature:
- They are temporarily unable to work if they are too cold.
- They are destroyed if they are too hot.

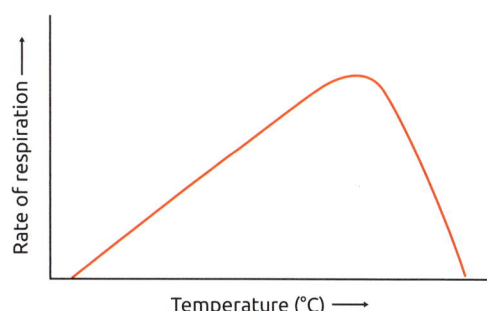

▶ Figure 7.2 Respiration is controlled by enzymes, so the rate of respiration depends on the temperature within the cell.

▶▶ Experiment 7.1

www.folensonline.ie/for-students

To investigate how temperature affects respiration

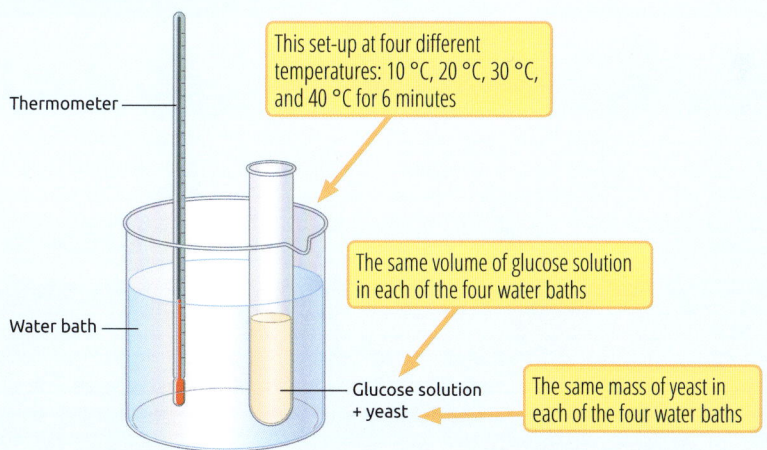

▶ Figure 7.3 Four water baths at four different temperatures

Result: Different heights of foam (indicating rate of activity) are produced at the different temperatures.

Conclusion: An increase in temperature from 10 °C to 40 °C causes an increase in the rate of respiration.

Note: If the temperature is too high, the enzyme will be destroyed and will not work.

▶▶ Science Self-Assessment

Now I am able to:	🟢	🟠	🔴
Define respiration			
Explain why organisms need respiration			
Explain how respiration is a chemical process			
Explain how respiration is a biological process			
List the factors that affect respiration			
Investigate how temperature affects respiration			

08 Photosynthesis

The Biological World strand

Main topics in this chapter:
- How Earth is dependent on photosynthesis
- What is photosynthesis?
- Why photosynthesis is both a chemical process and a biological process
- The factors affecting photosynthesis
- Investigating how light is necessary for photosynthesis
- Crop yields and photosynthesis

8.1 How Earth is dependent on photosynthesis
- To provide food to eat
- To provide oxygen to breathe
- To clean the air of carbon dioxide

8.2 What is photosynthesis?

Photosynthesis is the way green plants make their own food using light.

Word equation for photosynthesis:

$$\text{Carbon dioxide} + \text{water} \xrightarrow[\text{sunlight}]{\text{chlorophyll}} \text{glucose} + \text{oxygen}$$

Chemical equation for photosynthesis:

$$6CO_2 + 6H_2O \xrightarrow[\text{sunlight}]{\text{chlorophyll}} C_6H_{12}O_6 + 6O_2$$

The Sun is an essential source of energy for photosynthesis.

All life on Earth depends on the Sun's energy.

▶ Figure 8.1 Photosynthesis is essential for life on Earth.

How do plants photosynthesise?

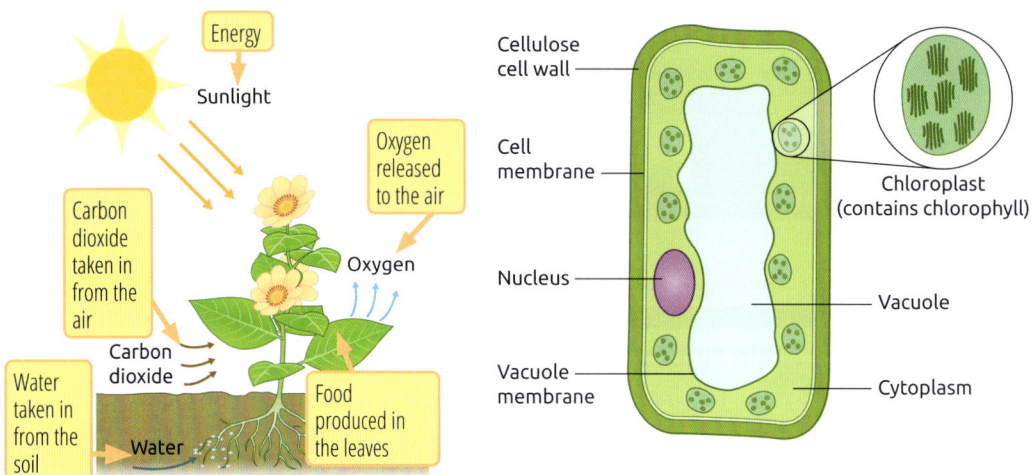

▶ Figure 8.2 Photosynthesis

▶ Figure 8.3 Plant cell showing a chloroplast

For photosynthesis to take place:
- Plants take in carbon dioxide from the air through tiny pores on their leaves called stomata (singular stoma).
- Plants take in water from the soil through their roots.
- Sunlight is absorbed by the chlorophyll in the chloroplasts in the cells of the leaves of the plant, Figure 8.3.
- The carbon dioxide and the water combine in the chloroplasts to form glucose. The energy for this reaction to happen comes from sunlight.
- Oxygen is released from the reaction and given off as a waste product.

Photosynthesis is a *chemical process* because:

It involves a *number of steps* where *new substances* are formed.

Photosynthesis is a *biological process* because:

It takes place in *living cells* and involves *enzymes.*

8.3 Factors affecting photosynthesis

The factors affecting photosynthesis are:
- **Carbon dioxide** because it reacts with water to form glucose and starch
- **Temperature** because the enzymes involved in photosynthesis are sensitive to temperature
- **Light** because light energy is converted to chemical energy during photosynthesis

▶▶ Experiment 8.1

To show that light is necessary for photosynthesis

- A plant is placed in darkness for 24 hours – to remove all starch (destarch it).
- A leaf is covered with aluminium foil – to prevent light from shining on it, Figure 8.4 (a).
- The plant is put in bright light for at least 6 hours – to allow photosynthesis to take place.
- Two leaves are tested for starch – one that was exposed to light and one that was shielded from light.

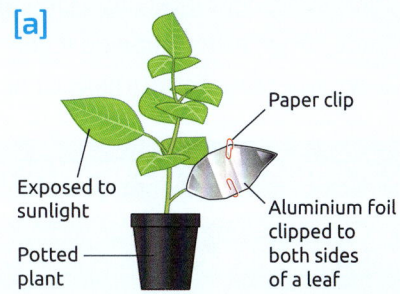

▶ Figure 8.4 (a) A destarched plant exposed to light, with one leaf covered from light

Each leaf is tested for starch to see if photosynthesis has taken place:
- Each leaf is placed in boiling water – to soften it, Figure 8.4 (b).
- Each leaf is then placed in hot alcohol – to remove the chlorophyll, Figure 8.4 (c).
- Each leaf is then put back in the hot water – to remove the alcohol.

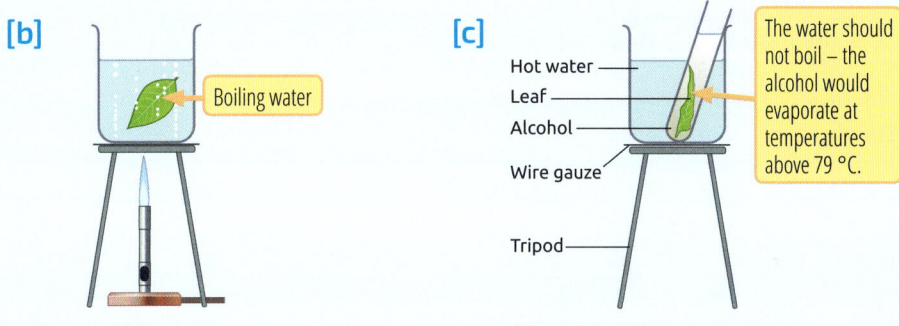

▶ Figure 8.4 (b) Leaf placed in boiling water

▶ Figure 8.4 (c) Leaf placed in hot alcohol to remove chlorophyll

- The leaf is placed on a white tile – to see any colour change clearly.
- Iodine solution is placed on the leaf – to test for starch, Figure 8.4 (d).

The results are summarised in Figure 8.4 (d).

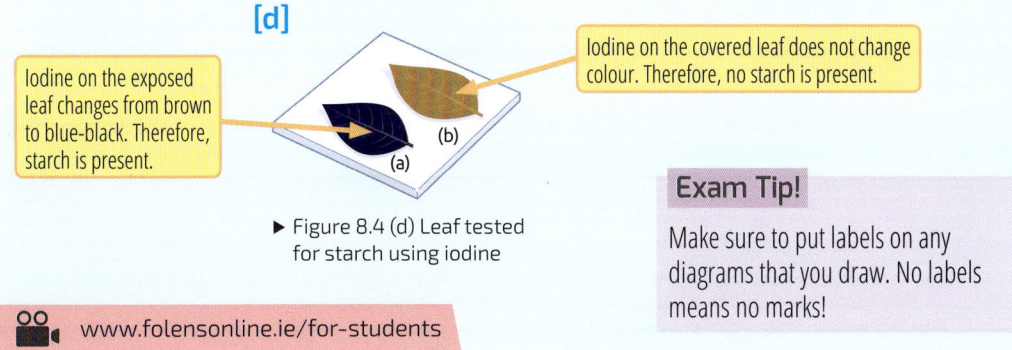

▶ Figure 8.4 (d) Leaf tested for starch using iodine

Exam Tip!
Make sure to put labels on any diagrams that you draw. No labels means no marks!

www.folensonline.ie/for-students

8.4 Crop yields and photosynthesis

Crop yields may be increased by increasing the rate of photosynthesis by:
- Increasing light intensity using artificial lighting
- Increasing carbon dioxide levels by burning gas in greenhouses
- Increasing temperatures with heaters

▶▶ Science Self-Assessment

Now I am able to:	🟢	🟠	🔴
List the ways in which Earth is dependent on photosynthesis			
Describe photosynthesis			
Explain how photosynthesis is a chemical process			
Explain how photosynthesis is a biological process			
Name the factors affecting photosynthesis			
Investigate if light is necessary for photosynthesis to take place			

09 Human reproduction

The Biological World strand

Main topics in this chapter:
- Reproduction – understanding the term
- The structure and functions of the human male and female reproductive systems
- The menstrual cycle
- Fertilisation, implantation and development of the baby
- Birth, breastfeeding and contraception
- *In vitro* fertilisation, hormonal replacement therapy and assisted human reproduction

9.1 Reproduction

Reproduction is the way that new individuals are produced from their parents.

Sexual reproduction, e.g. human reproduction, involves a cell from each parent joining to form a baby.

Gametes are sex cells – the sperm and the egg.

Fertilisation happens when the nucleus of the sperm joins with the nucleus of the egg to form a zygote, Figure 9.1.

A **zygote** is a fertilised egg.

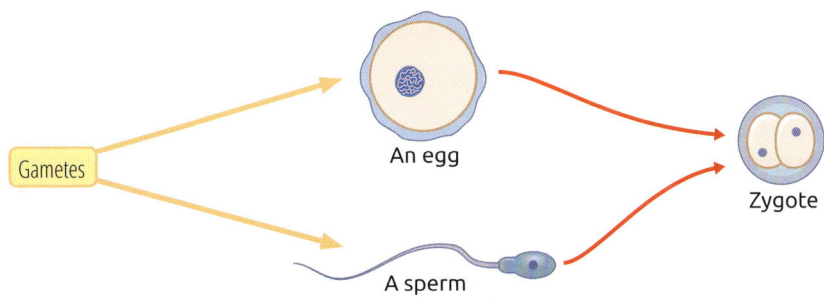

▶ Figure 9.1 Fertilisation

9.2 The human male reproductive system

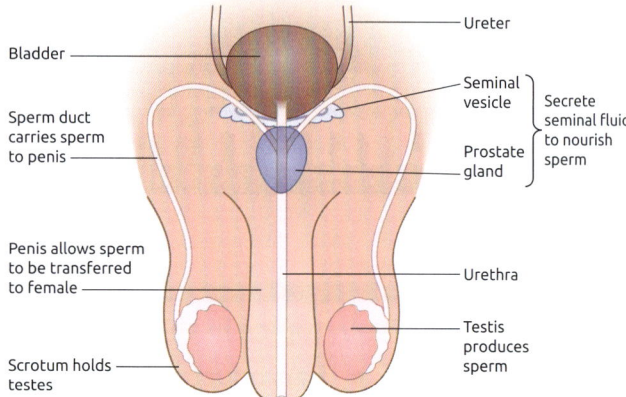

▶ Figure 9.2 Human male reproductive system, parts and functions

9.3 The human female reproductive system

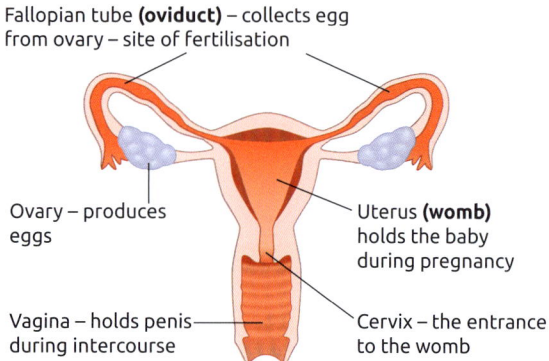

▶ Figure 9.3 Human female reproductive system, parts and functions

9.4 The menstrual cycle

The **menstrual cycle** is the monthly series of changes a woman's body goes through in preparation for the possibility of pregnancy.

Days	Ovary	Uterus
1–5	Egg(s) matures	Menstruation – blood and tissue lost through the vagina
5–14	Egg continues to mature	Blood and tissue are building up in the uterus again
14	Egg is released from the ovary – ovulation (It will die soon if it is not fertilised)	Blood and tissue continue to build up in the uterus
14–28	Hormones are released	Blood and tissue remain built up in the uterus
1–5	Another egg(s) starts to mature	Menstruation – blood and tissue lost from uterus – through the vagina

▶ Table 9.1 Summary of what happens in the ovary and in the uterus in one 28-day cycle

9.5 The fertile period

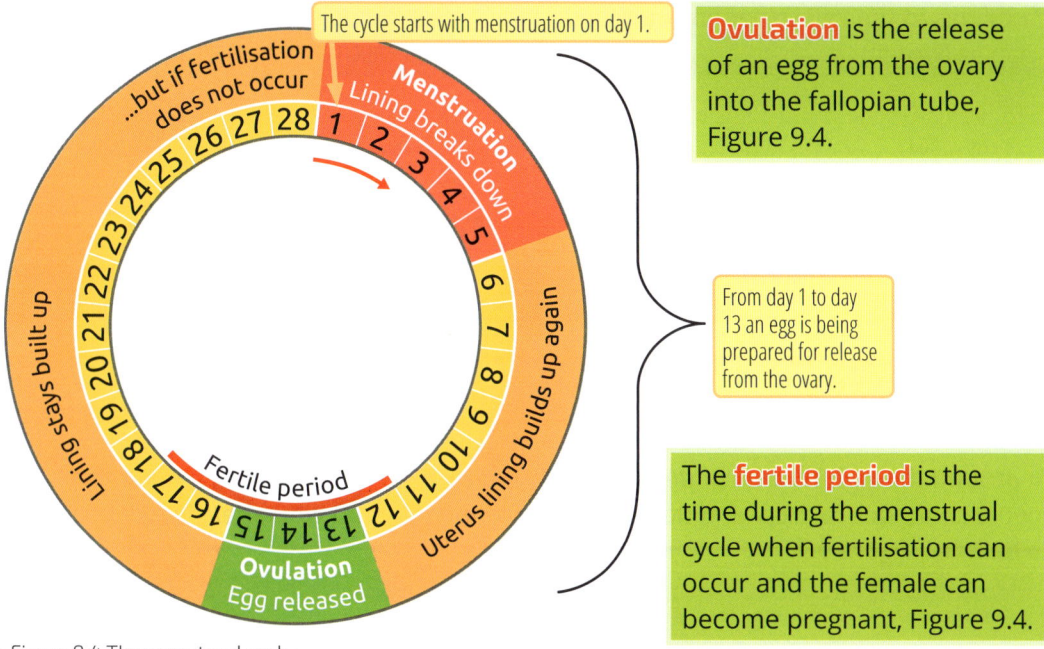

Ovulation is the release of an egg from the ovary into the fallopian tube, Figure 9.4.

From day 1 to day 13 an egg is being prepared for release from the ovary.

The fertile period is the time during the menstrual cycle when fertilisation can occur and the female can become pregnant, Figure 9.4.

▶ Figure 9.4 The menstrual cycle

9.6 Sexual intercourse and fertilisation

Sexual intercourse takes place when the penis is placed in the vagina.

Fertilisation will only occur if the egg and sperm are in the fallopian tube at the same time.

Fertilisation takes place when the nucleus of the egg and the nucleus of the sperm join together to form a fertilised egg known as a zygote.

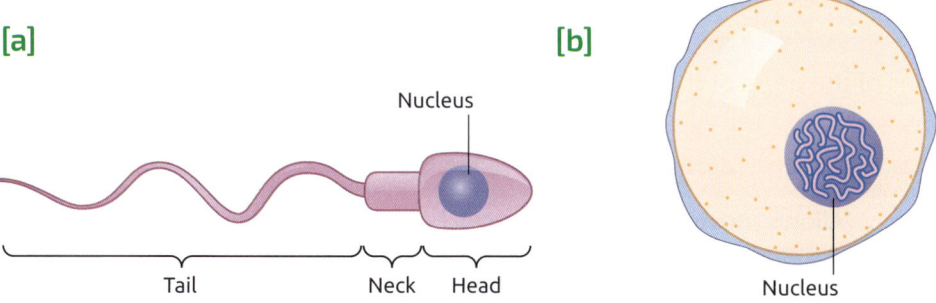

▶ Figure 9.5 (a) Sperm (b) Egg

9.7 Implantation and the development of the baby

The zygote divides many times to eventually become the **embryo**, Figure 9.6.

Once the embryo arrives in the uterus (about nine days after fertilisation) it **attaches** to the lining of tissue that has built up in the uterus. This is known as **implantation**.

39

Implantation occurs when the embryo attaches to the lining that has built up in the uterus (womb).

Exam Tip!
Ensure that you know the difference between fertilisation and implantation.

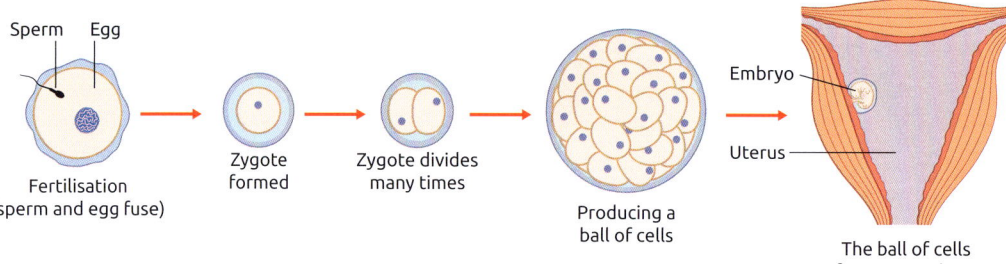

▶ Figure 9.6 The fertilised egg divides many times to form the embryo in the uterus.

At around the eighth week of development, the embryo is known as a foetus. The foetus continues to grow and develop until around week 40 when he/she will be ready to be born, Figure 9.7.

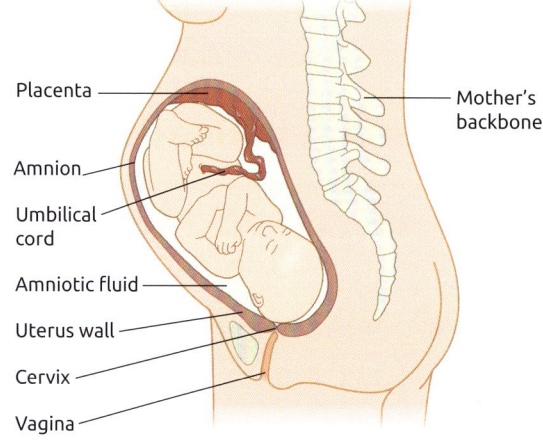

▶ Figure 9.7 Baby in the uterus

The functions of the parts of the uterus shown in Figure 9.7 are summarised in Table 9.2.

Part	Function
Placenta	Allows movement of substances between mother and foetus
Amnion	Holds fluid surrounding the foetus
Umbilical cord	Has blood vessels connecting baby to mother
Amniotic fluid	Protects the baby from shock and infection
Uterus wall	Muscular wall that will help push the baby out during birth
Cervix	A plug of mucus here seals the entrance to the uterus during pregnancy
Vagina	The canal through which the baby is born

▶ Table 9.2 The functions of the parts of the uterus during pregnancy

9.8 Birth

Giving birth to a baby involves three stages:
1. **Labour**
   The amniotic fluid passes out of the uterus; the cervix dilates (becomes wider); the muscle wall of the uterus starts contracting.
2. **Birth**
   As the uterus wall contracts, the baby is pushed through the birth canal to the outside.
3. **Removal of the placenta**
   The placenta is pushed out of the uterus by the muscles contracting once more.

9.9 Breastfeeding

Once the baby is born, the mother's body produces a hormone that causes milk to be produced by the mammary glands (the breasts).

Advantages of breastfeeding a baby:
- In the first days after birth, the milk has extra nutrients and antibodies.
- Breast milk contains the correct balance of nutrients.
- Antibodies continue to pass from the mother to the baby in the breast milk.
- Breastfeeding promotes a bond between mother and baby.
- Breastfeeding lowers the baby's risk of getting gastroenteritis (infection of stomach and gut).

9.10 Contraception

Contraception means preventing pregnancy by preventing fertilisation or implantation.
- **Natural contraception** means using knowledge of the female's menstrual cycle to estimate ovulation and avoiding sexual intercourse at that time.
- **Artificial contraception** means using mechanical or chemical methods to prevent pregnancy.

Method	How it works
Condom	A sheath is placed over the penis to collect sperm and prevent sperm from entering the female body
Diaphragm	A specially fitted device is placed in the vagina to prevent sperm passing into the uterus

▶ Table 9.3 Mechanical methods of contraception

Method	How it works
The contraceptive pill	A pill with a hormone to prevent the release of eggs each month
The bar	A small rod that is implanted under the skin of the woman; it releases a hormone that prevents the release of eggs each month

▶ Table 9.4 Chemical methods of contraception

9.11 Medical, ethical and societal issues in human reproduction

Medical issues include **hormone imbalances** in both males and females. These imbalances are treated with **hormone replacement therapy (HRT)**.

Medical issue	Symptoms	Possible cause	Possible treatment
Absence of ovulation	No eggs released from ovary	Low hormone levels	HRT
Low sperm count	Insufficient sperm for fertilisation to occur	Low hormone levels Alcohol abuse Smoking	HRT Stop drinking Stop smoking

▶ Table 9.5 Medical issues in human reproduction

Ethical issues include *in vitro* **fertilisation (IVF)**, which can also be considered a medical issue.

In vitro fertilisation involves eggs being collected from the woman and sperm being collected from the man. Figure 9.8 shows the next steps in the procedure.

A question of ethics – *in vitro* fertilisation (IVF)

Some ethical issues have arisen since the introduction of IVF in 1978:
- What happens to the frozen embryos if they are no longer needed?
- Will the excess embryos be used in stem cell research?
- Is it acceptable for couples to choose certain traits that they do or do not want in their baby?

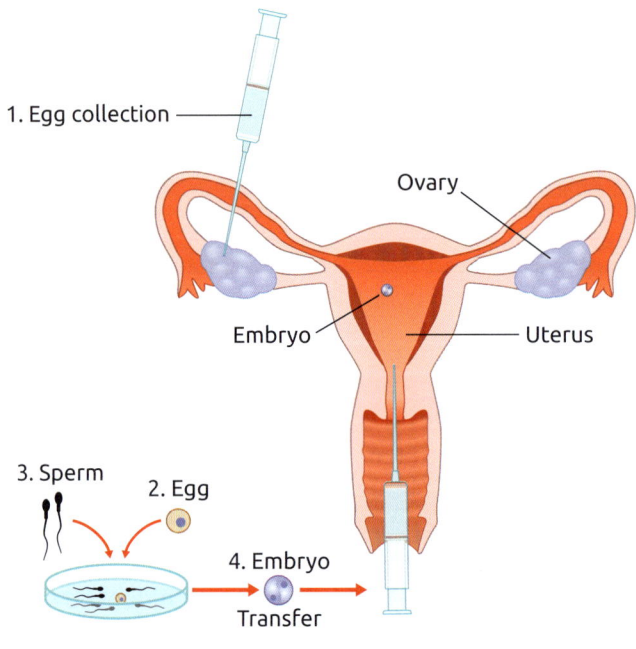

▶ Figure 9.8 Steps involved in carrying out *in vitro* fertilisation

Societal issues include any **assisted human reproduction (AHR) treatments**.

Questions for society:
- Who pays for these treatments?
- Will only the rich be able to get them?
- Should governments assist people who want these treatments but cannot afford them?

▶▶ Science Self-Assessment

Now I am able to:	🟢	🟠	🔴
Explain what is meant by *reproduction*			
Label the male and female reproductive systems			
State the functions of the organs of the male and female reproductive systems			
Describe the menstrual cycle			
Explain fertilisation, implantation and the development of the embryo			
Explain birth, breastfeeding and contraception			
Discuss medical, ethical and societal issues in human reproduction			

10 Inheritance and variation

The Biological World strand

Main topics in this chapter:
- Sexual and asexual reproduction
- Variation in species
- DNA, chromosomes and genes
- Mendelian inheritance and crosses

10.1 Sexual and asexual reproduction

Sexual reproduction involves two parents where the male and female gametes join together to form a zygote.

The offspring will be very like the parents but they will have characteristics that differ from both.

Asexual reproduction involves just one parent with the offspring identical to the parent.

Offspring produced by sexual reproduction show much greater variation than the offspring produced by asexual reproduction.

Some examples of asexual reproduction in plants are shown in, Figures 10.1 and 10.2.

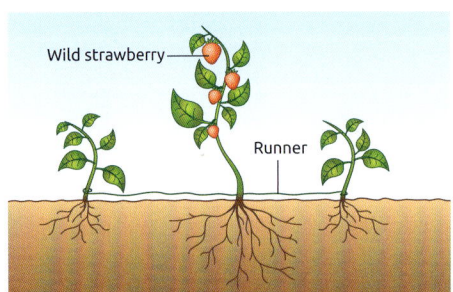

▶ Figure 10.1 Strawberry plants reproduce asexually by sending out runners that produce roots and grow into new plants identical to the parent.

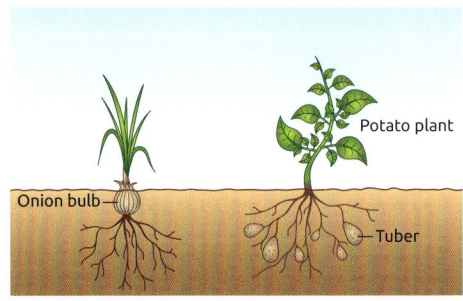

▶ Figure 10.2 Onions reproduce asexually using bulbs. Potatoes reproduce asexually using tubers. The offspring are identical to the parent.

Asexual reproduction takes place in many one-celled organisms, e.g. amoeba, Figure 10.3.

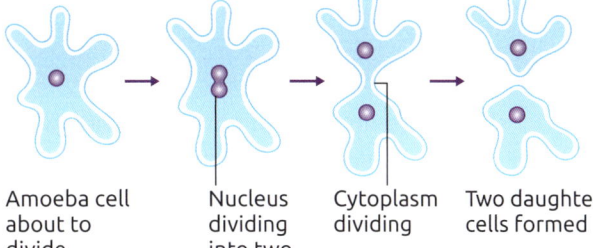

▶ Figure 10.3 Amoeba, a one-cell organism, dividing into two offspring, identical to each other and to the parent

Amoeba cell about to divide | Nucleus dividing into two | Cytoplasm dividing | Two daughter cells formed

10.2 Variation

▶ Figure 10.4 Same **species** – lots of **variation**!

The way members of the same species differ is known as **variation**. Variations are a result of changes in DNA. Changes in DNA are called **mutations**.

A **species** is a group of organisms that can breed with each other and produce fertile offspring.

Fertile means that an organism is capable of producing young.

10.3 Deoxyribonucleic Acid (DNA)

▶ Figure 10.5 Francis Crick and James Watson discovered the structure of DNA in 1953.

▶ Figure 10.6 Rosalind Franklyn's X-rays of DNA inspired Crick and Watson.

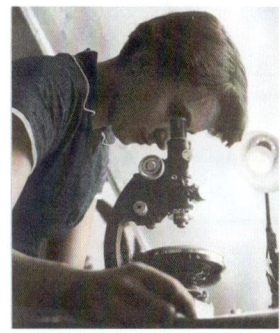

DNA has the structure of a double helix, Figure 10.7.

10.4 Chromosomes and genes

Chromosomes are made up of lengths of DNA wrapped around protein.

Table 10.1 shows the number of chromosomes present in each cell of various species. **Cells of humans contain 46 chromosomes in each cell**, Figure 10.8.

Species	Number of chromosomes	Species	Number of chromosomes
Fruit fly	8	Chimpanzee	48
Pea plant	14	Amoeba	50
Crayfish	>100	Human	46
Mallard	80	Mosquito	6
Rat	42	Horse	64
Toad	22	Redwood	22
Wheat	42	Earthworm	36
Chicken	78	House cat	32

▶ Table 10.1 Numbers of chromosome in each cell of some species

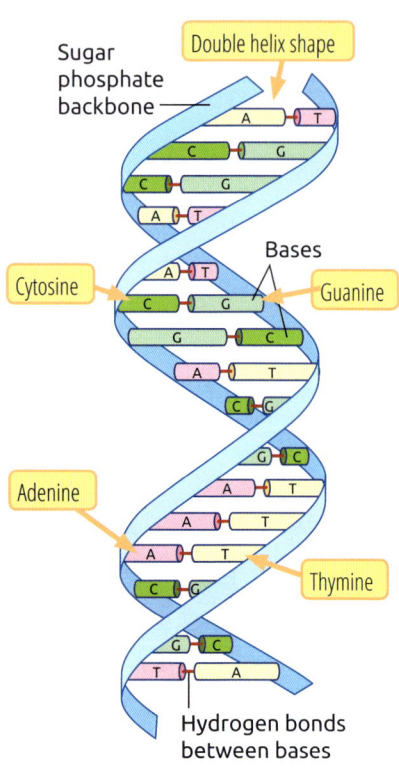

▶ Figure 10.7 Structure of DNA

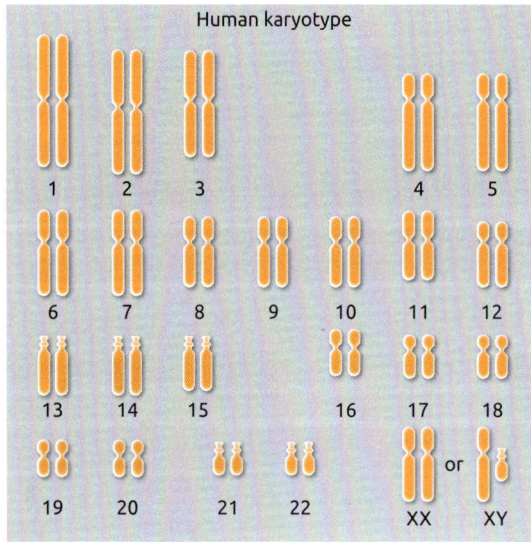

▶ Figure 10.8 Human chromosomes: 22 pairs of chromosomes are the same in both males and females. Females have two X chromosomes and males have one X chromosome and one Y chromosome.

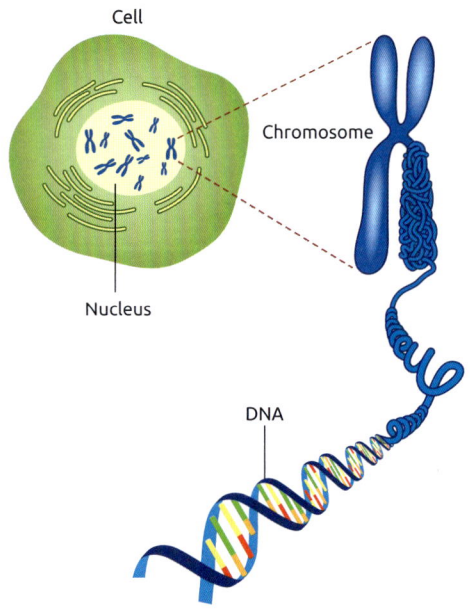

▶ Figure 10.9 Supercoiling in DNA – to allow it to fit in the nucleus

Genes are lengths of DNA along a chromosome. Each gene controls the making of a particular protein.

The traits or characteristics of an organism (e.g. hair colour) are controlled by pairs of genes – one gene from the mother and one gene from the father, Figure 10.10.

Question: Where are the pairs of genes controlling a particular trait located?

Answer: Each gene on a chromosome has a corresponding gene controlling the same trait on the same place on its partner chromosome.

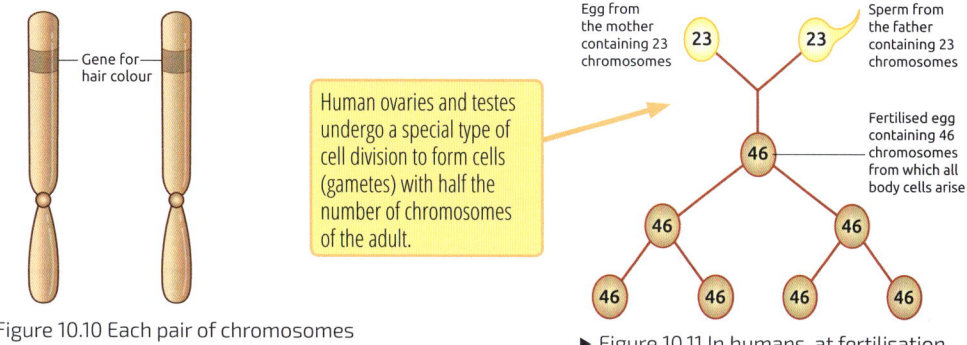

▶ Figure 10.10 Each pair of chromosomes carries genes for the same traits on the same locations.

▶ Figure 10.11 In humans, at fertilisation, the egg (23 chromosomes) and the sperm (23 chromosomes) fuse to form a zygote (46 chromosomes).

10.5 Mendelian inheritance

Inheritance is the way traits are passed from parents to offspring.

Gregor Mendel, Figure 10.12, discovered that:
- Cells of an organism carry two factors for the control of each trait.
- Gametes carry only one factor for each trait.
- When gametes fuse during fertilisation, the factors are in pairs again in the zygote.
- When an individual develops from the zygote, all the cells in the body have two factors controlling each trait, Figure 10.11.

What Mendel called 'factors' are now called 'genes'.

▶ Figure 10.12 Gregor Mendel – father of genetics (1822–1884)

10.6 Mendelian crosses

Terms used in genetics:
- **Expressed**: This is when the protein that a gene is controlling is actually made, e.g. when the gene for blue eyes causes the pigment in blue eyes to be made.
- **Genotype**: The genes that an organism possesses, e.g. two genes for brown eyes.
- **Phenotype**: The traits that can be seen in the organism, e.g. brown eyes.

47

- **Dominant**: A gene that prevents another gene from working (being expressed), e.g. the gene for brown eyes prevents the gene for blue eyes from working.
- **Recessive**: A gene that is prevented from being expressed (working), e.g. the gene for blue eyes is prevented from working by the gene for brown eyes.

Also note:
- **Letters** are used in genetic crosses to denote **genes**.
- **Dominant** genes are given **capital** letters.
- **Recessive** genes are given the **small** version of the letter that is given to the dominant trait.
- For example: if brown eyes are dominant to blue eyes, then:

  B = brown eyes and **b** = blue eyes.

Examples of genetic crosses

Example 1

In cats, coat colour is controlled by two different genes. The gene for black coat (B) is dominant to the gene for white coat (b). What colour coats would be possible in a cross between two cats if the mother has black coat (BB) and the father has white coat (bb)?

	Mother	X	Father
Phenotype	Black coat	X	White coat
Genotype	BB	X	bb
Gametes	B	X	b
Possible genotypes of kittens:		Bb	
Possible phenotypes of kittens:		black coat	

▶ Table 10.2 A genetic cross

Therefore, the only possible coat colour is black.

> **Exam Tip!**
> Practise genetic crosses using each of the steps used in the two examples here.

Example 2

In cats, coat colour is controlled by two different genes. The gene for black coat (B) is dominant to the gene for white coat (b). What colour coats would be possible in a cross between two cats if the mother has black coat (Bb) and the father has black coat (Bb)?

		Mother	X	Father
Phenotype		Black coat	X	Black coat
Genotype		Bb	X	Bb
Gametes		B or b	X	B or b
Possible genotypes of kittens:	BB	Bb	Bb	bb
Possible phenotypes of kittens:	Black coat	Black coat	Black coat	White coat

▶ Table 10.3 A genetic cross

Therefore, the possible coat colours are black coat and white coat.

▶▶ Experiment 10.1

To extract DNA from kiwi fruit

www.folensonline.ie/for-students

1. Extraction solution: salt, washing up liquid and water

2. Full kiwi peeled and mashed

3. Kiwi added to the extraction solution

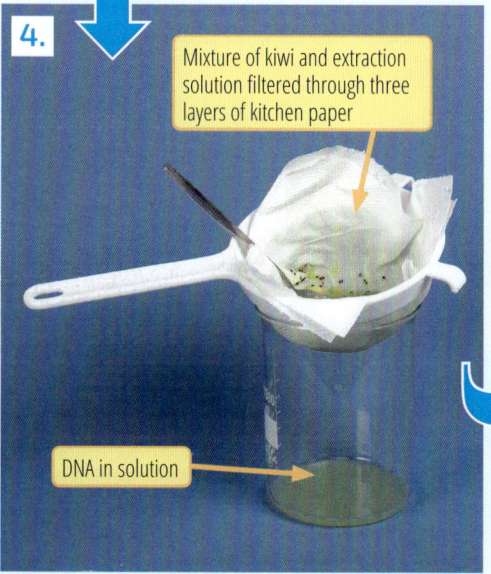

4. Mixture of kiwi and extraction solution filtered through three layers of kitchen paper

DNA in solution

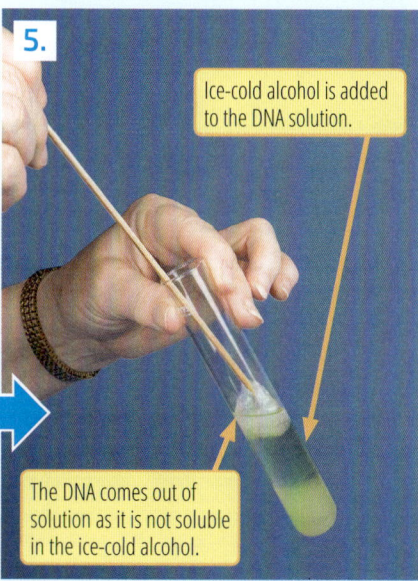

5. Ice-cold alcohol is added to the DNA solution.

The DNA comes out of solution as it is not soluble in the ice-cold alcohol.

10 Inheritance and variation

49

▶▶ Science Self-Assessment

Now I am able to:	🟢	🟠	🔴
Explain sexual and asexual reproduction			
Explain what is meant by *variation*			
Describe DNA, chromosomes and genes			
Explain Mendelian inheritance and carry out a simple genetic cross			
Extract DNA from kiwi fruit			

11 Evolution

The Biological World strand

▶▶ **Main topics in this chapter:**
- Evolution
- Natural selection
- Diversity of living things
- The difference between variation and biodiversity

11.1 Evolution

Evolution is the gradual changes that occur in a species over many generations.

Small-scale evolution involves changes over a **few** generations but no new species develops.

A **species** is a group of organisms that can breed with each other and produce fertile offspring.

Fertile means that an organism is capable of producing young.

The peppered moth is an example of small-scale evolution.
- The peppered moth flies at night but settles on trees during the day.
- Figure 11.1 shows how the peppered version of the moth was naturally camouflaged against the lichens on the trees.
- However, the black version of the moth was easily picked off by predators. Therefore, peppered moths were more plentiful.
- Figure 11.2 shows that pollution caused the barks of trees to turn black. As a result, the black moth was now camouflaged, and the peppered moth was obvious to predators and was eaten. Therefore, black moths became more plentiful.
- When the pollution was cleaned up, the barks of the trees recovered their normal, light colour.
- The peppered moth was again better camouflaged than the black moth. The peppered moth became more plentiful. The black moth, once again, became rare.

Lichens are an example of **mutualism** between an alga and a fungus. (See Chapter 13 for more information about mutualism.)

▶ Figure 11.1 The black version of the moth is easily seen against the lichens.

Lichens on the bark of the tree are a very light colour.

The peppered moth is well camouflaged and is not seen by predators.

The black moth is easily seen and is eaten by birds.

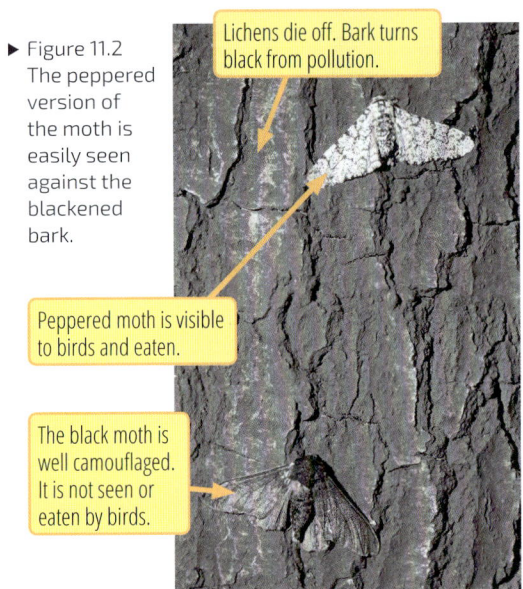

▶ Figure 11.2 The peppered version of the moth is easily seen against the blackened bark.

Lichens die off. Bark turns black from pollution.

Peppered moth is visible to birds and eaten.

The black moth is well camouflaged. It is not seen or eaten by birds.

So, it is the type of moth that is *best adapted to its environment* that will survive to breed and pass its genes on to its offspring.

This is known as **natural selection**.

> **Natural selection** is the way that organisms that are best adapted to their environment survive and live long enough to breed.

Organisms that are not well adapted to their environment become extinct, e.g. the black version of the peppered moth is facing extinction because of unsuitable habitats.

Natural selection is also known as 'survival of the fittest'.

> **Extinction** means that a particular species no longer exists.

Large-scale evolution involves changes over **many** generations and a **new species** develops, e.g. the modern horse.

In the evolution of the horse *great changes occurred in the DNA* to give rise to new species, Figure 11.3.

Horse evolution	Time period	Height
 Modern horse	1 million years ago	1.6 metres
 Pliohippus	10 million years ago	1.3 metres
 Miohippus	35 million years ago	1.0 metres
 Mesohippus	40 million years ago	0.6 metres

▶ Figure 11.3 The evolution of the horse

11.2 Charles Darwin

▶ Figure 11.4 Charles Darwin (1809-1882)

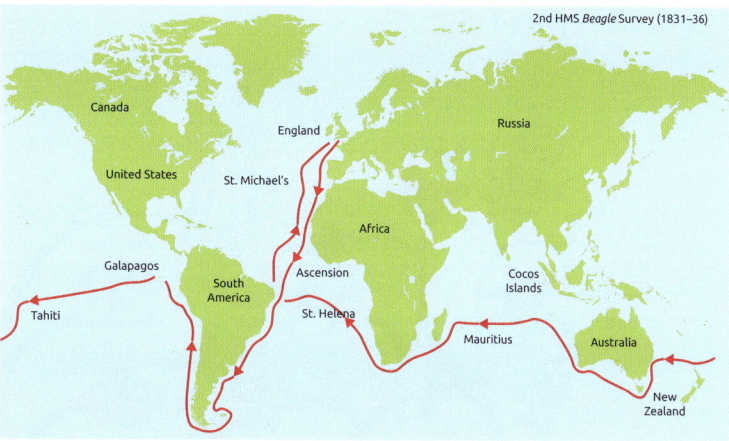

▶ Figure 11.5 Charles Darwin's journey on HMS *Beagle* (1831-6)

During his time in the Galapagos Islands off the coast of Ecuador, Figure 11.5, Charles Darwin closely studied the various forms of finches found there.

Darwin's finches very clearly illustrate natural selection:

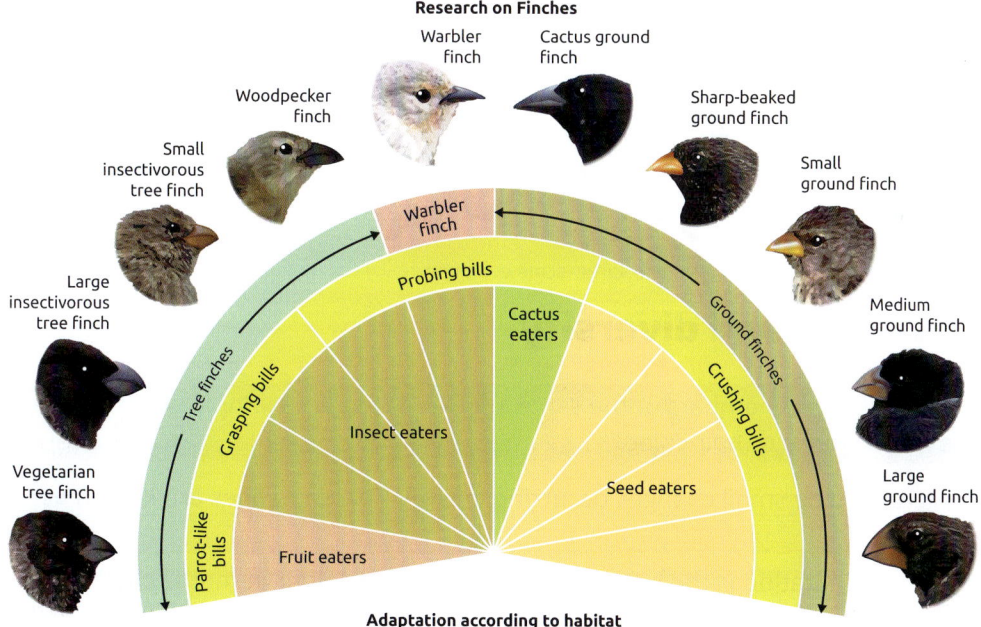

▶ Figure 11.6 Ten of Darwin's thirteen finches

- There are 21 islands in the Galapagos Islands.
- Charles Darwin noticed that the finches on the various islands were very similar to one another but differed greatly in one feature – their beaks!
- Darwin also noticed that the finches on each island had beaks that were perfectly designed to feed on the particular food source of the island, Figure 11.6.

53

Darwin said that all living things had a common ancestor. He also suggested that they did not follow a straight line of descent but that there were numerous branches in the Tree of Life, Figure 11.7.

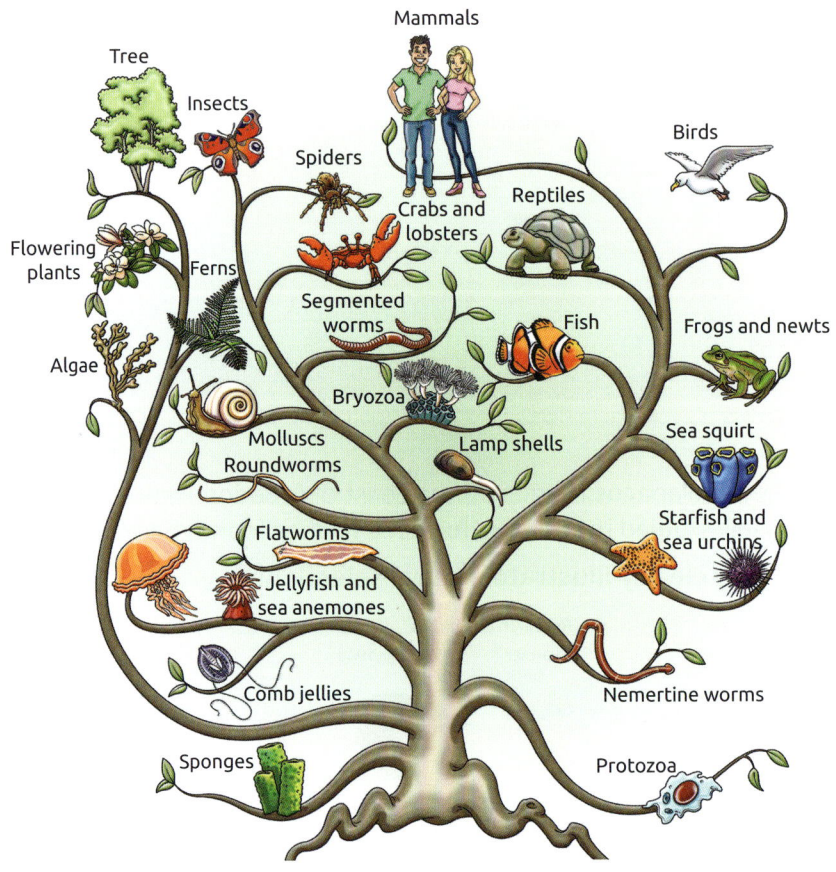

▶ Figure 11.7 The Tree of Life: large-scale evolution

11.3 Variation and diversity

Variation is the way members of the same species differ. An example of variation in humans is eye colour or hair colour.

Variation is caused by small changes occurring in DNA. These changes are known as **mutations**.

An example of a mutation is the gene (DNA) for peppered colour in moths **changing** to a gene for black colour; or the gene for brown eyes changing to a gene for blue eyes.

A **mutation** is a change in DNA.

Note: A mutation can be bad and leave an organism less well adapted to its environment – or a mutation can be good and leave an organism better adapted to its environment.

The word *diversity* means differences. In biology, the word means all the different species of living organisms on Earth and is more commonly referred to as *biodiversity*.

> Exam Tip!
>
> Remember: **Variation** is about **one** species only. **Diversity** is about **all** species.

> **Biodiversity** is the word used to describe the vast number of different species living on Earth.

▶ Figure 11.8 Biodiversity

How does natural selection explain diversity?

- Natural selection is the way that living organisms that are best adapted to their habitat are the ones that will survive and breed to pass on their traits to their offspring.
- There are so many different habitats on Earth that organisms are required to have very different traits to survive in them.
- Therefore, organisms have evolved very differently from each other in order to be able to survive in the very different habitats in which they live.

In fact, it is when a habitat changes drastically, e.g. large-scale felling of trees, that organisms are no longer well adapted to their environment and they become **extinct**.

▶▶ Science Self-Assessment

Now I am able to:	🟢	🟠	🔴
Outline evolution by natural selection			
Describe how natural selection affects which colour of peppered moth survives			
Explain what is meant by *variation* and *diversity*			
Describe how natural selection explains the diversity of living organisms			

12 Human health

The Biological World strand

Main topics in this chapter:
- Inherited factors in human health
- Environmental factors in human health
- Effects of nutrition on human health
- Effects of lifestyle choices on human health

12.1 What is meant by human health?

Human health is not just the absence of disease. It is a state of complete physical, mental and social wellbeing.

12.2 Human health and inherited factors

Every process that goes on in the body is controlled by chemicals such as enzymes and hormones.

There is a gene controlling the making of each enzyme and each hormone in the body (Chapter 10).

Therefore, the ability to produce enzymes and hormones is inherited.

Enzymes are proteins that speed up chemical reactions, e.g. digestion and respiration.

Hormones are proteins that bring about responses in the body, e.g. growth and development of sex characteristics.

If the gene for the production of a particular hormone or enzyme is not working properly (because of damaged DNA), then that enzyme or hormone will not be produced by the body. This can lead to very serious health issues such as cystic fibrosis or haemophilia, Table 12.1.

Inherited disorders	Mutated gene	Symptoms	Treatment
Cystic fibrosis	The gene that makes a protein to control salt coming out of cells	Respiratory system can become clogged with mucus	Physiotherapy Antibiotics
Haemophilia	The gene for making clotting factor 8	Excessive bleeding	Injections of factor 8

▶ Table 12.1 Some inherited human disorders

Table 12.2 shows how cystic fibrosis is inherited.

Inheritance of cystic fibrosis (cf) N = Normal gene (dominant) n = cf gene (recessive)

Parents' phenotype	Normal mother	X	Normal father
Parents' genotype	Nn	X	Nn
Gametes' genotype	N, n	X	N, n
Children genotype	NN	Nn	Nn	nn
Children phenotype	Normal	Normal (carrier)	Normal (carrier)	Cystic fibrosis

▶ Table 12.2 Inheritance of cystic fibrosis

In this particular case, Table 12.2, both parents are carriers of the cf gene but do not suffer from the disorder. However, as can be seen from the cross, there is a 1 in 4 chance that a child could inherit two cf genes.

Genetic crosses are explained in Chapter 10.

Less serious health issues can result from the lack of a particular enzyme. For example, lactose intolerance is caused when the enzyme lactase is not produced by the body and, therefore, lactose sugar cannot be digested.

12.3 Human health and environmental factors

Nutrition

Nutrition is concerned with how an organism gets its food and what type of food it eats.

A balanced diet is required for health.

A balanced diet includes the correct amounts of:

- Protein
- Carbohydrate
- Fat
- Minerals
- Vitamins
- Water

The correct amounts of each food type depend on:

- Age
- Gender
- Activity

The benefits of eating well are:

- A lower risk of heart disease, cancer and diabetes
- Stronger muscles and bones
- A healthy body mass
- Feeling better (wellbeing)

The food pyramid shows the recommended number of servings to be eaten per day from each food group.

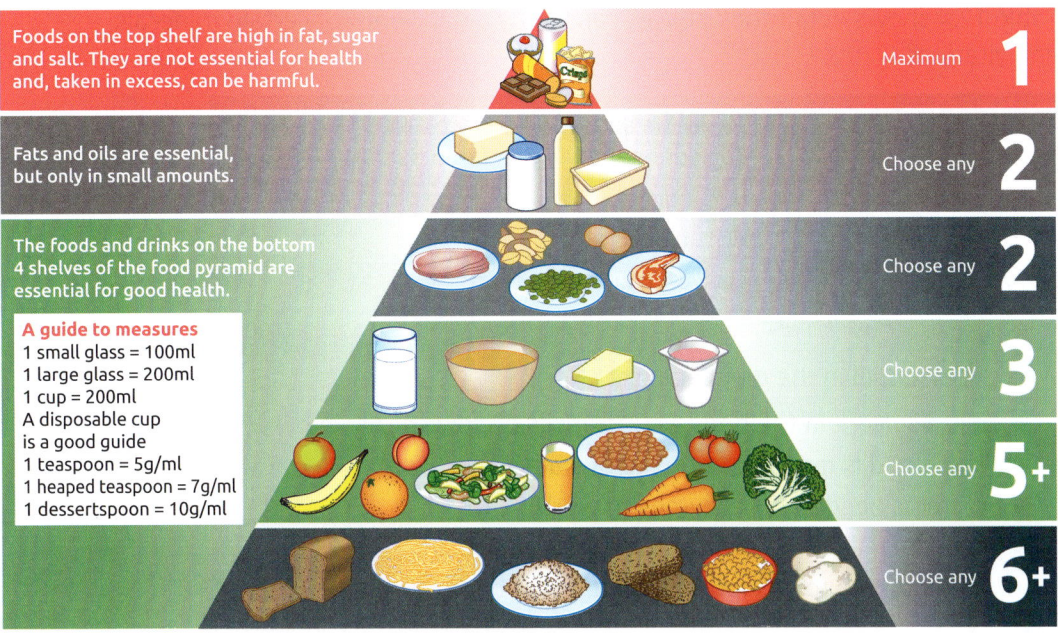

▶ Figure 12.1 The food pyramid helps you to follow a balanced diet.

Some information about the different food types is summarised in Table 12.3.

Food type	Healthy source	Function in body	Deficiency diseases
Protein	Lean meat, poultry, fish, eggs, beans, lentils	Growth Repair of tissue	
Carbohydrate Starch Fibre	Brown bread, pasta, rice, potatoes Fruit, vegetables, wholemeal cereal	Energy Persistalsis in the digestive system	
Fat	Vegetable oils, oily fish	Cell membranes	
Vitamins Vitamin C Vitamin D	Citrus fruits, kiwi, blackcurrants Sunlight, dairy foods, supplements	Making new cells Healthy bones, wellbeing	Scurvy Rickets
Minerals Calcium Iron	Dairy foods, tinned fish Red meat, green vegetables	Bones and teeth Part of haemoglobin	Osteoporosis Anaemia

▶ Table 12.3 Different food types and their sources and functions

Deficiency diseases are diseases caused by the lack of a particular food.

Table 12.4 shows details of diseases caused by a deficiency of certain minerals and vitamins.

Deficiency disease	Result of deficiency
Scurvy	Lack of healing in damaged tissue
Rickets	Soft bones
Osteoporosis	Brittle bones
Anaemia	Lack of iron in the blood

▶ Table 12.4 Results of deficiency diseases

Water is essential in the diet because:

- It is a solvent in the body – substances dissolve easily in it.
- The blood is mostly composed of water.
- Water is needed for enzymes to work.
- It helps maintain body temperature at 37° C.
- It helps flush toxins (poisons) out of the body.

Lifestyle choices

Lifestyle choices include the following:

- Eating a balanced diet – or not eating a balanced diet
- Avoiding alcohol, drinking alcohol in moderation – or drinking too much alcohol
- Not smoking – or smoking cigarettes, Figure 12.2
- Not taking illegal drugs – or taking illegal drugs
- Being active and taking part in exercise – or being inactive

Being active for young people means taking part in moderate to vigorous activity for a minimum of 60 minutes each day, Figure 12.3.

▶ Figure 12.2 Easier to say 'no' now rather than trying to say 'no' later

▶ Figure 12.3 Suitable activities to help young people to keep healthy

12.4 Food tests

The following tests may be carried out on food samples to see what particular food type they contain.

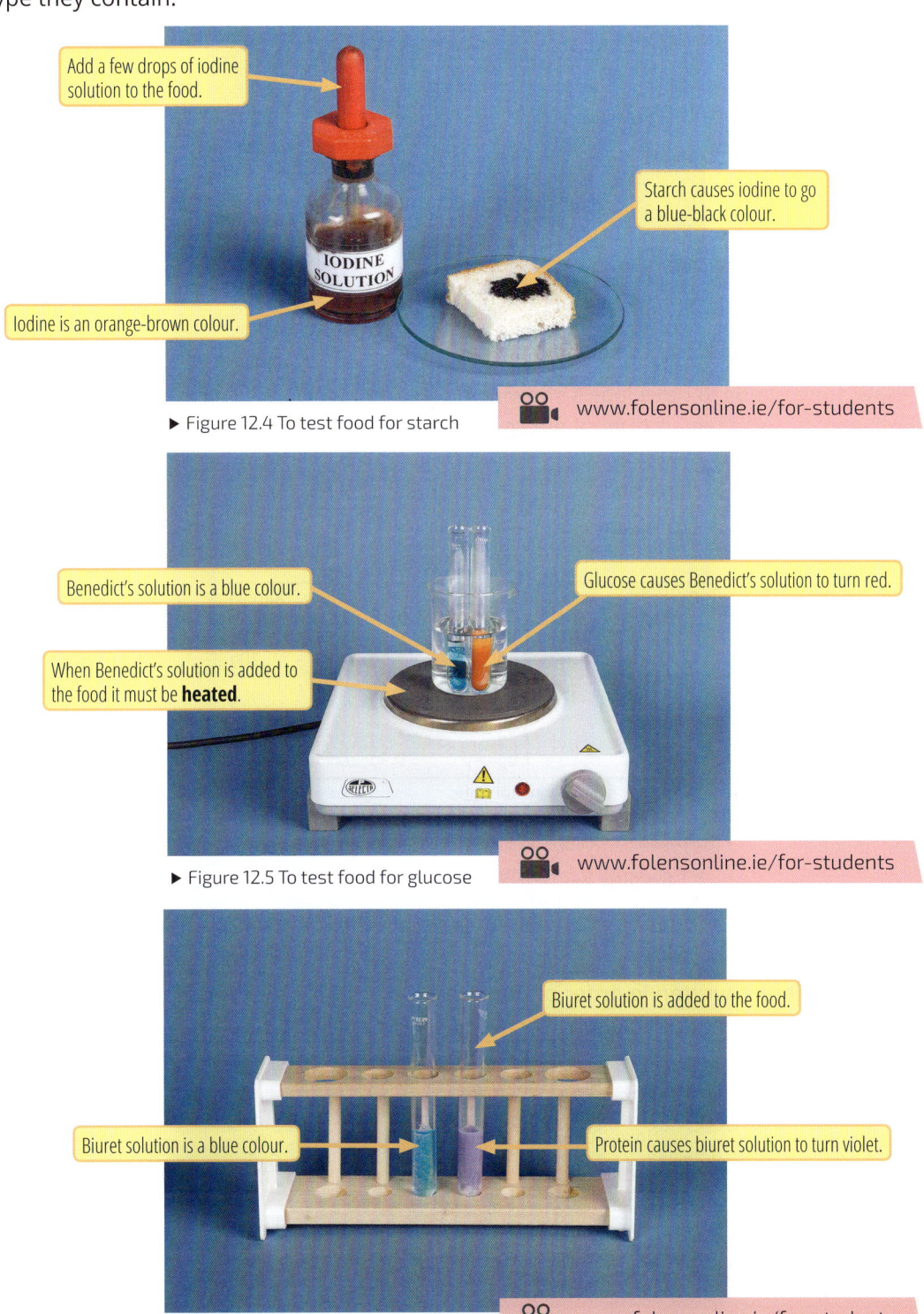

▶ Figure 12.4 To test food for starch

▶ Figure 12.5 To test food for glucose

▶ Figure 12.6 To test food for protein

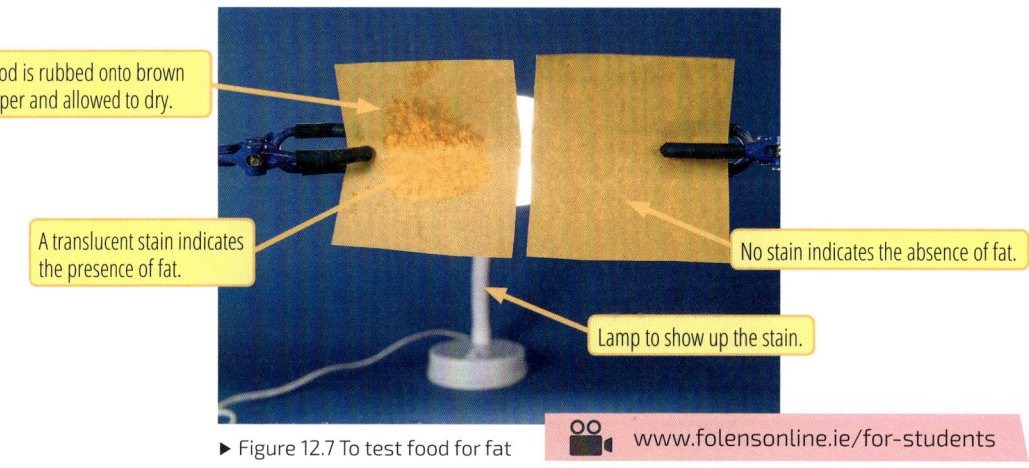

▶ Figure 12.7 To test food for fat

www.folensonline.ie/for-students

12.5 Labelling on food

By law, food needs to have labels showing its nutritional value, i.e. the amount of each food type in it and the amount of energy it contains, Figure 12.8.

Nutrition

Typical values	100g contains	Each slice (typically 44g) contains	% RI*	RI* for an average adult
Energy	985kj 235kcal	435kj 105kcal	5%	8400kj 2000kcal
Fat	1.5g	0.7g	1%	70g
of which saturates	0.3g	0.1g	1%	20g
Carbohydrate	45.5g	20.0g		
of which sugars	3.8g	1.7g	2%	90g
Fibre	2.8g	1.2g		
Protein	7.7g	3.4g		
Salt	1.0g	0.4g	7%	6g

This pack contains 16 servings
* Reference intake of an average adult (8400kj/2000kcal)

▶ Figure 12.8 Nutrition label on a loaf of white bread

In order to know what foods are in any prepared foods that you buy, you will need to read the food label, Figure 12.9.

Each ingredient is written in order of decreasing mass. In this example, after water, carrots are in the greatest amount and parsley is in the least amount.

INGREDIENTS

Water, Carrots, Onions, Red Lentils (4.5%), Potatoes, Cauliflower, Leeks, Peas, Cornflower, **Wheat**flour, Cream (**milk**), Yeast Extract, Concentrated Tomato Paste, Garlic, Sugar, **Celery** Seed, Sunflower Oil, Herb and Spice, White Pepper, Parsley

ALLERGY ADVICE

For allergens, see ingredients in **bold**

▶ Figure 12.9 Ingredients in a can of soup

▶▶ Science Self-Assessment

Now I am able to:	🟢	🟠	🔴
Explain some inherited factors in human health			
Explain some environmental factors in human health			
Describe the part played by the various food types in human health			
Explain how lifestyle choices can influence health			
Describe how to test food for the presence of different food types			

13 Microorganisms

The Biological World strand

Main topics in this chapter:
- What are microorganisms?
- Mutualism between humans and microorganisms
- Importance of microorganisms in human health

13.1 Microorganisms

Microorganisms are very tiny living things that usually can only be seen using a microscope.

Microorganisms, Figure 13.1, include:
- Viruses
- Bacteria
- Microscopic fungi

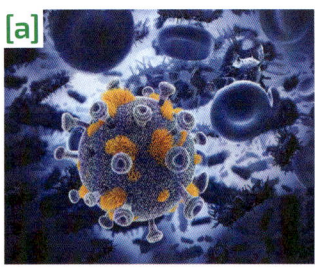
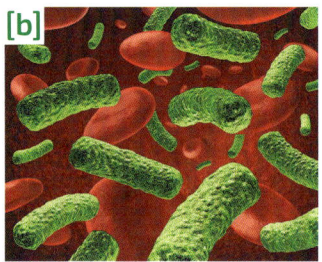

▶ Figure 13.1 (a) Virus, (b) bacteria and (c) fungus

13.2 Viruses

Human diseases caused by viruses:
- Colds
- Influenza (flu)
- Chicken pox

Viruses are not affected by antibiotics, Figure 13.2.

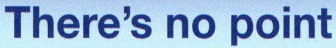

▶ Figure 13.2 Antibiotics cannot fight a virus.

Our greatest weapon against viral infections is vaccination.

> **Vaccination** is when a harmless version of a disease is introduced into a person in order to stimulate the production of antibodies and white blood cells against the disease.

After a person is vacccinated, if they come into contact with the actual disease, their body will be able to fight it.

Useful viruses:

- Some viruses kill bacteria that are harmful to humans.
- Viruses are used in genetic engineering, e.g. engineering bacteria to produce substances such as insulin (to treat diabetes).

13.3 Bacteria

Human diseases caused by bacteria:

- Cholera
- Tetanus
- Tuberculosis (TB)
- Tooth decay
- Strep throat
- Food poisoning

> **Exam Tip!**
> There is no need to know all the diseases listed! Make sure you know two diseases caused by each of the different types of microorganisms.

There are trillions of **useful** bacteria in the human gut (intestines).

- These bacteria are mainly found in the colon (large intestine).
- They are described as **mutualistic bacteria** because they benefit from us and we benefit from them, Figure 13.3.

> **Mutualism** is when two organisms live in close association and both of them benefit from the arrangement.

Benefits of mutualistic bacteria in the human gut:

- They help in the digestion of some foods.
- They produce vitamin B (for energy) and vitamin K (for clotting of blood).
- They help prevent harmful bacteria from surviving in the gut.
- They boost our immune system by keeping harmful populations of bacteria under control.

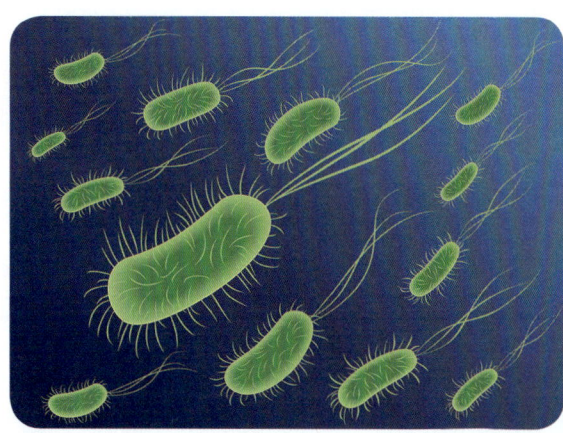

▶ Figure 13.3 Mutualism in the human gut

Probiotics

Probiotics are bacteria that improve human health.

Probiotics are taken as food supplements in the form of yogurts, drinks or capsules.
Other postive uses of bacteria:
- Break down dead matter (decomposers)
- Help recycle carbon and nitrogen
- Are involved in the production of antibiotics

13.4 Fungi

Human diseases caused by fungi:
- Athlete's foot
- Ringworm

Useful fungi:
- Fungi, along with bacteria, help with the recycling of carbon and nitrogen in the carbon cycle and the nitrogen cycle (Chapter 38).
- Fungi provide powerful medicines such as medicines to control cholesterol and medicines to help prevent rejection of transplanted organs (e.g. transplanted liver, heart and kidneys).
- Most antibiotics are based on chemicals that are produced by fungi.

13.5 Food spoilage and avoiding it

Food spoilage is caused by bacteria and fungi.

Protecting food from bacteria and fungi is a very important factor in human health.

Table 13.1 summarises ways of preserving food from attack by bacteria and fungi.

Preservation method	How it works
Refrigeration	The temperature is too low for microorganisms to grow
Freezing	There is no water available to the microorganisms so they cannot work
Pickling	The acidity of the vinegar destroys microorganisms
Salting and syrup	The salt or sugar draws water out of the microorganisms and they die
Drying	There is no water so microorganisms cannot survive
Pasteurisation	The food (e.g. milk/orange juice) is heated to a high temperature in order to kill microorganisms

▶ Table 13.1 Methods of food preservation

▶▶ Experiment 13.1

To show that microorganisms are present in air

- Two sterile agar plates are placed on a bench.
- The lid of one plate is removed and left on the bench, Figure 13.4.
- The uncovered plate is exposed to the air for about 5 minutes.
- The lid is put back on the petri dish and sealed with tape.
- The second petri dish is left unopened and sealed with tape. This is the control.
- The plates are labelled 'exposed' and 'control'.
- Both plates are placed upside down in an incubator at room temperature (20 °C) for 48 hours.

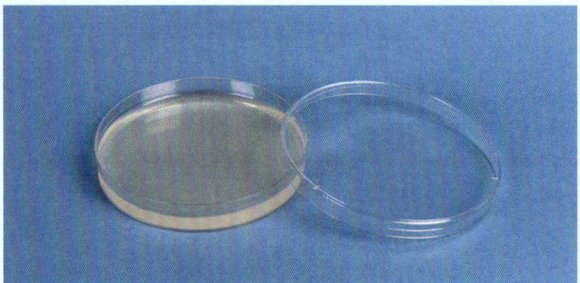

▶ Figure 13.4 Agar plates

Result

The exposed plate has bacterial and fungal colonies growing on it, Figure 13.5. The control, the unopened plate, will have no growth on it.

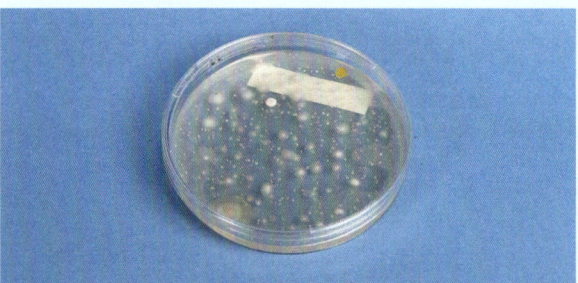

▶ Figure 13.5 Colonies of bacteria and fungi growing on the exposed plate

Safety

After the experiment, these plates will be placed in an incubator or autoclave at 120 °C for at least 30 minutes. They may then be placed in the general waste bin.

This is carried out because some of the microorganisms that grow on the plates may be disease-causing.

 www.folensonline.ie/for-students

▶▶ Science Self-Assessment

Now I am able to:	🟢	🟠	🔴
Explain the word *microorganisms*			
Explain how bacteria, fungi and viruses can have negative effects on human health			
Explain how bacteria, fungi and viruses can have positive effects on human health			
Discuss the benefits of mutualistic bacteria in the human gut			
Carry out an experiment to show that there are microorganisms in the air			

14
Habitat study

The Biological World strand

Main topics in this chapter:
- What is ecology?
- How to conduct a habitat study
- How to investigate adaptation, competition and interdependence in a specific habitat

14.1 What is ecology?

Ecology is the branch of biology that studies the relationships of organisms to one another and to their physical surroundings (their environment).

Why is ecology important?
- It provides knowledge about the way the Earth works.
- It provides evidence of the interdependence between people and the natural world.
- A better understanding of ecological systems will allow scientists to predict the consequences of human activity on the environment.
- It gives scientists a systematic way to monitor the effect of industrial developments on local habitats.

Some aspects of ecology are summarised in Figure 14.1.

▶ Figure 14.1 Ecology

14.2 Habitat

A **habitat** is the natural environment where a particular organism **lives**.

Every organism has a unique habitat that provides for its needs.
- The habitat is where organisms get food, water and shelter.
- Organisms also breed in their natural habitat.

The climate of a habitat, the food available in the habitat, and competition from other species – these are some of the factors that determine *whether a species will survive or not*. Some examples of habitats are shown in Figure 14.2.

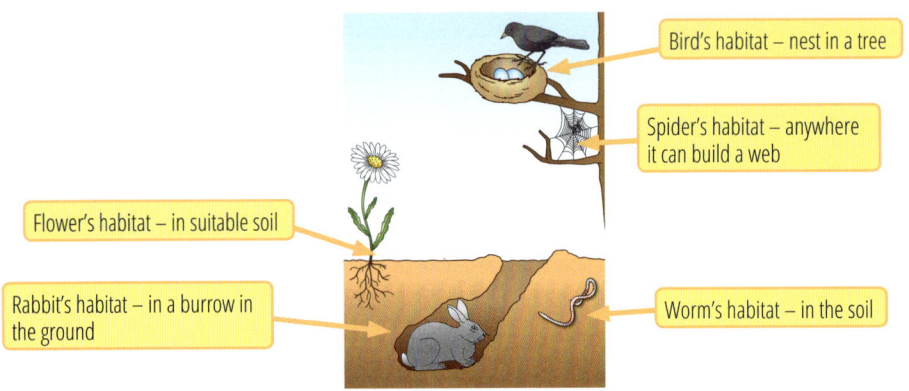

▶ Figure 14.2 Some examples of habitats

14.3 Community

- An ecological community is a group of interacting species living in the same place, Figure 14.3.

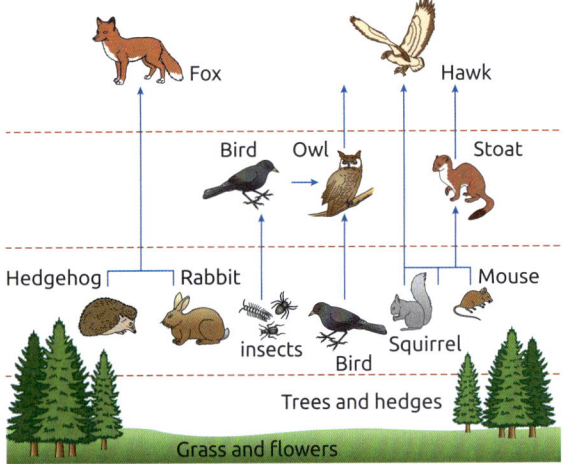

▶ Figure 14.3 A community

A **community** is all the animals and plants that live in a particular area (habitat) and share the resources in that area.

The ecological **niche** of a species is its role in a community, how it fits in and how it interacts with other organisms.

- A community is bound together by the effects that species have on one another.
- Within a community, organisms all have a unique niche, or role, they fill to keep the community healthy.

Examples of niches:

- A rabbit's niche is that it eats grass and it may be eaten by the fox.
- A stoat's niche is that it feeds on mice and it may be eaten by a hawk.

14.4 Steps in a habitat study

Step 1: Which habitat?

We are studying a grassland – it could be school field, park or garden.

Step 2: How much of the habitat?

You only need to study a section of the habitat – perhaps 100 m x 20 m.

Step 3: Measure the abiotic factors affecting the habitat

> **Abiotic factors** are the non-living influences that affect organisms in their habitats, e.g. air temperature, soil temperature, soil pH and light intensity.

Some abiotic factors in a habitat are summarised in Table 14.1.

Factor	Apparatus	Method
Air temperature	Thermometer/ temperature sensor	Place a thermometer or temperature sensor in the air.
Soil temperature	Soil thermometer/ temperature probe	Place a soil thermometer or a temperature probe in the soil.
Soil pH	Universal indicator/ pH sensor	Collect some soil and test with universal indicator or a pH sensor.
Light intensity	Light meter/light sensor	Expose a light meter and take the reading.

▶ Table 14.1 Some abiotic factors in a habitat

Step 4: Identify the producers

> **Producers** are green plants that can make their own food using the process of photosynthesis.

Producers may be identified using a key for the particular habitat in which they are found.

A key asks questions about the organism that you want to identify. By answering the questions, you are led to the identity of the organism.

For example, you could use the questions in the key in Figure 14.4 to name the trees from which the leaves in Figure 14.5 come.

1. Are the leaves single (not divided into leaflets)?   Go to 2
   Are the leaves divided into leaflets?   Go to 4
2. Are the leaves divided into many lobes (rounded parts)?   Oak
   Are the leaves not divided into many lobes?   Go to 3
3. Is the edge of the leaf smooth?   Beech
   Is the edge of the leaf spiked?   Holly
4. Are the leaves arranged like the fingers of a hand?   Horse chestnut
   Are the leaves arranged in pairs?   Ash

▶ Figure 14.4 Key to identify trees

 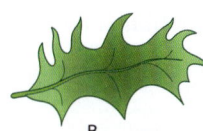   

A   B   C   D   E

▶ Figure 14.5 Leaves of trees to be identified

Step 5: Identify the consumers

> **Consumers** are organisms (mostly animals) that feed on other organisms for their food.

- Some consumers eat plants only – **herbivores**.
- Some consumers eat animals only – **carnivores**.
- Some consumers eat both animals and plants – **omnivores**.

Consumers may also be identified using an appropriate key. Table 14.2 shows the ways of catching animals in the field in order to identify them.

Apparatus	How it is used	Used to collect	
(1) Pooter	One tube is placed over the organism and you suck through the second tube with gauze (prevents you swallowing the organism).	Small insects (such as greenfly) and spiders.	Suck in through this tube. The insect is pulled in through this tube. Gauze. Insect.
(2) Beating tray	A white sheet/tray is held under the leaves of a tree or shrub. The branches are shaken or beaten with a stick (this dislodges the animals and they fall onto the sheet).	Insects and small animals that live on the leaves of shrubs and trees.	Beating stick. Sheet.
(3) Pitfall trap	A jar is sunk into the ground (the mouth of the jar must be level with the soil). A flat stone supported by small stones forms a lid (the lid prevents rain getting in).	Animals, e.g. ground beetles, that walk along the surface of the ground. Useful to compare animals that are out at night with those around during the day.	Flat stone. Stone. Jar. Soil.

▶ Table 14.2 Methods of collecting animals

Step 6: Identify the decomposers

Decomposers may be identified using a key for the particular habitat being studied.

> **Decomposers** are organisms that break down dead plants and animals into materials that go back into the soil.

Step 7: Adaptation

Adaptation is the way an organism is suited to survive in its environment.

Table 14.3 shows some organisms and how they are adapted to their particular environment.

Habitat	Plant adaptation and benefit	Animal adaptation and benefit
Hedgerow	**Nettles** have stinging hairs to prevent them being eaten by certain animals	**Peacock butterflies** have long tube-like mouthparts that allow them to suck nectar.
Grassland	**Buttercups** have bright yellow petals to attract insect pollinators.	**Earthworms** are a dark colour for camouflage.
Woodland	**Primroses** flower early in the spring and get more light, before the leaves come out on the trees.	**Sparrowhawks** have large feet with needle-sharp talons for catching their prey.
Rocky sea shore	**Seaweeds** produce a slimy mucilage that prevents them drying out at low tide.	**Limpets** have a muscular foot to anchor themselves to the rocks and prevent them from being swept away.
Pond	**Common water-crowfoot** has two types of leaf: one for under water, the other for above.	**Dragonflies** have huge eyes and keen eyesight to identify their insect prey.

▶ Table 14.3 Examples of plant and animal adaptations in different habitats

Step 8: Competition

Competition is the interaction between members of the same species (intraspecific) or members of different species (interspecific) for resources that are in short or limited supply.

- Plants may compete for light, water and space.
- Animals may compete for food, shelter, mates and territory (e.g. grey squirrel and red squirrel).

[a]  [b]

▶ Figure 14.6 (a) Grey squirrel and (b) red squirrel

Although there is not great aggression between these two species, the grey squirrel is bigger and stronger than the red squirrel and is generally the winner when it comes to food and territory.

Red squirrels usually disappear from woodland areas within 20 years of the arrival of the grey squirrel.

An example of competition between two plants is grass and daisies – both will be trying to get water from the ground.

Step 9: Interdependence

When we speak of interdependence in ecology, we are speaking of how one living organism is dependent on another.

> **Interdependence** is the way one thing relies on another.

Some examples of interdependence are shown in Figure 14.7.

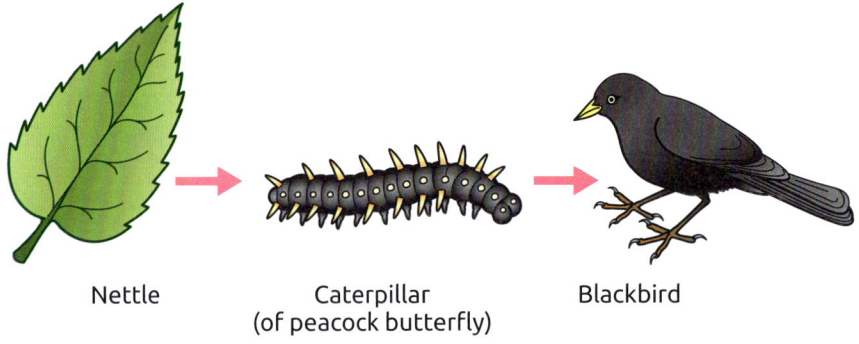

Nettle   Caterpillar   Blackbird
(of peacock butterfly)

▶ Figure 14.7 A food chain

Exam Tip!

Make sure you know **two** examples each of **adaptation**, **competition** and **interdependence** from the particular habitat that you studied.

- If the producer at the beginning of a food chain dies off, the rest of the organisms in the food chain are in danger of dying off because of a lack of food.
- Animals depend on plants for their food: either directly, by feeding on the plant; or indirectly, by feeding on an animal that feeds on the plant.
- Some plants depend on animals to pollinate their flowers: animals carry pollen from one flower to another for sexual reproduction.
- Some plants depend on animals to disperse their seeds.
- The control of one population of animals may be dependent on the predation by another population of animals. For example, foxes keep rabbit numbers under control by catching and killing them for food.

▶▶ Experiment 14.1

To investigate the frequency of a particular plant species in a habitat

Frequency is the percentage chance of finding a particular organism in one throw of a quadrat.

A **quadrat** is an open square of wood, usually 50 cm square, i.e. 0.5 m × 0.5 m = 0.25 m².

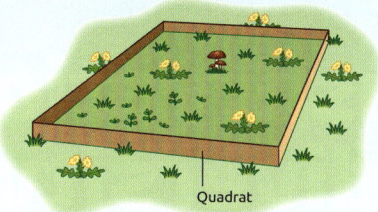

▶ Figure 14.8 A quadrat

- The species to be counted is chosen and identified.
- A pencil is thrown randomly over the shoulder.
- A quadrat is placed where the pencil lands.
- If the plant is in the quadrat, a tick is placed under quadrat 1 in the table of results, Table 14.4.
- If the plant is not in the quadrat, the box under quadrat 1 in the table of results remains empty.
- The quadrat is placed randomly, as above, ten times.
- The presence/absence of the plant is recorded under each quadrat number.
- The frequency of the plant is calculated as below.

Plant	Quadrat number										Frequency = $\frac{\text{Total}}{10}$	Per cent frequency = $\frac{\text{Total}}{10} \times 100$
	1	2	3	4	5	6	7	8	9	10		

▶ Table 14.4 This type of table may be used to record the results of a quadrat survey.

▶▶ Science Self-Assessment

Now I am able to:	🟢	🟠	🔴
Explain the term *ecology*			
Conduct a habitat study			
Explain the terms *producer*, *consumer*, *decomposer*, *adaptation*, *competition* and *interdependence*			
Give two examples of each of the above			

15 Conservation of biodiversity

The Biological World strand

Main topics in this chapter:
- What is an ecosystem?
- How energy and matter flow through ecosystems
- Benefits people get from ecosystems
- Ecological biodiversity and how humans can conserve it
- How humans can contribute to global food production

15.1 What is an ecosystem?

An **ecosystem** is a community of organisms that interact with each other and are affected by the abiotic, biotic, climatic and edaphic factors surrounding them.

The size of an ecosystem can vary enormously:
- The bark of a tree or an entire rain forest
- A pond or an ocean
- 1 m of a hedgerow or all the hedgerows in Ireland
- The entire planet Earth!

Usually, when we are studying an ecosystem, it is on a small scale, e.g. a school garden, a small area within a woodland, or a short width of rocky sea shore.

Table 15.1 shows the factors that are usually measured when an ecosystem is being studied.

Factor	Meaning	Examples
Abiotic	Non-living	Temperature, pH, wind speed, light intensity
Biotic	Living	Predation, competition, disease
Climatic	Weather over a long period	Rainfall, sunlight, temperature
Edaphic	To do with the soil	Type of soil, moisture content of soil, pH of soil

▶ Table 15.1 Factors affecting ecosystems

15.2 Energy flow in an ecosystem

The energy needed for an ecosystem to function comes mostly from the **Sun,** Figure 15.1.

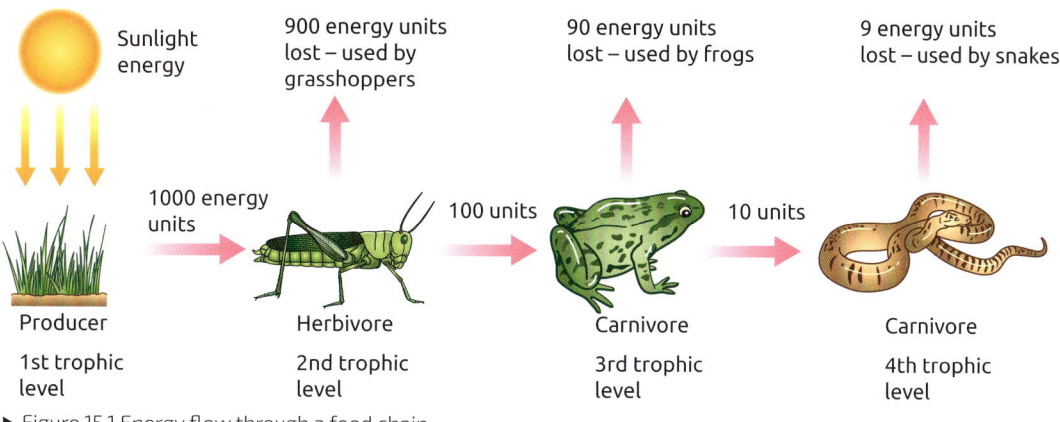

▶ Figure 15.1 Energy flow through a food chain

All the organisms in an ecosystem that belong to the same species are referred to as a **population** of those organisms, e.g. all the foxes or all the oak trees.
All the different populations together in an ecosystem are referred to as a **community**.

A **trophic** level is the position an organism occupies in a food chain.

Light energy is trapped for the ecosystem during the process of **photosynthesis** (Chapter 8).

All the other living organisms in an ecosystem depend on the producers for energy. In this way:

- **Producers** get their energy from the Sun by photosynthesis.
- **Primary consumers** get their energy from producers by eating them.
- **Secondary consumers** get their energy from primary consumers by eating them.
- **Tertiary consumers** get their energy from secondary consumers by eating them.
- **Decomposers** make sure that vital elements such as carbon, nitrogen and calcium are recycled.

Note: Figure 15.1 shows that a lot of energy is lost between one trophic level and the next. Only about 10 per cent of energy from one trophic level is actually gained by the next level. The other 90 per cent is used by the organisms for growth, reproduction, movement and some is also lost as heat.

15.3 Flow of matter in an ecosystem

Details of the cycling of **carbon** and **water** are covered in Chapter 38.
Nitrogen is also cycled through ecosystems.
Plants need nitrogen to convert the starch that is made during photosynthesis to protein.
Plants cannot take in nitrogen from the air. The nitrogen needs to be in the form of nitrate salts which are produced during the nitrogen cycle.

15.4 Benefits people get from ecosystems

Some of the benefits that people get from ecosystems are summarised in Table 15.2.

Benefit	Details
Food	- Seafood comes from oceanic ecosystems. - Many agricultural crops are derived from wild species of plants. - Pollination of crops is dependent on wild species of insects.
Water	- Trees take water from the soil and release this water into the air as vapour from their leaves. - Large forests contribute an enormous volume of water to clouds which in turn will release fresh water into rivers and lakes.
Medicines	Most medicines are derived from plants, e.g. - Morphine from the poppy - Aspirin from the willow - Medicines from animals include AZT, which is used to treat HIV. AZT comes from a marine sponge, Figure 15.2. - We get a powerful painkiller from the cone snail, Figure 15.3. ▶ Figure 15.2 Marine sponge ▶ Figure 15.3 Cone snail
Recreation	Forest walks, swimming facilities in oceans, lakes and rivers, sailing, etc.
Spiritual and aesthetic effects	Many ecosystems provide people with uplifting and healing benefits.

▶ Table 15.2 Benefits people get from ecosystems

15.5 Ecological biodiversity

Ecological biodiversity refers to all the different types of ecosystems on Earth.

Why is there a need for ecological biodiversity?

- Totally different organisms require totally different habitats. Therefore, there is a **need for very different types of ecosystems** to accommodate them all.
- Each species has a niche (Chapter 14) in its ecosystem that helps **keep the ecosystem healthy**.
- We are learning about new species every day and we are realising the role they play in ecosystems. By **studying and maintaining biodiversity** we help to keep our planet healthy.

Some examples of different types of ecosystems are summarised in Table 15.3 and shown in Figures 15.4 and 15.5.

Types of ecosystems			
Terrestrial		Aquatic	
Forest	Grassland	Salt water	Fresh water
• High density of living organisms • Teeming with life • Easily upset with small changes	• Grazing animals • Lots of insects • Lots of animals that feed on insects	• Covers 71 % of Earth's surface • 97 % of Earth's water • Large amounts of minerals dissolved in these waters	• Covers 0.8 % of Earth's surface • 0.009 % of Earth's water • Home to about 41 % of all fish species

▶ Table 15.3 Some examples of ecosystems

▶ Figure 15.4 Marine ecosystem – ocean

▶ Figure 15.5 Freshwater ecosystem – river

15.6 Conserving ecological biodiversity

Some examples of conservation are shown in Figures 15.6 and 15.7.

Conservation is the **wise management** of a natural resource to prevent exploitation, destruction or neglect.

▶ Figure 15.6 Replanting forests

▶ Figure 15.7 Young trees planted on the surface of an unused coal mine

Methods of ecological conservation

- Forest management/replanting
- Plans to prevent over-harvesting of algae (seaweed)
- Plans to prevent over-harvesting of fish
- Plans to prevent inappropriate hunting of wild game such as hunting of monkeys
- Global initiatives to stop emissions that cause dangerous climate change
- Mine rehabilitation, Figure 15.7
- Local plans to prevent pollution
- Reduced consumption of resources and problems associated with waste management by:
  - Reducing
  - Reusing
  - Recycling

> **Exam Tip!**
> When there is a long list of examples (such as the above), instead of trying to recall the entire list, choose **three** that are easy for you to remember.

15.7 Global food production

Scientists tell us that if we can improve food production methods and increase efficiency in distributing it, along with reducing food wastage, Figure 15.8, we can produce enough food for everyone in the world by 2050, Figure 15.9.

▶ Figure 15.8 Good food is being thrown away.

▶ Figure 15.9 Sustainable food production is needed.

We need to improve how we **grow**, **transport** and **consume** food, Table 15.4. Sustainability is covered in depth in Chapters 27 and 32.

Benefit	Details
Growing	• Fertilise land without leaching minerals into waterways • Breed good-quality seed • Reuse land • Employ cooperative measures where growers help each other
Transport	• Rely less on food from far away • Consume foods that are in season • Rely on local growers
Consumption	• Lessen our food portions • Eat healthier food • Stop wasting food – it is estimated that one-third of food produced globally is wasted

▶ Table 15.4 Improving sustainable food production

▶▶ Science Self-Assessment

Now I am able to:	🟢	🟠	🔴
Explain what an ecosystem is			
Describe how energy flows through an ecosystem			
Explain how people benefit from ecosystems			
Describe how humans can protect biodiversity			
Explain how humans can contribute to an improvement in sustainable global food production			

16 Materials

The Chemical World strand

Main topics in this chapter:
- Properties of the states of matter
- The particle theory
- Change of state: melting, evaporation, boiling and condensation

16.1 States of matter

The general word that scientists use for what materials are made of is **matter**.

> **Matter** is anything which occupies space and has mass.

- Every substance in the world around us exists either as a solid, a liquid or a gas.
- Wood is a solid, water is a liquid, and air is a gas.
- These three forms of matter are known as the **states of matter**.

> The three **states of matter** are solid, liquid and gas.

Properties of the states of matter

The word *property* means how a substance appears or behaves.

The properties of solids, liquids and gases are summarised in Table 16.1.

Solids	Liquids	Gases
Definite shape	No definite shape	No definite shape
Definite volume	Definite volume	No definite volume
Hard to compress	Hard to compress	Easy to compress
Do not flow	Flow easily	Diffuse to fill all available space

▶ Table 16.1 Summary of the properties of solids, liquids and gases

16.2 The particle theory

Scientists have developed a theory to explain the properties of solids, liquids and gases. The theory is called the **particle theory**.

- We imagine solids, liquids and gases being made up of tiny particles.
- The particles are so tiny that they can only be seen with special types of microscopes. These microscopes are much more powerful than the ones in your school laboratory.
- In a **solid** the particles are in fixed positions and do not move about but can vibrate, Figure 16.1.
- The particles are packed closely together. There are strong forces holding the particles together.
- Because the particles are in fixed positions, the solid has a definite shape.
- In a **liquid** the particles have more freedom of movement than in a solid.
- The particles in the liquid can slide over each other, Figure 16.2.
- This is why a liquid can flow.
- Since there is no regular arrangement of particles, the liquid has no shape of its own.
- A liquid always takes up the shape of its container.
- In a **gas** the particles are much farther apart than in a liquid or a solid, Figure 16.3.
- Particles in a gas can move quickly into all the space available.
- There are only very weak forces between the particles.

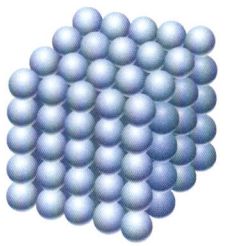

▶ Figure 16.1 The arrangement of particles in a solid: the particles are in fixed positions.

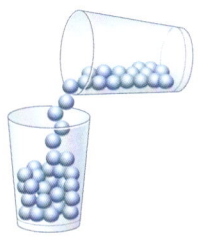

▶ Figure 16.2 The arrangement of particles in a liquid: the particles can slide over one another. Therefore, liquids can flow.

▶ Figure 16.3 The particles in a gas are farther apart than in a solid or liquid. They are continuously moving around in all the space available.

> **Exam Tip!**
> Make sure that you can distinguish between diagrams representing the arrangement of particles in solids, liquids and gases.

- The particles in solids and liquids are very close together.
- This means that it is difficult to squash solids and liquids into a smaller volume.
- Since the particles in a gas are much farther apart, it is easy to squeeze them into a smaller volume, Figure 16.4.

 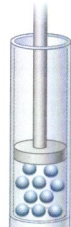

▶ Figure 16.4 Gases can be compressed (squashed) because there is space between the particles of a gas. Solids and liquids are difficult to compress (squash) because the particles are already very close to each other.

- Diffusion takes place quickly with gases because the particles of the gas are moving fast and there are only weak forces between the particles.

> **Diffusion** is the spreading out of materials because of the movement of their particles.

- Diffusion is much slower in liquids because the particles are moving more slowly.
- In solids, because the particles are not free to move about, any diffusion that occurs is much too slow to be easily seen.

16.3. Change of state

Melting

- When a solid is heated, the heat energy causes the particles to vibrate.
- As heating continues, the particles vibrate faster and faster.
- Eventually, the particles break free and begin to slide over each other.
- The solid has now melted to form a liquid, Figure 16.5.

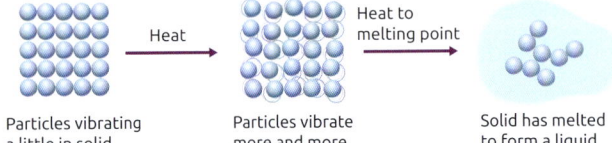

> The **melting point** is the temperature at which a solid changes to a liquid.

Particles vibrating a little in solid → Particles vibrate more and more → Solid has melted to form a liquid

▶ Figure 16.5 When a solid melts, the particles vibrate so much that they break away from their fixed positions. The solid now begins to change into a liquid.

▶▶ Experiment 16.1

To measure the melting point of a solid

In this experiment a sample of a solid material (e.g. benzoic acid) is heated and the temperature at which it turns into a liquid is measured.

- A melting-point tube is sealed at one end by holding it in a Bunsen burner.
- A small amount of benzoic acid is placed in the melting-point tube.
- An aluminium melting-point block is placed on a hotplate, Figure 16.6.
- The melting-point tube is placed in the aluminium block.
- The aluminium block is heated using a hotplate.
- At a certain temperature, the white powder changes to a colourless liquid.
- The solid benzoic acid has melted to liquid benzoic acid.
- The temperature at which the solid melts is read from the digital thermometer.

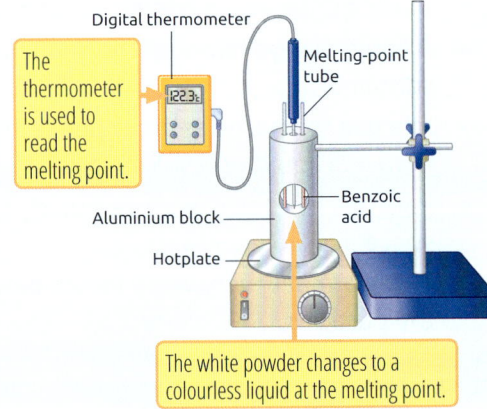

▶ Figure 16.6 Measuring the melting point of benzoic acid using an aluminium melting-point block

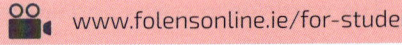

www.folensonline.ie/for-students

A small number of solids change directly from a solid to a gas when heated. This occurrence is known as **sublimation**.

Evaporation

- Puddles on the road dry up quickly on a sunny day, Figure 16.7.
- Heat from the sun gives some particles **near the surface** of the liquid extra energy.
- These particles now have enough energy to escape from the liquid into the air.
- We say that some of the liquid has **evaporated** to form a gas.

▶ Figure 16.7 Heat from the Sun causes the particles near the surface to escape into the air. Evaporation is now taking place and puddles of water soon 'disappear' on a sunny day.

> **Evaporation** is the changing of a liquid to a gas at the surface of the liquid.

Boiling

- When a liquid is heated, the particles get more energy and move faster and faster.
- Eventually, the particles break away from the liquid state and form a gas.
- When a certain temperature is reached, particles of gas form throughout the liquid and not just at the surface. The liquid is now boiling.
- When a liquid is boiling, the particles are escaping from all parts of the liquid very quickly.
- Bubbles of gas are seen forming **inside the liquid**. In the case of water, these bubbles of gas consist of water vapour. The boiling point of the liquid has now been reached, Figure 16.8.

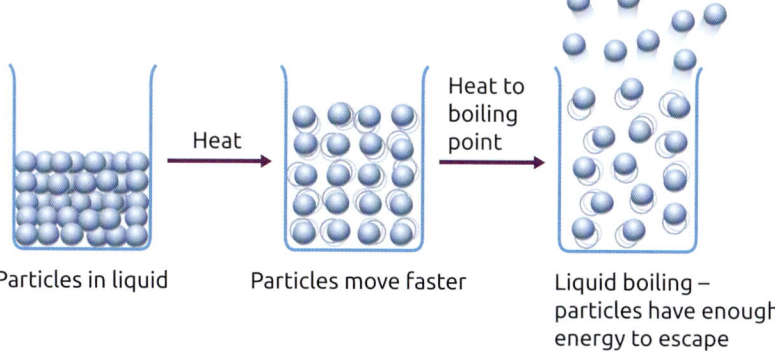

Particles in liquid → Heat → Particles move faster → Heat to boiling point → Liquid boiling – particles have enough energy to escape

▶ Figure 16.8 At the boiling point of a liquid, the particles break away from all parts of the liquid and form a gas.

> The **boiling point** of a liquid is the temperature at which a liquid changes to a gas throughout the liquid. The boiling point of water is 100 °C.

Condensation

- When a gas is cooled, the particles slow down and a liquid is formed.
- Condensation is often seen in a kitchen or bathroom when steam (gas) meets the much colder glass in a window.

Condensation is the changing of a gas to a liquid.

When a solid melts to form a liquid or a liquid evaporates to form a gas, we say that there is a **change of state**. The various changes of state are summarised in Figure 16.9.

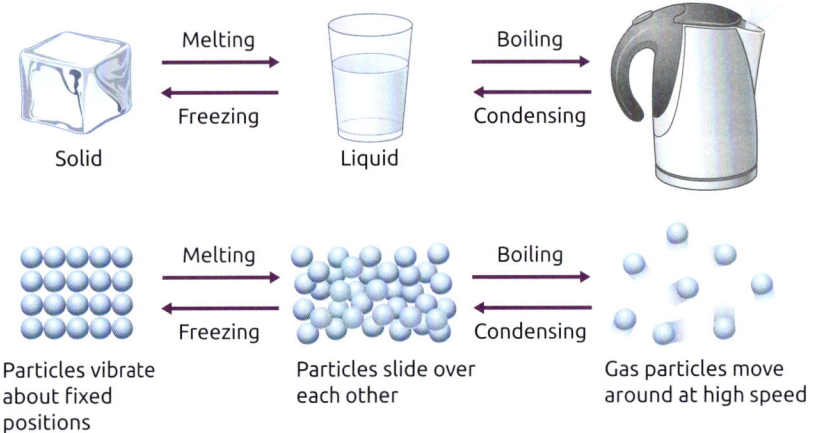

Particles vibrate about fixed positions

Particles slide over each other

Gas particles move around at high speed

▶ Figure 16.9 The state of a substance can be changed by heating or cooling.

Exam Tip!

Make sure that you can identify the various changes of state in diagrams similar to Figure 16.9.

▶▶ Science Self-Assessment

Now I am able to:	🟢	🟠	🔴
Name the three states of matter			
Describe the properties of solids, liquids and gases			
Carry out an experiment to measure the melting point of a solid			
Distinguish between evaporation and boiling			
Use the particle theory to explain the properties of the three states of matter			

17 Elements, compounds and mixtures

The Chemical World strand

▶▶ **Main topics in this chapter:**
- Elements: meaning, names and symbols
- Formation of compounds when elements combine together
- Differences between mixtures and compounds

17.1 Elements – simple substances

Robert Boyle, an Irish scientist, introduced the word *element* into the language of chemistry.

> An **element** is a substance that cannot be split up into simpler substances by chemical means. Elements contain only one type of atom.

Copper is an example of an element.
- It consists of only one type of atom, i.e. atoms of copper.
- It cannot be split into anything simpler: it contains copper atoms and nothing else.

There are many other examples of elements, Figure 17.1.
- All the known elements are listed in a table called the **Periodic Table of the Elements** (printed on page 264 of this book).
- To find out if a substance is an element, just examine the Periodic Table. If the substance is an element, it will be listed there.

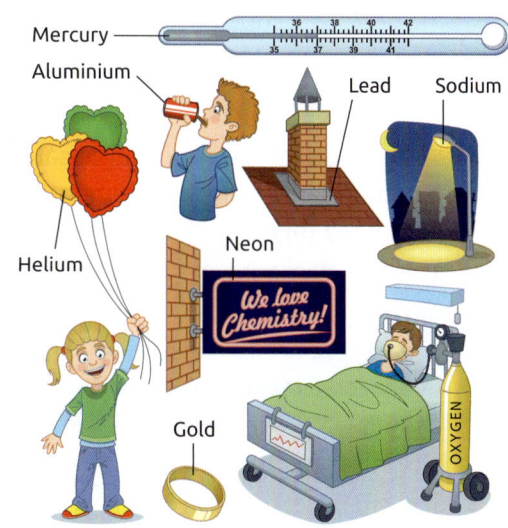

▶ Figure 17.1 Elements are the simplest substances. They have many uses in our everyday lives.

- Each element has its own symbol. The symbol is a shorthand way of representing the element.
- The symbol for some elements is simply the first letter of the name of the element, Table 17.1.
- The symbol for other elements is the first letter plus another letter, Table 17.2. The first letter is always a capital letter. The second letter is always a small letter.
- Sometimes the symbol for the element is taken from the Latin name for the element. Examples of these are listed in Table 17.3.

Element	Symbol
Hydrogen	H
Carbon	C
Nitrogen	N
Oxygen	O
Fluorine	F
Phosphorus	P
Sulfur	S

▶ Table 17.1 The symbol for some elements is simply the first letter of the name of the element.

Element	Symbol
Helium	He
Neon	Ne
Magnesium	Mg
Aluminium	Al
Silicon	Si
Chlorine	Cl
Calcium	Ca
Manganese	Mn
Zinc	Zn

▶ Table 17.2 The symbol for some elements is the first letter of the name plus another letter.

Element	Symbol
Sodium (*natrium*)	Na
Iron (*ferrum*)	Fe
Copper (*cuprum*)	Cu
Silver (*argentum*)	Ag
Gold (*aurum*)	Au

▶ Table 17.3. Some unusual symbols of elements. The Latin name is indicated in brackets.

17.2 Compounds

Substances such as salt, sugar and water are composed of more than one element. Substances made by joining together two or more elements are called **compounds**.

A **compound** is a substance that is made up of two or more different elements combined together chemically. Compounds contain two or more different types of atoms.

- Water is called a compound because it contains two different elements combined together chemically.
- The two elements are hydrogen and oxygen, Figure 17.2.
- Since there are two atoms of hydrogen for every atom of oxygen, chemists say that water has the **chemical formula** H_2O.
- The chemical formula H_2O is just a shorthand method used by chemists to represent water.

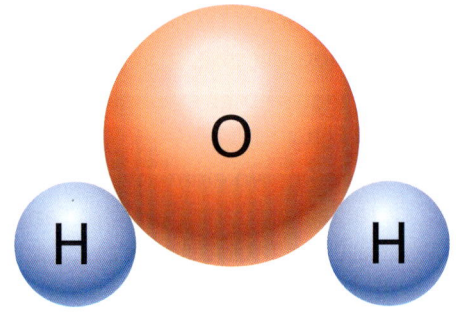

▶ Figure 17.2 Water is a compound. It is made up of the elements hydrogen and oxygen combined together chemically.

Compounds: points to note

- Although there are only about one hundred elements, there are millions of compounds.
- Compounds are made when elements combine together in a **chemical reaction** (Chapter 21).

17.3 Mixtures

Many of the ordinary things we see around us are made up of two or more elements or compounds which are just mingled or jumbled up together. Such substances are known as **mixtures**.

> A **mixture** consists of two or more different substances mingled with each other but not chemically combined.

Some examples of mixtures are shown in Figure 17.3.

[a]

[b]

[c]

[d]

▶ Figure 17.3 Examples of mixtures include: (a) Air (b) Crude oil (c) Toothpaste (d) Cement

Mixtures: points to note

- The substances in the mixture are just mingled together. They are not chemically combined.
- In a mixture, the substances which make up the mixture can be present in any amounts.

▸▸ Experiment 17.1

To make a mixture using iron and sulfur and then change the mixture into the compound iron sulfide

- Iron filings and sulfur are placed in a mortar and the mixture is ground very well using the pestle and mortar, Figure 17.4.
- The mixture is divided into two parts.
- A bar magnet is used to separate the iron filings from the sulfur in the first part of the mixture.
- The other part of the mixture is placed in a test tube and heated in the fume cupboard using a Bunsen burner.
- When iron filings and sulfur are mixed together, no new substance is formed. The individual pieces of iron and sulfur may still be seen in the mixture. The iron may easily be separated from the mixture with a magnet.
- When iron filings and sulfur are mixed together and heated, the mixture glows. This indicates that a chemical reaction is taking place and that heat is being given off.
- A dark-grey solid substance called iron sulfide is formed. Iron sulfide is a compound.

$$Fe + S \longrightarrow FeS$$
$$iron + sulfur \longrightarrow iron\ sulfide$$

- Iron sulfide looks different from the mixture of iron and sulfur. Iron sulfide cannot be separated into iron and sulfur using a magnet.
- Iron sulfide has different properties to the elements from which it is made. Iron sulfide is not attracted to a magnet.

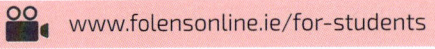
www.folensonline.ie/for-students

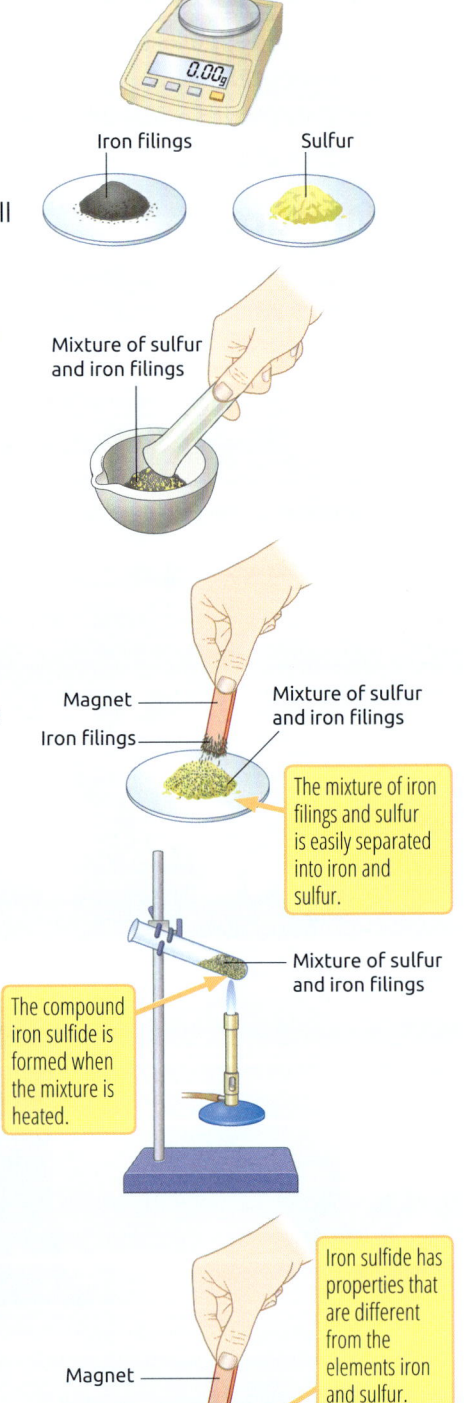

▶ Figure 17.4 Investigating the properties of a mixture of iron and sulfur and of the compound iron sulfide

A summary of some particle theory diagrams is shown in Figure 17.5.

Solids, Liquids and Gases

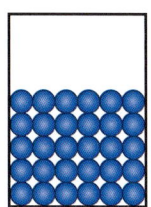 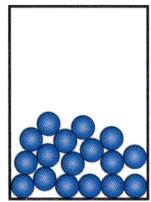 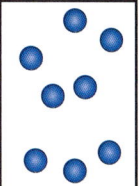

In a solid, the particles are in fixed positions and can only vibrate about these fixed positions.

In a liquid, the particles can slide over each other.

In a gas, the particles have complete freedom of movement and move around at high speed.

Elements

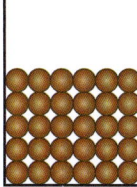 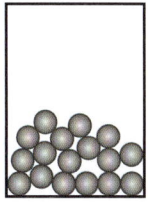 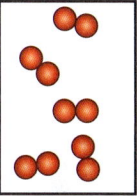

Particles (atoms) of a solid element, e.g. copper. An element consists of only one type of atom.

Particles (atoms) of a liquid element, e.g. mercury. Note that all the atoms are the same.

Particles (molecules) of a gaseous element, e.g. oxygen. Note that since oxygen is an element, the two atoms in the molecule are the same.

Compounds

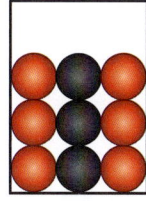 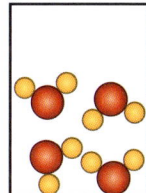 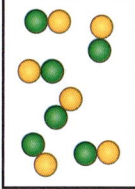

Molecules of a solid compound, e.g. solid carbon dioxide ('dry ice'), CO_2. Note that compounds consist of different atoms joined together.

Molecules of a liquid compound, e.g. water. A molecule of water consists of one atom of oxygen joined to two atoms of hydrogen.

Molecules of a gaseous compound, e.g. hydrogen chloride, HCl.

Mixtures

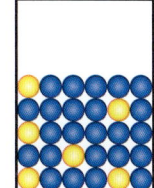 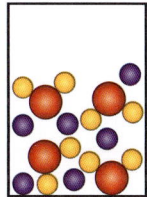 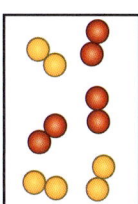

A mixture of two solids, e.g. a mixture of iron filings and sulfur.

A mixture of two liquids, e.g. a mixture of water and methylated spirits. For simplicity, the particles of methylated spirits are represented as purple spheres.

A mixture of two gases, e.g. a mixture of hydrogen and oxygen.

▶ Figure 17.5 Summary of particle theory diagrams

The differences between mixtures and compounds are summarised in Table 17.4.

Mixture	Compound
1. The amounts of the substances in the mixture can vary.	The elements in a compound are always present in the same amount.
2. A mixture contains two or more substances.	A compound is a single substance.
3. The properties of a mixture are similar to those of the substances in the mixture.	The properties of a compound are different to those of the elements which reacted to form the compound.
4. It is usually easy to separate the parts of a mixture	It is usually difficult to separate the elements in a compound. This is only possible using suitable experiments.
5. There are almost no energy changes when a mixture is made.	Heat is usually given out or taken in when a compound is formed.

▶ Table 17.4 The differences between mixtures and compounds

▶▶ Science Self-Assessment

Now I am able to:	🟢	🟠	🔴
Explain the terms *element*, *compound* and *mixture*			
Recall that all known elements are listed in the Periodic Table			
Write the symbols of common elements			
Describe an experiment to make a mixture of iron and sulfur and also to make the compound iron sulfide			
Discuss the differences between elements, mixtures and compounds			

18
Solutions and formation of crystals

The Chemical World strand

▶▶ **Main topics in this chapter:**
- Dilute and concentrated solutions
- Crystal formation
- Solubility curves

18.1 Water as a solvent

Water is an excellent **solvent**, i.e. a very large number of substances dissolve in it.

> A **solvent** is a substance that dissolves other materials to form a solution.

Some important terms are highlighted in Figure 18.1.

- When a substance such as salt or sugar is added to water, the substance seems to vanish or disappear in the water.
- We know, however, that the substance is still present, since the solution has the taste of salt or sugar.
- A solution is a perfect mixture because, when you look at a solution, you cannot see the individual solute and solvent.
- Solutions are always clear, i.e. if you hold them up to the light, the light passes through them.

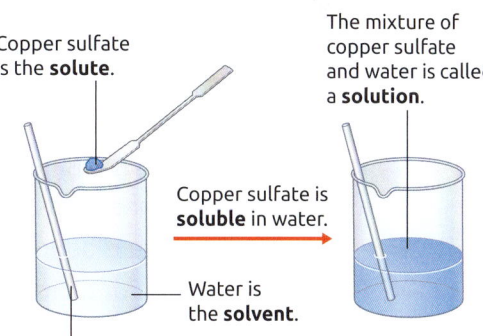

▶ Figure 18.1 A solute (copper sulfate) is being added to a solvent (water) to form a solution of copper sulfate in water.

In some cases, fine particles of a solid or liquid are spread throughout a liquid. They are not dissolved and do not settle to the bottom: the mixture has a cloudy appearance. The mixture is known as a **suspension**. Examples include muddy water and Milk of Magnesia.

> A **suspension** is a mixture in which small solid or liquid particles are suspended in a liquid (or gas).

18.2 Dilute and concentrated solutions

If a small amount of solute is dissolved in the solvent, the solution is said to be dilute.

If a large amount of solute is dissolved in the solvent, the solution is said to be concentrated.

> A **dilute solution** is one in which there is a small amount of solute in a large amount of solvent.

> A **concentrated solution** is one in which there is a large amount of solute in a small amount of solvent.

18.3 Crystal formation

Crystals have a definite shape and are usually shiny. If you examine a crystal closely, you will see definite angles between the faces. However, non-crystalline solids (e.g. flour) have no definite shape and are usually dull.

> A **crystal** is a solid with a regular shape. The particles inside the crystal are arranged in a regular pattern.

▶▶ Experiment 18.1

To grow crystals of copper sulfate

- Some copper sulfate is ground up using a pestle and mortar.
- The powdered substance is added to water in a beaker. A stirring rod is used to help the powder to dissolve more quickly, Figure 18.2.
- Copper sulfate is continually added until the solute no longer dissolves but settles at the bottom of the beaker.
- The temperature of the water is read using a thermometer.
- The water is heated to about 60 °C. It is observed that the undissolved copper sulfate now dissolves.
- More copper sulfate is added.
- The water is heated until no more copper sulfate will dissolve.
- About half the solution is placed in a warm evaporating basin and put aside to cool slowly.
- The other half is cooled quickly by holding the beaker under running water from the tap.
- Large crystals are formed in the evaporating basin.
- Smaller crystals are formed in the beaker.
- We conclude that more copper sulfate dissolves at the higher temperature.
- We also conclude that crystals are formed when a hot, concentrated solution is cooled.

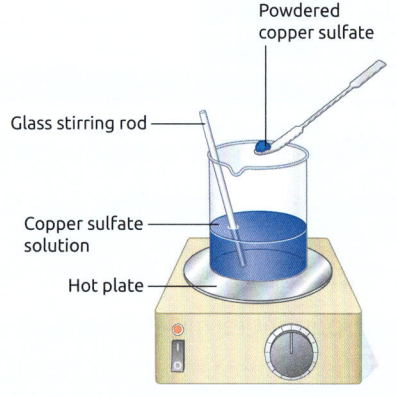

▶ Figure 18.2 Making a saturated solution of copper sulfate using powdered copper sulfate. Crystals of copper sulfate are formed as this hot saturated solution cools.

A solution that contains the maximum amount of solute is called a **saturated solution**.

> A **saturated solution** is one that contains as much dissolved solute as possible at a given temperature.

Crystals are formed when a hot, saturated solution is cooled.

Note: A solution that has not dissolved the maximum amount of solute at a given temperature is called an **unsaturated** solution.

18.4 Solubility and solubility curves

Chemists use the term **solubility** for the amount of solute that will dissolve in a certain amount of solvent.

> The **solubility** of a substance is the mass of it (in grams) that will dissolve in 100 grams of solvent at a fixed temperature.

For example, the solubility of copper sulfate is 40 g/100 g water at 60 °C. This means that 40 g of copper sulfate will dissolve in 100 g of water at 60 °C.

▶▶ Experiment 18.2

To investigate the effect of temperature on solubility

- A sample of copper sulfate is ground up with a pestle and mortar.
- 100 g of the copper sulfate is weighed out on an electronic balance.
- 100 cm³ of water is placed in a beaker and the water is heated to about 30 °C.
- The exact temperature of the water is measured using a digital thermometer.
- Some copper sulfate is added to the water with stirring after each addition, Figure 18.3.
- The copper sulfate is added until no more will dissolve, i.e. until a few grains remain undissolved at the bottom of the beaker.
- The amount of copper sulfate that has **not** been added to the water is weighed.
- The amount of the copper sulfate that has dissolved in the water is calculated by subtraction.
- The procedure is repeated at various other temperatures.
- The results are summarised in a table and also by means of a graph on graph paper.

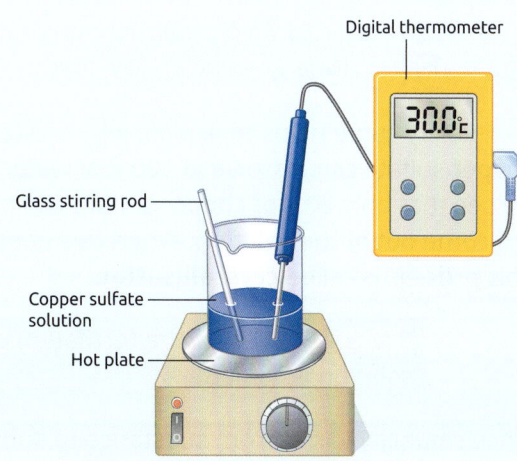

▶ Figure 18.3 Apparatus to investigate the effect of temperature on solubility

Sample results

Some sample results are given in Table 18.1.

Temperature (°C)	Solubility, i.e. mass of copper sulfate (g) that will dissolve in 100 g of water
0	14
10	17
20	20
30	25
40	29
50	34
60	40
70	47
80	56
90	68

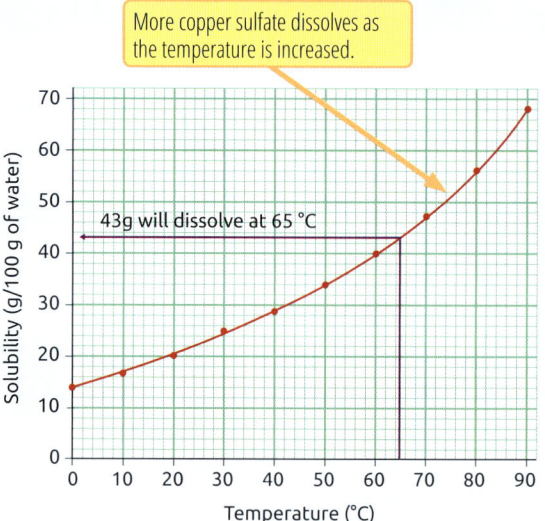

▶ Table 18.1 This table shows how the solubility of copper sulfate changes with temperature. These results are also shown on the graph in Figure 18.4.

▶ Figure 18.4 The solubility curve for copper sulfate. A solubility curve shows how solubility changes with temperature. In this case, we see that more copper sulfate dissolves at a higher temperature.

The graph shown in Figure 18.4 is called a solubility curve.

> A **solubility curve** is a graph showing how the solubility of a substance varies with temperature.

Exam Tip!
It is important that you can graph a solubility curve using data given to you. Also, you must be able to use a solubility curve to deduce certain information.

A solubility curve helps to explain why crystals are formed. At 80 °C we see that 56 g of copper sulfate can dissolve in 100 g of water. However, if the solution is cooled to 20 °C, we see that only 20 g of copper sulfate can now dissolve. Therefore, 56 g – 20 g = 36 g will come out of the solution. When this happens, crystals are usually formed. This process is called **crystallisation**.

> **Crystallisation** is the formation of crystals when a hot saturated solution is cooled.

Since solubility varies from substance to substance, each substance has its own solubility curve.

Solubility curves are very useful to chemists. For example, suppose you wanted to know how much copper sulfate will dissolve in 100 g of water at 65 °C. The mass of copper sulfate (43 g) can be read off the graph, as shown in Figure 18.4.

Electrical conductivity

- Substances such as copper sulfate do not conduct electricity in the solid state.
- This is because the charged particles in the crystals are locked in fixed positions and cannot carry the electric current through the crystal.
- When the crystals are dissolved in water, these charged particles are now free to move and can carry an electric current.
- We say that copper sulfate solution displays electrical conductivity.
- We use the apparatus in Figure 18.5 to test for the ability of a solution to carry an electric current.
- If we investigate electrical conductivity in a sugar solution, we find that the bulb does not light, Figure 18.6.
- This tells us that sugar does not produce any charged particles when dissolved in water.

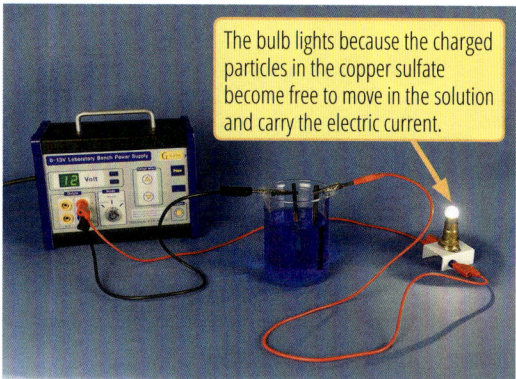

The bulb lights because the charged particles in the copper sulfate become free to move in the solution and carry the electric current.

▶ Figure 18.5 Investigating electrical conductivity in a copper sulfate solution

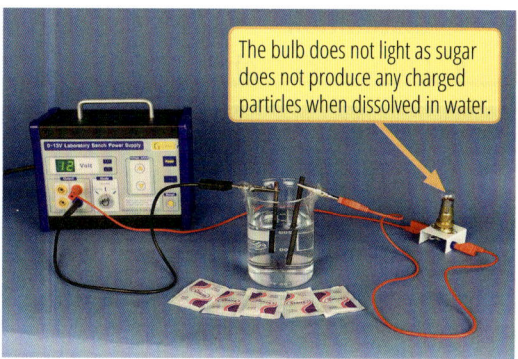

The bulb does not light as sugar does not produce any charged particles when dissolved in water.

▶ Figure 18.6 Investigating electrical conductivity in sugar solution

▶▶ Science Self-Assessment

Now I am able to:	🟢	🟠	🔴
Explain the differences between a dilute, a concentrated and a saturated solution			
Investigate the solubility of a variety of substances in water			
Investigate the effect of temperature on solubility			
Draw and interpret solubility curves			
Describe how to investigate electrical conductivity in various solutions			

19 Separating mixtures

The Chemical World strand

Main topics in this chapter:
- Filtration
- Evaporation
- Distillation
- Chromatography

19.1 Filtration

Filtration is used in coffee filters to separate the coffee solution from the ground coffee. It is also used in the operating theatre to let the air through but trap the germs. Filtration is used in a colander when separating cooked vegetables from the cooking liquid.

Filtration is a method of separating an insoluble solid from a liquid, using a material that allows the liquid to pass through but not the solid.

▶▶ Experiment 19.1

To separate a mixture of water and soil using filtration

- The filter paper allows the salt solution to pass through it.
- The soil remains behind on the filter paper.

Glass rod helps prevent splashing

Glass rod

Muddy water

Filter paper

Soil

Funnel supports the filter paper

Filter paper keeps the soil behind (residue) and allows the water (filtrate) to flow through it

RESIDUE

FILTRATE

Water

▶ Figure 19.1 Apparatus to separate water and soil. The soil remains behind on the filter paper. The water passes through the filter paper.

The **filtrate** is the liquid that has been filtered, i.e. the liquid that has passed through the filter paper.

19.2 Evaporation

▶▶ Experiment 19.2

To separate sodium chloride from a solution of sodium chloride in water

> **Evaporation** is the changing of a liquid to a gas at the surface of a liquid.

- Salt solution is heated in an evaporating basin, Figure 19.2.
- The water evaporates.
- Pure salt is left behind, Figure 19.3.

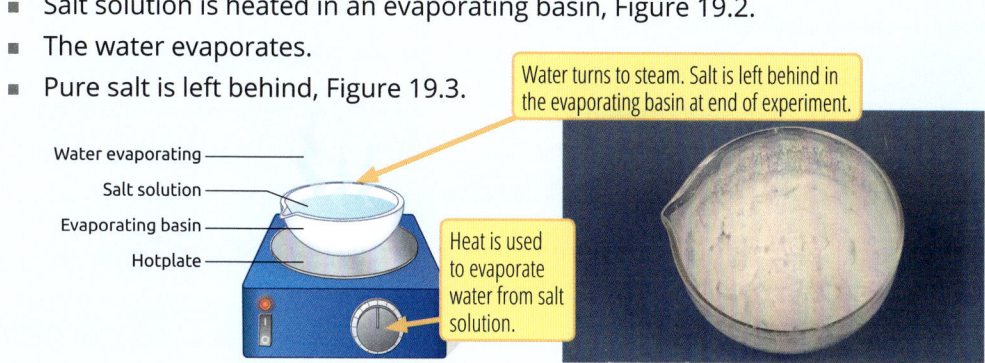

▶ Figure 19.2 Evaporation is a very useful way of separating salt from water.

▶ Figure 19.3 The white solid is pure salt that has been separated from the solution of salt and water, using evaporation.

19.3 Separating mixtures using both filtration and evaporation

Rock salt consists of salt (sodium chloride) mixed with sand and soil.
To obtain pure salt from rock salt, we make use of filtration and evaporation.

▶▶ Experiment 19.3

To separate salt from rock salt using filtration and evaporation

[1] Pestle and mortar are used to crush lumps of rock salt.

[2] Salt dissolves in water. Sand does not dissolve in water.

[3] Heating helps to dissolve more salt. Stirring helps to dissolve salt more quickly.

[4] Salt solution passes through the filter paper. Sand remains behind on filter paper.

[5] Salt solution is poured from conical flask into evaporating basin and heated.

[6] Water is evaporated from the salt solution. Pure salt is obtained.

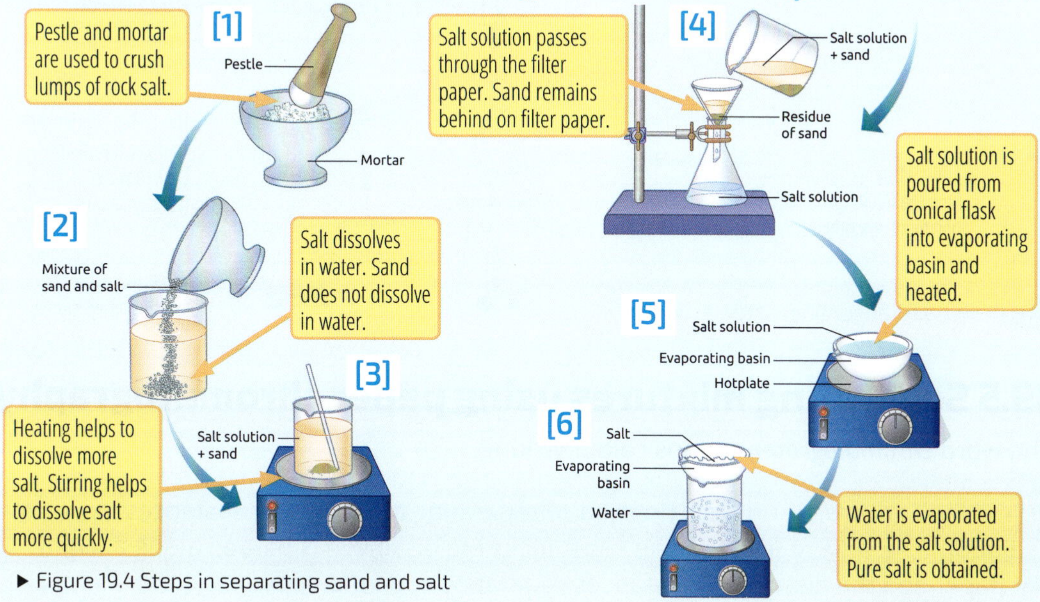

▶ Figure 19.4 Steps in separating sand and salt

19.4 Separating mixtures using distillation

It would be difficult to use evaporation alone to obtain pure water from sea water. We need to have some method of changing the vapour back to a liquid again. Changing a vapour back to a liquid is called **condensation** (Chapter 16). The apparatus that cools the vapour to a liquid is called a condenser. In the laboratory, we use a special type of condenser called a Liebig condenser. Evaporating a liquid followed by condensing the vapour is called distillation.

> The **distillate** is the purified liquid produced by condensation from a vapour during distillation, i.e. the product of distillation.

> **Distillation** is the vaporising of a liquid by boiling it and then condensing the vapour by cooling it.

In this experiment, the distillate is pure water (distilled water). Note the direction in which cold water from the tap enters and leaves the Liebig condenser.

Exam Tip!
Make sure you can label the various parts of the distillation apparatus. Also, note where the water enters and leaves the Liebig condenser.

▶▶ Experiment 19.4

To obtain a sample of pure water from sea water

- Some sea water is heated in a distillation apparatus, Figure 19.5.
- The water is converted to steam.
- The steam is condensed back to water using a Liebig condenser.
- Pure water called **distilled water** is obtained from the sea water.

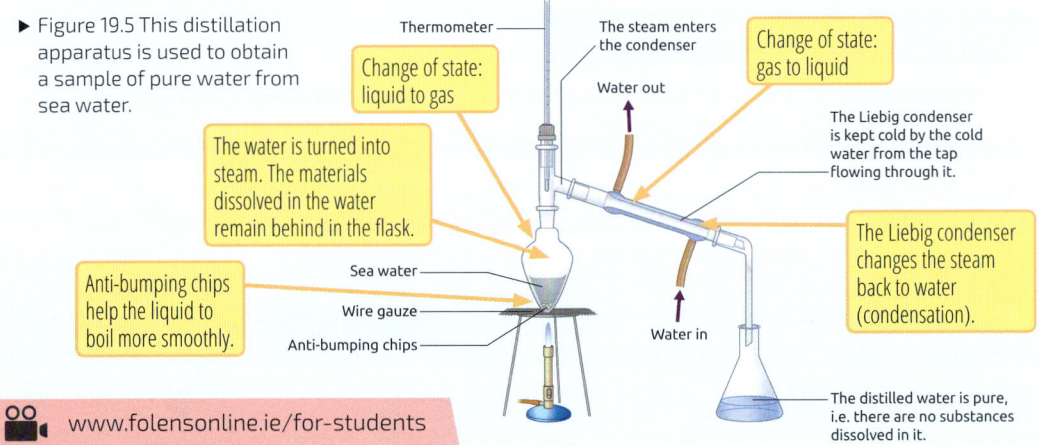

▶ Figure 19.5 This distillation apparatus is used to obtain a sample of pure water from sea water.

www.folensonline.ie/for-students

19.5 Separating mixtures using paper chromatography

The word *chromatography* means colour writing.

> **Paper chromatography** is a method of separating mixtures of substances in solution. The solvent in which the substances are dissolved is passed along a length of paper and the dissolved substances separate out on the paper.

▶▶ Experiment 19.5

To separate the dyes in a sample of ink using chromatography

- A spot of ink from a marker is placed on paper.
- A suitable solvent is allowed to soak through the chromatography paper.
- If the ink is water soluble, water is used as the solvent. If the ink does not dissolve in water, another solvent (e.g. nail varnish remover, alcohol) is used.
- The mixture of inks used to make the ink in the marker will separate out into various colours on the chromatography paper.
- If the ink in the marker consists of just a single colour, then no separation will be observed.

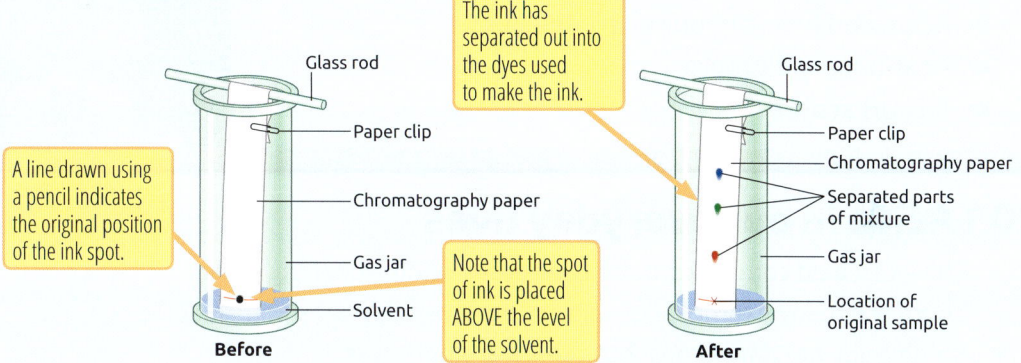

▶ Figure 19.6 An experiment to separate the various colours in a dye using paper chromatography. Note that the sample is placed just above the level of the solvent.

The paper showing the separated colours is called a **chromatogram**.

> A **chromatogram** is the strip of paper on which the parts of a mixture have been separated by chromatography.

▶▶ Science Self-Assessment

Now I am able to:	🟢	🟠	🔴
Describe how to separate the parts of a mixture using filtration			
Describe how to separate the parts of a mixture using evaporation			
Describe how to carry out a simple distillation to obtain a sample of pure water from sea water			
Describe how to separate the parts of a mixture using paper chromatography			

20 Acids and bases, pH

The Chemical World strand

Main topics in this chapter:
- Acids and bases in our everyday lives
- Acid-base indicators
- The pH scale

20.1 Acids in our everyday lives

- The word *acid* comes from the Latin word *acidus* meaning sour.
- There are many examples of acids in our everyday lives, Figure 20.1.
- Some acids are dangerous, but others are harmless.

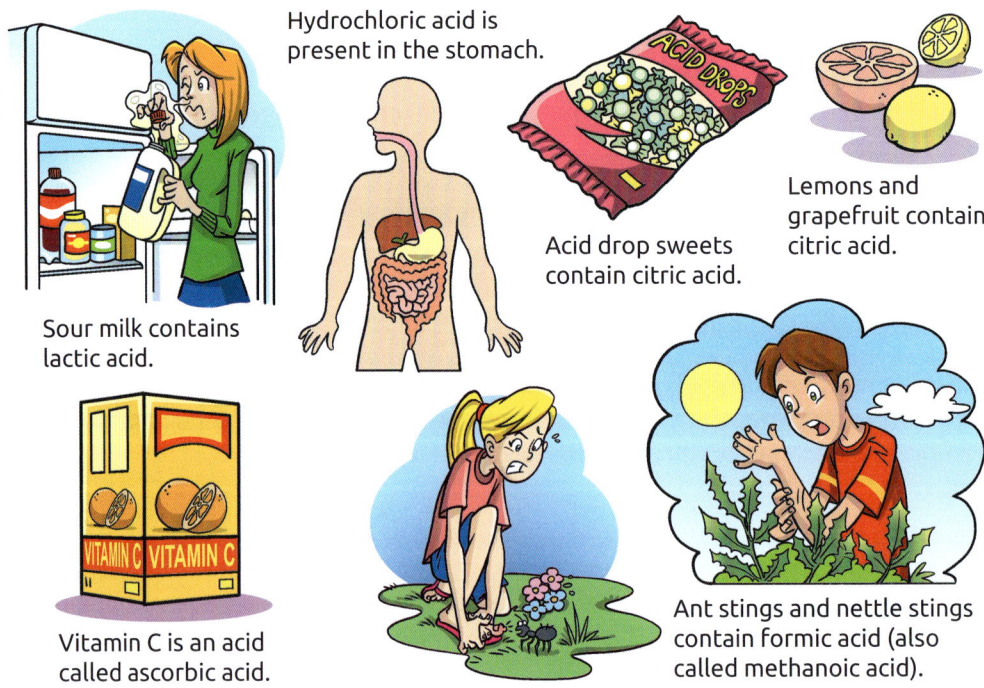

▶ Figure 20.1 Some examples of everyday substances that contain acids

20.2 Acid–base indicators

- It is very dangerous to taste certain acids.
- Instead, we use a substance called an **indicator** to test for the presence of an acid.
- Indicators tell us ('indicate') if a substance is an acid.
- An example of such a substance is litmus.
- Litmus turns red when mixed with an acid, Figure 20.2.

▶ Figure 20.2 The acid in the lemon turns litmus from blue to red.

Acids turn litmus from blue to red.

- Some substances turn litmus from red to blue. Such a substance is called a base.
- A base is the 'chemical opposite' to an acid
- Examples of common bases are shown in Figure 20.3.
- Bases that dissolve in water are called **alkalis**. Soap is an example of an alkali.

Bases turn litmus from red to blue.

- Litmus is commonly used in the laboratory to show (indicate) whether a substance is acidic or basic.
- Litmus is called an indicator.

An **indicator** is a compound which shows by means of a colour change whether a substance is acidic or basic.

If there is no colour change, we say that the substance is **neutral**.

- A neutral substance is neither an acid nor a base.
- Examples of neutral substances are water, sugar and salt.
- In neutral substances: red litmus stays red, and blue litmus stays blue.
- Litmus is found in laboratories as a solution or as litmus paper.

Drain cleaner contains a base called sodium hydroxide (caustic soda).

Indigestion tablets contain magnesium hydroxide. Milk of Magnesia also contains this base.

Bath salts contain a base called sodium carbonate.

Window cleaner and oven cleaners contain ammonia solution.

Toothpaste contains a base called sodium hydrogencarbonate.

▶ Figure 20.3 Some examples of everyday substances containing bases

20.3 The pH scale

- There are different levels of acidity and basicity. The acid in a car battery is highly acidic. The acid in orange juice is only mildly acidic.
- The **pH scale** is used to tell us how acidic or basic a substance is.
- The pH scale goes from 0 to 14. This scale indicates the level of acidity or basicity in a solution as follows:

> A solution whose pH is 7 is neutral.
> A solution whose pH is less than 7 is acidic.
> A solution whose pH is greater than 7 is basic (alkaline).

- The lower the pH value below 7, the more acidic the substance.
- The higher the pH value above 7, the more basic the substance.
- Litmus tells us if a substance is acidic or basic. It does not tell us the pH of the substance.
- To find the pH of a solution we use a pH sensor attached to a datalogger and a computer, Figure 20.4.

[a]
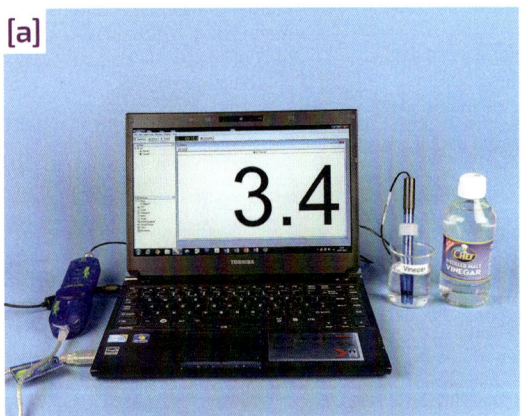

[b]

▶ Figure 20.4 (a) The pH of vinegar tells us that vinegar is an acid. (b) The pH of washing soda tells us that washing soda is a base.

- pH is also measured using pH paper or universal indicator solution.
- pH paper is universal indicator solution that has been soaked onto paper.
- A piece of pH paper or a few drops of universal indicator are placed in the solution whose pH is to be measured.
- The colour shown by the paper or indicator is then matched against a colour chart that comes with the indicator, Figure 20.5.

▶ Figure 20.5 This photograph shows the colour charts on rolls of pH universal indicator paper.

Some examples of common substances and their corresponding pH values are shown in Figure 20.6.

Exam Tip!

Make sure you can use pH values to classify substances as acidic, basic or neutral.

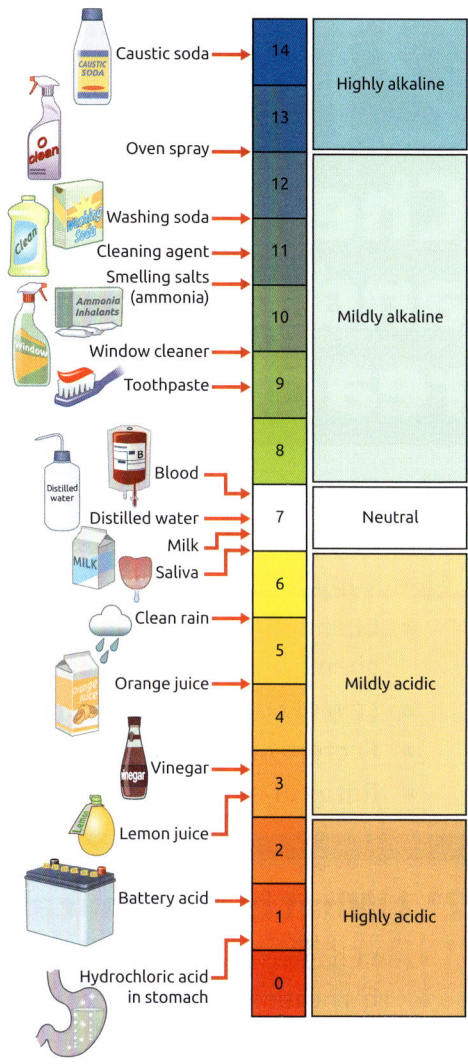

▶ Figure 20.6 The pH scale tells us the levels of acidity and basicity in a substance.

▶▶ Science Self-Assessment

Now I am able to:	🟢	🟠	🔴
Give examples of everyday acids and bases			
Describe how to test for an acid and a base			
Explain the term *indicator*			
Investigate the pH values of various substances and classify these substances as acidic, basic or neutral			

21 Chemical reactions and rates of chemical reactions

The Chemical World strand

Main topics in this chapter:
- Chemical reactions and writing balanced chemical equations
- Law of conservation of mass
- Factors affecting rates of reactions
- Rates of biochemical reactions

21.1 What is a chemical reaction?

- In Chapter 17 we heated a mixture of iron and sulfur.
- This heating resulted in the formation of a new substance called iron sulfide.
- The formation of iron sulfide is an example of a **chemical reaction**.

> A **chemical reaction** is a change that results in the formation of one or more new substances.

- When a chemical reaction has taken place, we could also say that a **chemical change** has taken place, i.e. the reactants have been changed into products.
- Chemical reactions are represented using equations.
- There are two types of equations in chemistry: **word equations** and **chemical equations**.

Note: If no new substance is formed, the change is called a **physical change**. For example, in Chapter 16 we learned about melting, boiling, evaporation and condensation. No new substance is formed when water is converted to steam, since water and steam are the same substance, i.e. they have the same chemical formula (H_2O).

> A **physical change** is a change that does not result in the formation of any new substance.

- The melting of wax is a physical change as no new substance is formed.
- However, the burning of wax is a chemical reaction as new substances (carbon dioxide and water vapour) are formed when wax is burned.
- The mixing of iron and sulfur is a physical change as no new substance is formed. However, when iron and sulfur are heated, a chemical reaction occurs as a new substance (iron sulfide) is formed.
- Other examples of physical changes are changes in shape or in size, e.g. crushing a can, breaking glass, chopping wood or cutting paper, Figure 21.1.

▶ Figure 21.1 These changes are examples of physical changes because no new substance is formed.

Word equation

iron + sulfur ⟶ iron sulfide

- Iron and sulfur are the chemicals that react together in the chemical reaction. These chemicals are called the **reactants**.
- The products are the chemicals that are produced in a chemical reaction. Iron sulfide is the **product** of the above reaction.

Chemical equation

A chemical equation is similar to a word equation except that it uses symbols (for elements) and formulas (for compounds) in the equation.

The chemical equation for the reaction of iron and sulfur is:

Fe + S ⟶ FeS

21.2 Writing balanced chemical equations

During a fireworks display, magnesium is burned to give a very bright light. The balanced equation for this reaction is:

magnesium + oxygen ⟶ magnesium oxide
$2Mg + O_2 \longrightarrow 2MgO$

- This balanced equation is illustrated in Figure 21.2.
- There are two oxygen atoms on the left-hand side and two oxygen atoms on the right-hand side. Oxygen is balanced.
- There are two magnesium atoms on the left-hand side and two magnesium atoms on the right-hand side. Magnesium is balanced.
- Therefore, the equation is balanced.

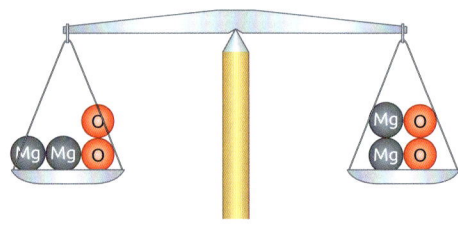

▶ Figure 21.2 The equation 2Mg + O_2 ⟶ 2MgO is an example of a balanced equation.

21.3 Law of conservation of mass

The French chemist Antoine Lavoisier was particularly interested in making careful measurements when chemical reactions occur. He found that when a chemical reaction occurs, the total mass of the reactants is always equal to the total mass of the products, Figure 21.3.

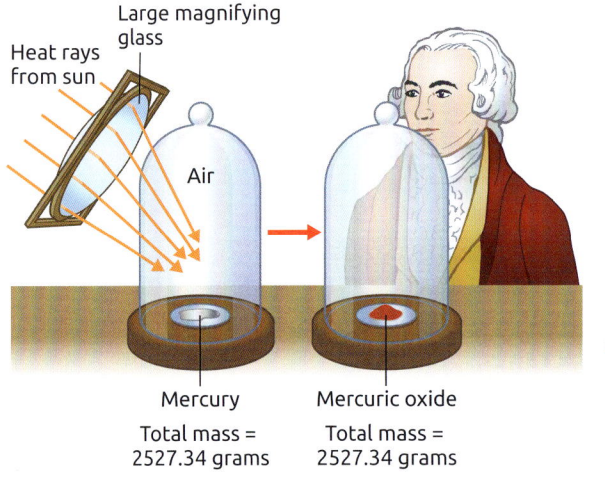

Mercury
Total mass = 2527.34 grams

Mercuric oxide
Total mass = 2527.34 grams

The **law of conservation of mass** states that when a chemical reaction occurs, the total mass of the reactants is always equal to the total mass of the products.

▶ Figure 21.3 Antoine Lavoisier heated mercury in a sealed bell jar full of air. He found that the total mass of the apparatus and chemicals at the beginning of the experiment was the same as the total mass at the end.

- Lavoisier explained his results by saying that the mercury had reacted with the oxygen in the air to form mercuric oxide.
- The following reaction had occurred:

2Hg + O_2 ⟶ 2HgO
mercury + oxygen ⟶ mercuric oxide
(silvery liquid)   (red powder)

- The law of conservation of mass was verified by many careful measurements.

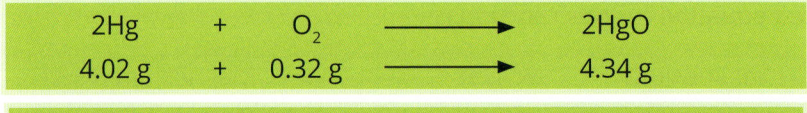

2Hg + O_2 ⟶ 2HgO
4.02 g + 0.32 g ⟶ 4.34 g

Total mass of reactants = 4.34 g   Total mass of product = 4.34 g

▶▶ Experiment 21.1

To investigate if mass is unchanged when a physical change takes place

- Some ice cubes are placed in a plastic container, Figure 21.4.
- A lid is placed on the container. The container is placed on a laboratory balance.
- The mass of the container and contents is noted at regular intervals of time.
- The ice melts to water.
- No change in mass is observed.
- We conclude that there is no change in mass when a physical change occurs.

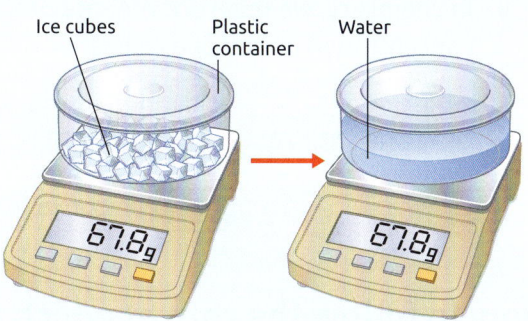

▶ Figure 21.4 A physical change takes place as the ice cubes melt. No change is observed in the total mass of the container and contents.

www.folensonline.ie/for-students

▶▶ Experiment 21.2

To investigate if mass is unchanged when a chemical reaction takes place

- Some sodium chloride solution is placed in a conical flask.
- A small test tube containing silver nitrate solution is carefully placed in the flask, Figure 21.5.
- A rubber bung is placed on the conical flask.
- The mass of the conical flask and contents is measured.
- The conical flask is shaken so that the two solutions are mixed.
- A chemical reaction takes place. A new white cloudy substance is formed in the flask.
- The mass of the conical flask and contents is measured after mixing.
- No change in mass is observed.
- We conclude that there is no change in mass when a chemical reaction occurs.
- The law of conservation of mass applies to chemical reactions.

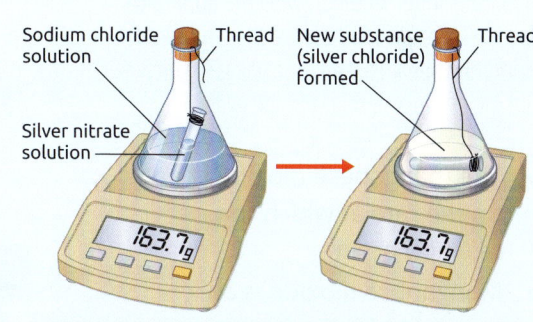

▶ Figure 21.5 A chemical reaction takes place when the two solutions are mixed. No change is observed in the total mass of the container and contents before or after the reaction has taken place. This verifies the law of conservation of mass.

www.folensonline.ie/for-students

21.4 Rate of reaction

- The term **rate of reaction** is used to describe how quickly chemical reactions occur.
- In chemistry, we measure the rate of a chemical reaction by measuring how the concentration of any one reactant or product changes with time.

The **rate of reaction** is defined as the change in concentration per unit time of any one reactant or product.

$$\text{Rate of reaction} = \frac{\text{Change in concentration of any one reactant or product}}{\text{Time taken}}$$

How to follow the rate at which a reaction occurs

Consider the reaction in which hydrogen peroxide decomposes to give off oxygen gas in the presence of manganese dioxide.

$$2H_2O_2 \xrightarrow{MnO_2} 2H_2O + O_2$$

hydrogen peroxide → water + oxygen

We can follow the rate at which this reaction occurs using the apparatus shown in Figure 21.6.

Exam Tip!

Do not forget to mark in the graduations on the graduated cylinder when drawing the apparatus shown in Figure 21.6. Otherwise the graduated cylinder might be mistaken for a gas jar, which would mean a loss of marks in the exam.

- The manganese dioxide speeds up the rate at which the reaction occurs.
- Manganese dioxide is an example of a catalyst.

A **catalyst** is a substance that alters the rate of a chemical reaction but is not used up in the reaction.

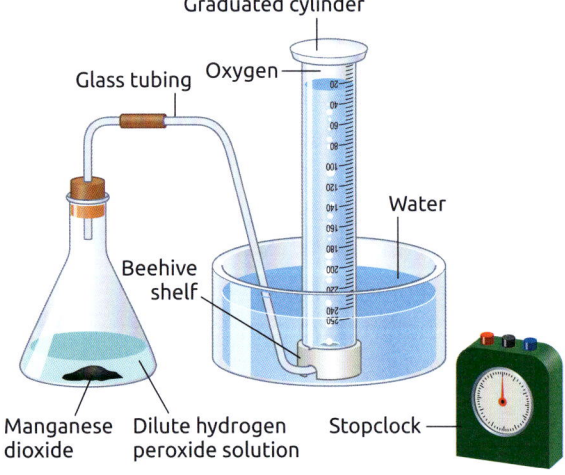

▶ Figure 21.6 This apparatus may be used to study the rate at which hydrogen peroxide breaks down to form oxygen and water. The manganese dioxide is added to the hydrogen peroxide and a stopclock is immediately started.

- Note that the word *alters* is used in the definition. The reason for this is that some catalysts can decrease the rate of reaction.
- If a graph of volume of oxygen (y-axis) against time (x-axis) is drawn on graph paper, a graph of similar shape to that shown in Figure 21.7 is obtained.

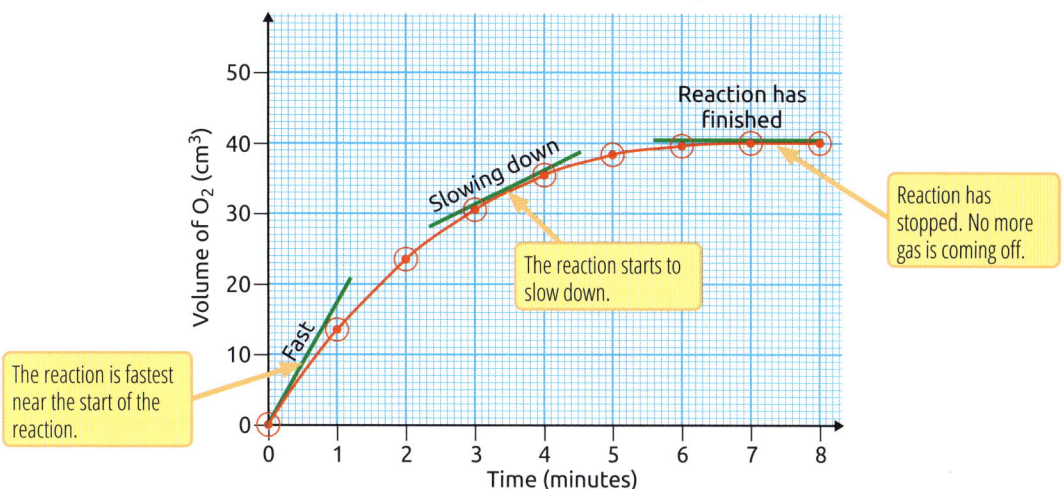

▶ Figure 21.7 When the volume of oxygen given off is plotted against the time, a graph similar to this one is obtained.

$$\text{Average rate} = \frac{\text{Total volume of oxygen}}{\text{Total time for reaction to take place}} = \frac{40 \text{ cm}^3}{6 \text{ mins}} = 6.67 \text{ cm}^3/\text{min}$$

21.5 Factors affecting rates of reaction

By experiment it is found that the rate of a reaction depends on five factors:
  (i) Types of reactants
  (ii) Particle size
  (iii) Concentration
  (iv) Temperature
  (v) Catalysts

(i) Types of reactants

▶▶ Experiment 21.3

To investigate the effect of types of reactants on the rate of a reaction

- The rate of reaction depends on the type of chemicals that react together.
- The phrase **nature of reactants** is often used to describe this effect.
- Magnesium metal reacts with hydrochloric acid to give off hydrogen gas.

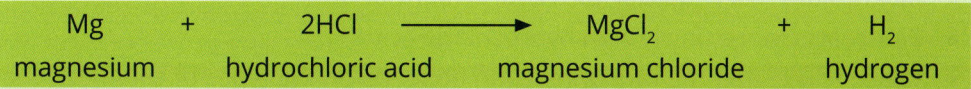

- Zinc metal reacts with hydrochloric acid to give off hydrogen gas.

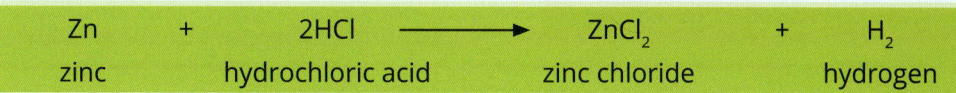

- The apparatus to study the reaction is shown in Figure 21.8.

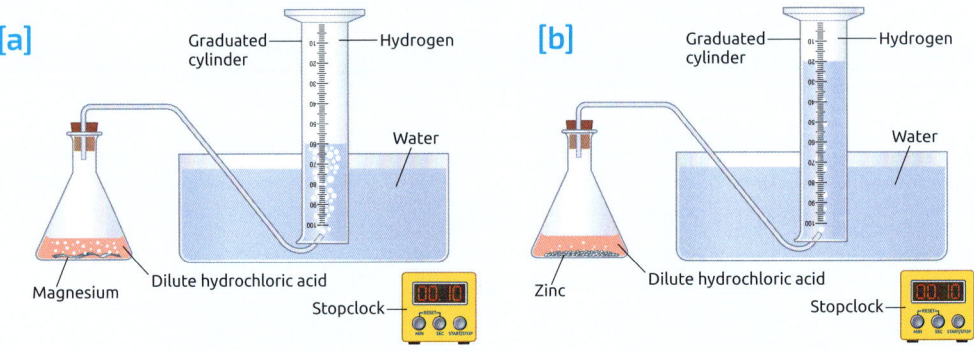

▶ Figure 21.8 (a) Magnesium reacts very quickly with hydrochloric acid to produce hydrogen gas. (b) If the magnesium metal is replaced by zinc metal, the reaction takes place much more slowly.

- The volume of hydrogen given off is measured at regular intervals until the reaction stops.
- The data are recorded in a table similar to Table 21.1.

Time (mins)	0	0.5	1.0	1.5	2.0	2.5	3.0	3.5
Volume of H_2 (cm³)								

▶ Table 21.1 The volumes of gas given off at regular time intervals are recorded in this type of table.

- The experiment is repeated with the same mass of zinc metal instead of magnesium metal.
- A graph of volume of hydrogen against time is plotted for each experiment on graph paper, Figure 21.9.

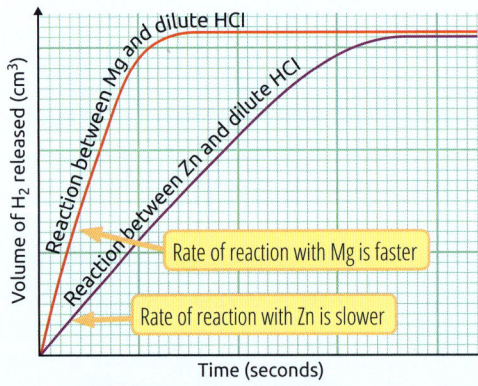

▶ Figure 21.9 The graphs show that Mg reacts faster than Zn with HCl. The steeper the slope, the faster the reaction.

▶ **Test for hydrogen gas**

Hydrogen burns with a pop when mixed with air.

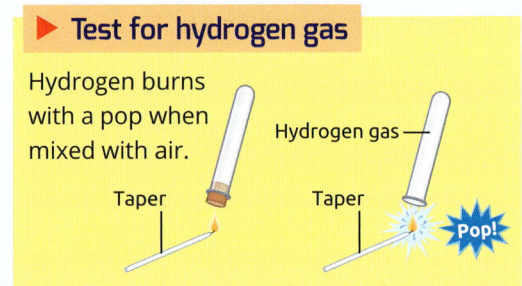

- Magnesium reacts quickly with hydrochloric acid.
- Zinc reacts more slowly with hydrochloric acid.
- We conclude that the rate of reaction depends on the types of chemicals that are reacting together.

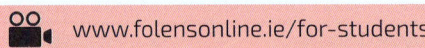
www.folensonline.ie/for-students

(ii) Particle size

▶▶ Experiment 21.4

To investigate the effect of particle size on the rate of a reaction

- We study the reaction between marble chips and dilute hydrochloric acid.
- We use small marble chips and large marble chips to compare the rates of reaction.
- The chemical name for marble is calcium carbonate.

$$CaCO_3 + 2HCl \longrightarrow CaCl_2 + H_2O + CO_2$$

calcium + hydrochloric → calcium + water + carbon
carbonate   acid   chloride   dioxide

- The apparatus is set up as shown in Figure 21.10.
- The total mass of the conical flask, marble chips, cotton wool, graduated cylinder and hydrochloric acid is noted.
- The acid is added to the marble chips and the flask is swirled to help mix the two chemicals.
- The stopclock is immediately started.
- The cotton wool plug is placed in the mouth of the conical flask.
- The cotton wool prevents any loss of acid spray during the experiment. The spray is caused by the fizzing that takes place when the marble reacts with the acid.

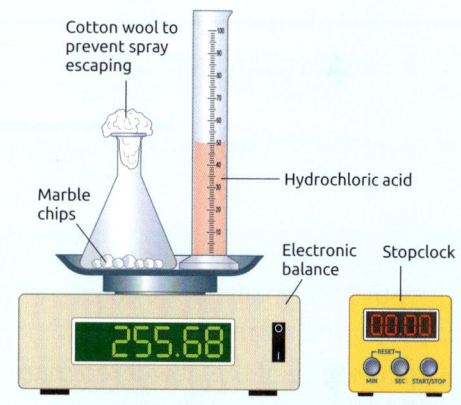

▶ Figure 21.10 Apparatus to study the effect of particle size on the rate of reaction. As the hydrochloric acid reacts with the marble, carbon dioxide is formed. This carbon dioxide escapes from the conical flask.

- If spray is lost, the result will be inaccurate. We wish to study the loss in mass due only to the carbon dioxide escaping.
- The cotton wool allows the carbon dioxide gas to escape.
- The conical flask and the empty graduated cylinder are again placed on the pan of the electronic balance.
- The mass displayed on the electronic balance is noted at regular intervals.
- The data are recorded in the form of a table similar to Table 21.2.

Time (mins)	0	0.5	1.0	1.5	2.0	2.5	3.0	3.5
Total mass (g)								
Loss in mass (g)								

▶ Table 21.2 The results of the experiment are recorded in this type of table.

- The loss in mass is calculated by subtracting each value of the mass from the mass before the acid was added to the marble, i.e. loss in mass at a given time = mass at start − mass at that time.
- It is observed that the mass decreases with time.
- The experiment is repeated with the same mass of smaller marble chips.
- It is noted that the loss in mass takes place at a faster rate.
- A graph of total mass against time is plotted for both experiments on graph paper, Figure 21.11.
- Alternatively, a graph of loss in mass against time is plotted, Figure 21.12.
- The experiment is repeated with very small marble chips or powdered marble.

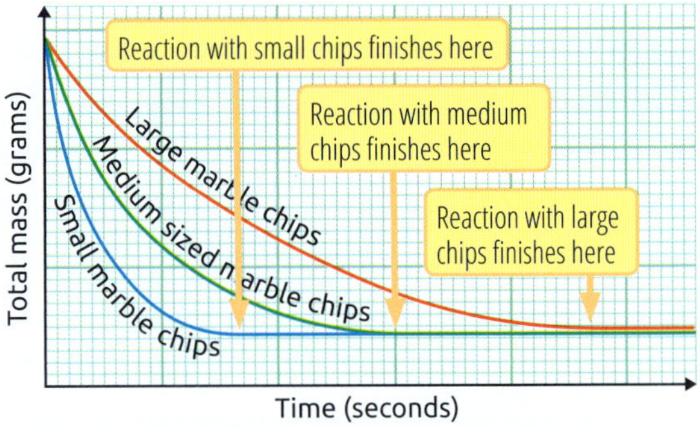

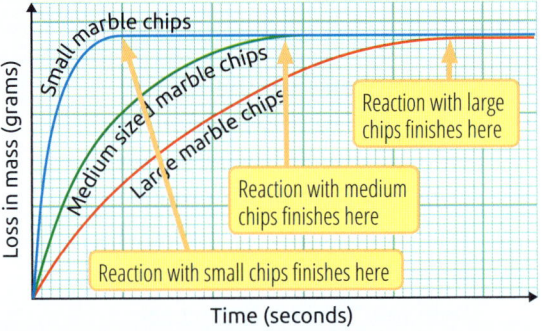

▶ Figure 21.11 The rate of reaction increases as the size of the marble chips gets smaller.

▶ Figure 21.12 The rate of loss of mass increases as the size of the marble chips gets smaller.

- In the case of the powdered marble, the rate of reaction is so fast that it cannot be measured accurately.
- We conclude that the rate of reaction depends on particle size.
- The smaller the particle size, the faster the rate.

 www.folensonline.ie/for-students

▶ **Test for carbon dioxide gas**

Carbon dioxide gas turns limewater milky. Also, a lighted taper is extinguished when placed in a container of carbon dioxide.

(iii) Concentration

▶▶ **Experiment 21.5**

To investigate the effect of concentration on the rate of reaction

- We react magnesium metal with different concentrations of hydrochloric acid in the apparatus shown in Figure 21.13.

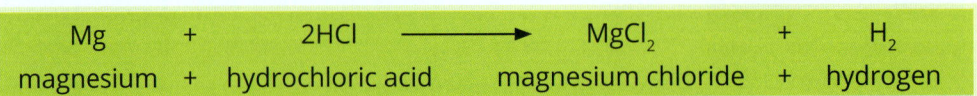

Mg + 2HCl ⟶ MgCl$_2$ + H$_2$
magnesium + hydrochloric acid ⟶ magnesium chloride + hydrogen

- A known mass of magnesium metal is added to the flask.
- The stopclock is immediately started.
- The stopper is placed on the conical flask.
- The volume of gas collected is recorded at regular time intervals, Table 21.3.

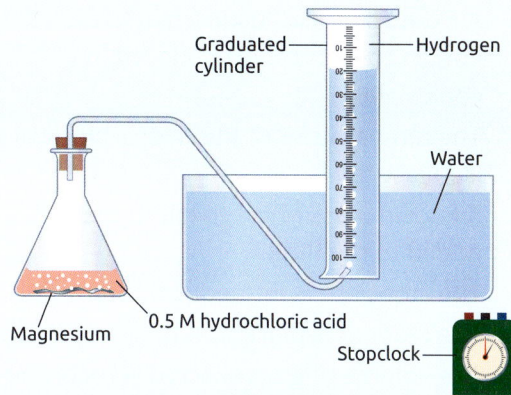

▶ Figure 21.13 This apparatus is used to study the effect of concentration on the rate of the reaction between magnesium and dilute hydrochloric acid.

Time (mins)	0	0.5	1.0	1.5	2.0	2.5	3.0	3.5
Volume of H_2 (cm³)								

▶ Table 21.3 The volumes of gas given off at regular time intervals are recorded in this type of table.

- The experiment is repeated with higher concentrations of acid.
- It is found that the rate of reaction increases as the concentration of hydrochloric acid increases.
- The results are plotted on graph paper of volume of H_2 given off versus time, Figure 21.14.
- We conclude that the rate of a reaction depends on concentration.
- The greater the concentration, the faster the rate.

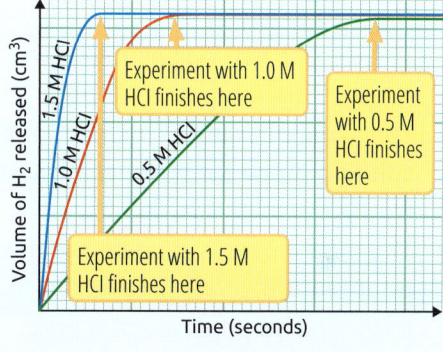

▶ Figure 21.14 The more concentrated the acid, the steeper the curve. This shows that, as the concentration of acid is increased, the rate of reaction also increases.

www.folensonline.ie/for-students

(iv) Temperature

▶▶ Experiment 21.6

To investigate the effect of temperature on the rate of reaction

- We react magnesium metal with a hydrochloric acid solution at different temperatures in the apparatus shown in Figure 21.15.

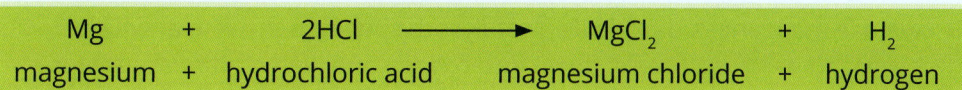

| Mg | + | 2HCl | → | MgCl$_2$ | + | H$_2$ |
| magnesium | + | hydrochloric acid | | magnesium chloride | + | hydrogen |

- A fixed volume of hydrochloric acid of known concentration is placed in a conical flask.
- The temperature of the hydrochloric acid is measured.
- A known mass of magnesium metal is added to the flask.
- The stopclock is immediately started.
- The stopper is placed on the conical flask.
- The volume of gas collected is recorded at regular time intervals, Table 21.4.

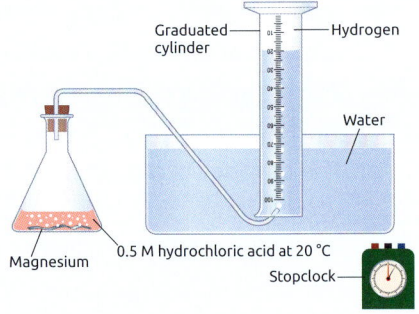

▶ Figure 21.15 This apparatus is used to study the effect of temperature on the rate of the reaction between magnesium and dilute hydrochloric acid.

Time (mins)	0	0.5	1.0	1.5	2.0	2.5	3.0	3.5
Volume of H_2 (cm³)								

▶ Table 21.4 The volumes of gas given off at regular time intervals are recorded in this type of table.

- The same quantity of hydrochloric acid solution of the same concentration is warmed to about 40 °C.
- The experiment is repeated with the hydrochloric acid at this temperature.
- The same quantity of hydrochloric acid solution of the same concentration is warmed to about 60 °C.
- The experiment is repeated at this temperature.
- It is found that the rate of reaction increases as the temperature increases.
- The results are plotted on graph paper of volume of H_2 given off versus time, Figure 21.16.
- We conclude that the rate of a reaction depends on temperature.
- The higher the temperature, the faster the rate.

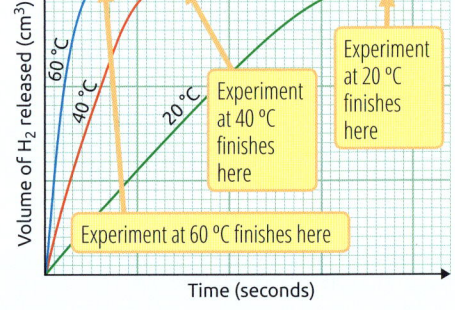

▶ Figure 21.16 The higher the temperature of the hydrochloric acid solution, the steeper the curve. This shows that, as the temperature of the acid is increased, the rate of reaction also increases.

www.folensonline.ie/for-students

(v) Catalysts

▶▶ Experiment 21.7

To investigate the effect of a catalyst on the rate of reaction

- We use manganese dioxide as a catalyst to speed up the rate at which hydrogen peroxide breaks down into oxygen and water in the apparatus shown in Figure 21.17.

- Some dilute hydrogen peroxide is placed in a conical flask.
- A small amount of manganese dioxide is quickly added to the hydrogen peroxide in the conical flask.
- The rubber stopper is immediately inserted in the conical flask.
- The stopclock is immediately started.
- The mixture is shaken briefly.
- The volume of gas in the graduated cylinder is measured at regular intervals, Table 21.5.

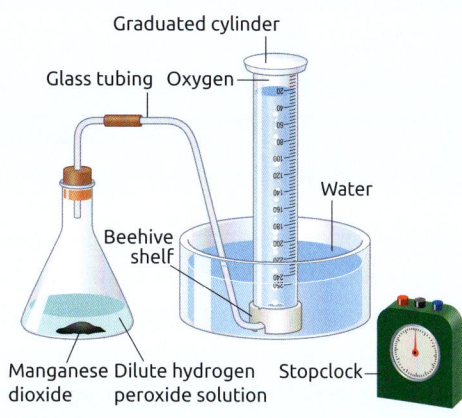

▶ Figure 21.17 This apparatus is used to study the rate at which hydrogen peroxide breaks down into oxygen and water. A catalyst called manganese dioxide is used to speed up the rate of reaction.

$$H_2O_2 \xrightarrow{MnO_2} H_2O + \tfrac{1}{2}O_2$$

hydrogen peroxide → water + oxygen

Time (mins)	0	0.5	1.0	1.5	2.0	2.5	3.0	3.5
Volume of O_2 (cm^3)								

▶ Table 21.5 The volumes of gas given off at regular time intervals are recorded in this type of table.

- A graph of volume of oxygen given off against time is drawn on graph paper, Figure 21.18.
- To illustrate the role of the catalyst, a graph for the uncatalysed reaction is also drawn. However, this is not drawn to scale as it could take many months for the hydrogen peroxide to completely break down if no catalyst were present.
- We conclude that the rate of a reaction is altered by the presence of a catalyst.
- The rate of decomposition of hydrogen peroxide is increased by the presence of manganese dioxide.

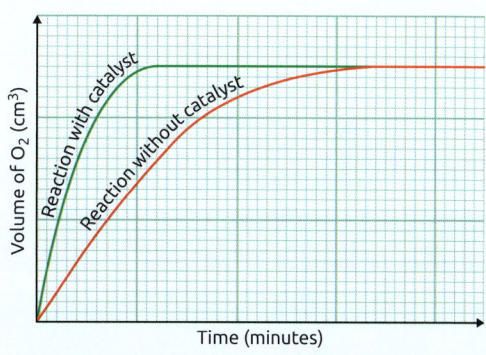

▶ Figure 21.18 The rate of reaction of the catalysed reaction is far greater than that of the uncatalysed reaction.

 www.folensonline.ie/for-students

▶ Test for oxygen gas

Oxygen rekindles a glowing wooden splint. Substances burn more vigorously in oxygen.

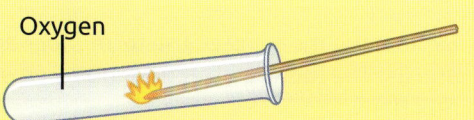

21.6 Rates of biochemical reactions

- The branch of science which studies the chemical reactions in living things is called **biochemistry**.

A **biochemical reaction** is a chemical reaction that takes place in living cells, i.e. a reaction in which new substances are formed.

There are many examples of biochemical reactions taking place inside animal and plant cells, e.g. cellular respiration, photosynthesis and digestion.

Enzymes are biological catalysts. These biological catalysts help biochemical reactions to take place at quite low temperatures inside cells, Figure 21.19.

The rates of biochemical reactions are affected by:

1. **Concentration** of enzymes and of the substances on which the enzymes are acting. The general name given to the substance on which an enzyme acts is the **substrate**.
2. **Temperature**: Many biochemical reactions only take place at specific temperatures.
3. **pH**: Many enzymes only work within specific pH ranges. Outside these pH ranges these enzymes become inactive.

▶ Figure 21.19 Liver contains an enzyme (biological catalyst) called catalase which speeds up the rate at which hydrogen peroxide is broken down in our bodies.

▶▶ Science Self-Assessment

Now I am able to:	🟢	🟠	🔴
Describe chemical reactions using word equations and balanced chemical equations			
Carry out an experiment to investigate if mass is unchanged when a chemical reaction takes place			
Investigate the five factors on which the rate of a reaction depends			
Interpret graphs obtained from investigating rates of reactions			
Explain the meaning of the term *biochemical reaction* and list the factors affecting the rates of biochemical reactions			

22
Reactions between acids and bases

The Chemical World strand

Main topics in this chapter:
- Common laboratory acids and bases
- Reaction of an acid with a base – neutralisation
- Acid rain – solving the problem

22.1 Common laboratory acids and bases

The two most common laboratory acids are hydrochloric acid (HCl) and sulfuric acid (H_2SO_4), Figure 22.1.

- Sulfuric acid and hydrochloric acid are **strong acids**.
- Strong acids are acids that break up (dissociate) almost completely when dissolved in water.

The most common bases that are used in the school laboratory are sodium hydroxide and calcium hydroxide.

- The chemical formula for sodium hydroxide is NaOH.
- Sodium hydroxide is commonly called caustic soda, Figure 22.2. The word *caustic* means it burns or destroys things. It is used to clear blocked drains.
- Sodium hydroxide is a **strong base**. Strong bases are bases that break up almost completely when dissolved in water. Sodium hydroxide dissolves in water to give a basic (alkaline) solution.
- Limewater is a chemical that is used to test for carbon dioxide.
- Limewater contains a base called calcium hydroxide.
- The formula for calcium hydroxide is $Ca(OH)_2$.

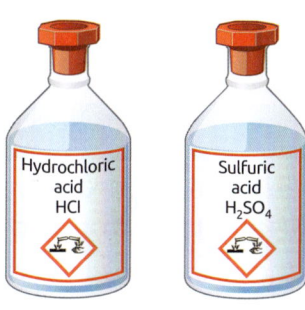

▶ Figure 22.1 Two common laboratory acids

▶ Figure 22.2 Sodium hydroxide is a common base. It is generally called caustic soda. It corrodes or 'eats away' the material that is blocking the drain.

119

22.2 Reaction of an acid with a base – neutralisation

The word *antacid* means against acid. Antacids are bases that cure stomach upsets by reacting with the excess acid in the stomach. Excess acid means that there is too much acid in your stomach, Figure 22.3.

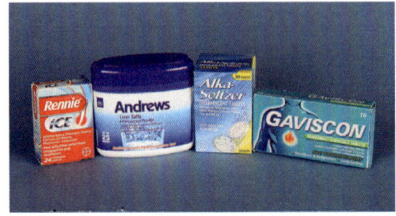

▶ Figure 22.3 Antacid tablets are used to react with excess acid in the stomach.

- The properties of an acid are counteracted or neutralised by a base.
- The reaction between an acid and a base is called a **neutralisation** reaction.
- The substance formed in a neutralisation reaction is often neutral (i.e. neither acidic nor basic).

When an acid and a base neutralise each other, a salt and water are formed.

$$\text{Acid + Base} \longrightarrow \text{Salt + Water}$$

There are lots of different salts but sodium chloride is the main one we meet in this course.

The most common example of a neutralisation reaction is the reaction between hydrochloric acid and sodium hydroxide.

$$\text{hydrochloric acid} + \text{sodium hydroxide} \longrightarrow \text{sodium chloride} + \text{water}$$
$$\text{HCl} + \text{NaOH} \longrightarrow \text{NaCl} + \text{H}_2\text{O}$$

▶▶ Experiment 22.1

To titrate hydrochloric acid (HCl) solution against sodium hydroxide (NaOH) solution and then to prepare a sample of sodium chloride (NaCl)

The method of adding one solution from a burette to another solution, in order to find out how much of the two solutions will just react with each other, is called a **titration**.

- The apparatus is set up as shown in Figure 22.4.
- Note that the acid is placed in the burette and the base is placed in the conical flask.
- A funnel is used to add the dilute hydrochloric acid solution to the burette.
- For safety reasons, a pipette filler is used to draw the base into the pipette.
- About three drops of methyl orange indicator are added to the conical flask.
- The acid is slowly added from the burette to the conical flask until one drop turns the indicator from orange to pink.
- During the titration, the inside wall of the conical flask is washed down with deionised water from a wash bottle. This ensures that any splashes of acid on the side of the flask are added to the base.

Exam Tip!
Remember: **A**CID **A**BOVE **B**ASE **B**ELOW

- The titration is repeated to check the accuracy of the result.
- The volume of hydrochloric acid found by titration is now added from the burette to a fresh portion of sodium hydroxide solution in the conical flask **without using an indicator**.
- The solution from the conical flask is emptied into an evaporating basin. The evaporating basin is placed on a hotplate.
- The solution is evaporated almost to dryness and is then allowed to cool.
- White crystals are formed in the evaporating basin. On analysis, these white crystals are found to be crystals of sodium chloride (common table salt).
- We conclude that hydrochloric acid and sodium hydroxide have reacted to form sodium chloride.

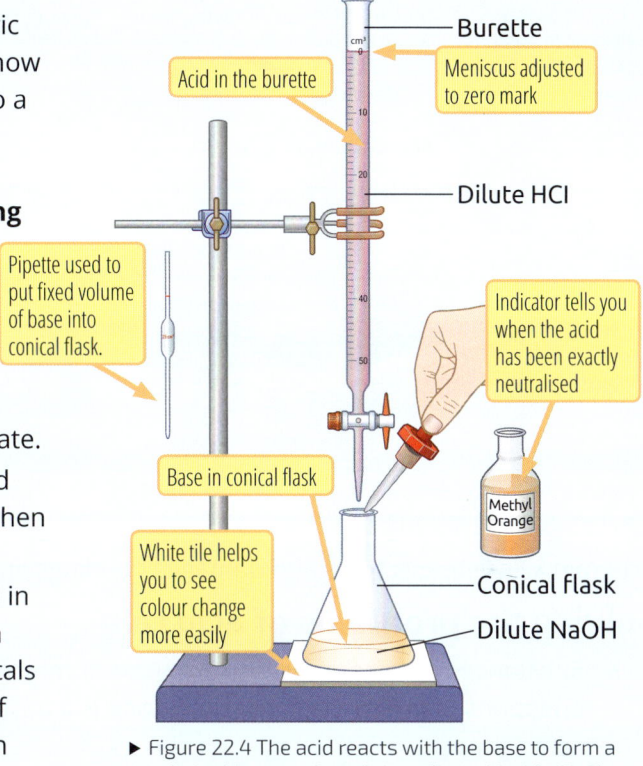

▶ Figure 22.4 The acid reacts with the base to form a salt. In this case, the salt is sodium chloride, NaCl.

22.3 Acid rain

- Rain is naturally slightly acidic because of dissolved carbon dioxide from the air.
- In some parts of Europe, rain is quite acidic with an average pH of around 4.1.
- Rainwater with a pH of less than 5.5 is described as **acid rain**.
- Acid rain contains sulfuric acid and nitric acid.
- Sulfuric acid comes from sulfur dioxide (SO_2) in the air. Most of the sulfur dioxide in the air comes from burning fossil fuels, Figure 22.5.
- The nitric acid in the air comes from the emissions of car exhausts.
- Car engines take in nitrogen and oxygen from the air. Car exhausts emit oxides of nitrogen.
- These oxides of nitrogen dissolve in water to form nitric acid.

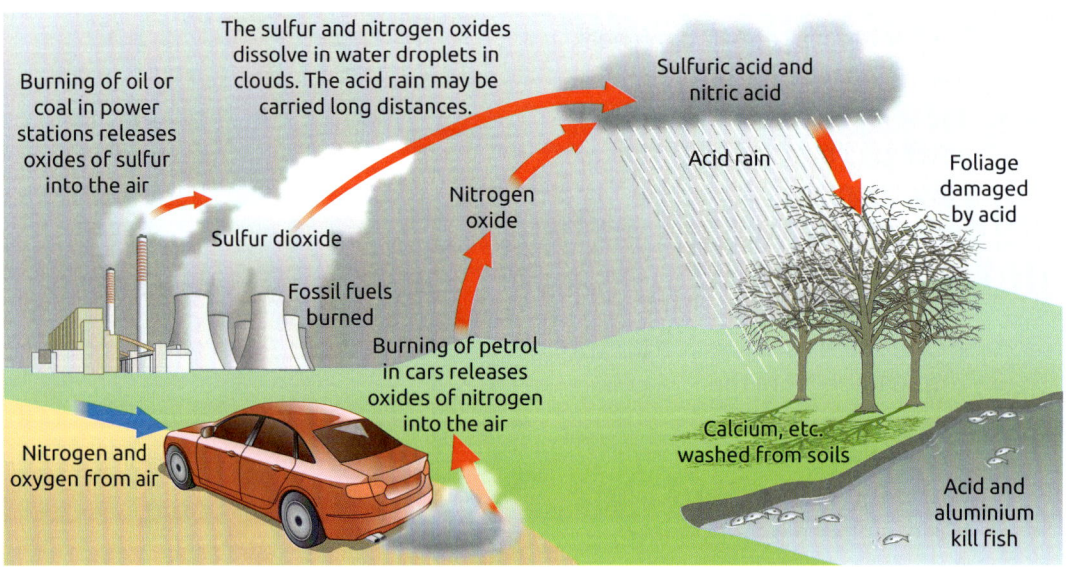

▶ Figure 22.5 Acid rain is formed when sulfur dioxide and oxides of nitrogen dissolve in water. Acid rain contains sulfuric acid and nitric acid.

Acid rain kills fish, kills trees and damages buildings and objects made of limestone.

Solving the problems of acid rain

- Substances such as limestone are used to remove the sulfur dioxide from the emissions of power stations. Limestone is a base and this neutralises the acidic gases.
- The sulfur content of fuels such as oil and gas is being reduced.
- Catalytic converters are now installed in the exhaust systems of cars. They contain catalysts that remove the harmful oxides of nitrogen from the exhaust fumes.
- Efforts are being made to burn less fossil fuel and to use other forms of energy instead, e.g. wind energy and hydroelectric energy.

▶▶ Science Self-Assessment

Now I am able to:	🟢	🟠	🔴
Name some common laboratory acids and bases			
Explain what happens when an acid and a base react with each other			
Carry out an acid–base titration and prepare a sample of a salt			
Discuss the problems caused by acid rain and explain the attempts being made to solve these problems			

23
Energy in chemical reactions

The Chemical World strand

Main topics in this chapter:
- Exothermic and endothermic reactions
- Activation Energy
- Energy profile diagrams

23.1 Heat changes in chemical reactions

- Almost all chemical reactions involve heat being given out or taken in.
- A chemical reaction which gives out heat is called an **exothermic** reaction.

An **exothermic reaction** is one that gives out heat.

Since heat is given out, a temperature rise is observed when an exothermic reaction takes place, Figure 23.1.
- All reactions which involve the burning of fuels are exothermic. For example, the burning of coal or natural gas are examples of exothermic reactions.

Some chemical reactions take in heat.

An **endothermic reaction** is one that takes in heat.

- A temperature drop is always observed when an endothermic reaction takes place, i.e. heat is taken in from the surroundings.
- When an endothermic reaction takes place in a test tube, heat flows from the surroundings into the test tube, Figure 23.2.
- An example of an endothermic reaction is the reaction of sherbet with water. This is why sherbet feels cold in your mouth when you eat it.

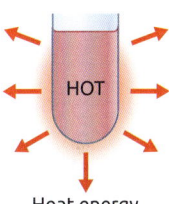

Heat energy is lost to the surroundings

▶ Figure 23.1 An exothermic reaction gives out heat, i.e. heat is lost to the surroundings.

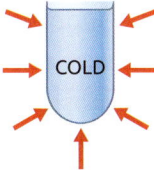

Heat energy is taken in from the surroundings

▶ Figure 23.2 An endothermic reaction takes in heat, i.e. the temperature falls at first and then heat is taken in from the surroundings.

23.2 Activation Energy

The Collision Theory states that:

- For a reaction to occur, the reacting particles must collide with each other.
- A collision will only result in the formation of products if a certain minimum energy is reached in the collision. This type of collision is called an effective collision.

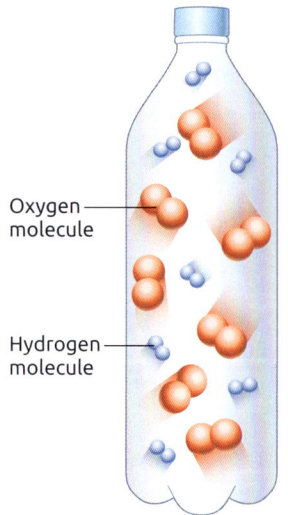

An **effective collision** is one that results in the formation of products.

Imagine a plastic bottle that has been filled with a mixture of hydrogen gas and oxygen gas, Figure 23.3.

- The particles of hydrogen gas consist of two hydrogen **atoms** joined together. This is called a **molecule** of hydrogen.
- The particles of oxygen gas consist of two atoms of oxygen joined together. This is called a **molecule** of oxygen.
- The plastic bottle contains millions of these molecules which are colliding with each other and with the walls of the bottle.

▶ Figure 23.3 This bottle contains a mixture of hydrogen gas and oxygen gas. The particles of hydrogen gas and oxygen gas are continually colliding with each other and with the walls of the bottle.

The **Activation Energy** is the minimum energy which colliding particles must have for a reaction to occur, i.e. the minimum energy required for effective collisions between particles to take place.

- Colliding particles have more energy at higher temperature as they are moving faster at the higher temperature.
- Therefore, there are more effective collisions at the higher temperature.
- Therefore, chemical reactions are faster at higher temperatures.
- In the mixture of hydrogen gas and oxygen gas in the bottle, extra energy needs to be supplied to cause the two gases to react.
- This extra energy is supplied by means of a lighted taper.
- An explosive reaction then takes place between the hydrogen and oxygen to form water.

$$2H_2 + O_2 \longrightarrow 2H_2O$$
hydrogen + oxygen ⟶ water

This explosive reaction launches a bottle containing a mixture of hydrogen and oxygen into the air!

23.3 Energy profile diagrams

Chemists use diagrams to represent the energy changes that take place when a chemical reaction takes place. An example of this type of diagram is shown in Figure 23.4. This type of diagram is called an **energy profile diagram** or a **reaction profile diagram**.

> An **energy profile diagram** is a graph which shows the change in energy of a chemical reaction with time as the reaction takes place.

An example of an energy profile diagram for a reaction with a small Activation Energy is shown in Figure 23.5.

- The size of the Activation Energy depends on the types of chemicals (reactants) reacting together.
- Some reactions have a large Activation Energy, i.e. a lot of energy must be supplied to get the reactants to react. Therefore, these reactions are slow or may not occur at all.
- Some reactions have a small Activation Energy, i.e. only a little energy must be supplied to get the reactants to react. Therefore, these reactions are fast.

An exothermic reaction may be represented on an energy profile diagram as shown in Figure 23.6. The energy given out is represented by the symbol ΔH pronounced 'delta H'. The symbol Δ stands for 'change'.

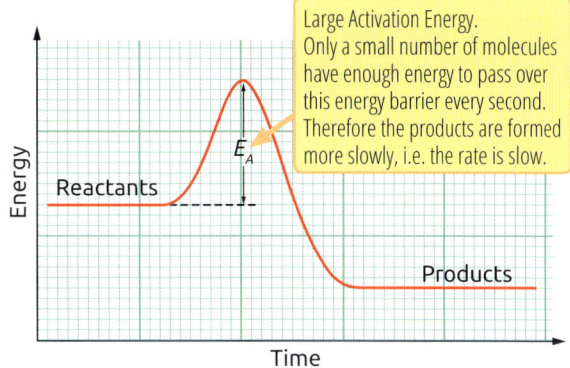

▶ Figure 23.4 An energy profile diagram for a reaction with a large Activation Energy.

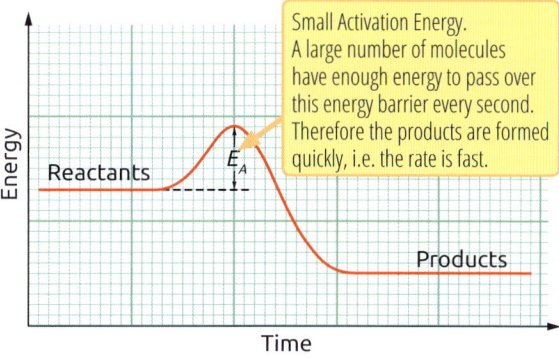

▶ Figure 23.5 An energy profile diagram for a reaction with a small Activation Energy.

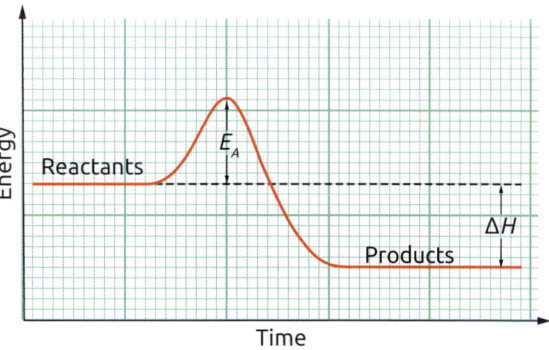

▶ Figure 23.6 An energy profile diagram for an exothermic reaction. Note that the products have less energy than the reactants. The energy given out is represented by the symbol ΔH.

An endothermic reaction may be represented on an energy profile diagram as shown in Figure 23.7.

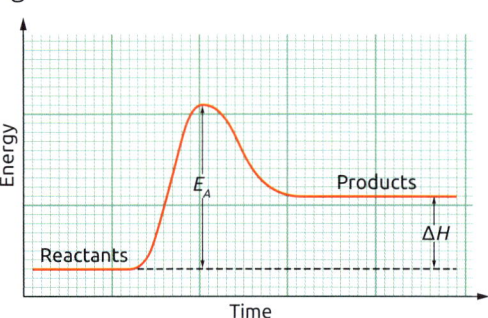

▶ Figure 23.7 An energy profile diagram for an endothermic reaction. Note that the products have more energy than the reactants. The energy taken in is represented by the symbol ΔH.

How do we explain why a catalyst affects the rate of reaction?

- A catalyst works by providing an alternative route for the reaction to occur.
- This alternative route has a lower Activation Energy, Figure 23.8.
- Due to the lower Activation Energy, more molecules now have the energy for effective collisions to occur, i.e. the rate of reaction increases.

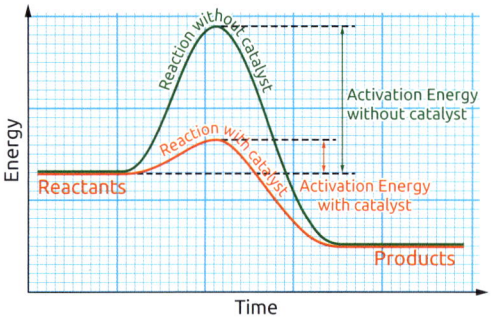

▶ Figure 23.8 A catalyst reduces the Activation Energy for a reaction. The diagram shows the energy profile diagram for a catalysed and uncatalysed **exothermic** reaction.

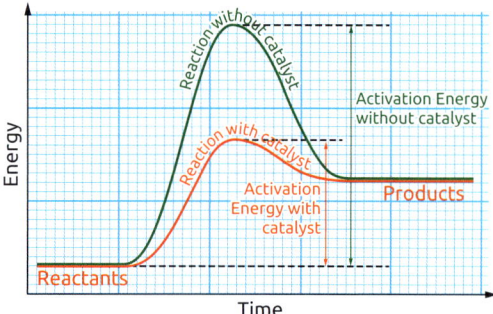

▶ Figure 23.9 The diagram shows the energy profile diagram for a catalysed and uncatalysed **endothermic** reaction.

It is also possible to represent a catalysed and uncatalysed endothermic reaction using an energy profile diagram, Figure 23.9.

▶▶ Science Self-Assessment

Now I am able to:	🟢	🟡	🔴
Explain exothermic and endothermic reactions			
Investigate exothermic and endothermic reactions in the laboratory			
Explain Collision Theory and Activation Energy			
Interpret energy profile diagrams			

24
Structure of the atom

The Chemical World strand

Main topics in this chapter:
- Atomic structure and subatomic particles
- Atomic number and mass number
- Atomic structures of some elements

24.1 The atom

Scientists have discovered that the materials around us are made up of millions of tiny particles. These particles are called **atoms**.

- John Dalton, Figure 24.1, was an English scientist who imagined atoms to be like very small marbles or billiard balls.
- He said that an atom of copper is the smallest piece of copper that shows all the properties of copper.

An **atom** is the smallest particle of an element which still has the properties of that element.

▶ Figure 24.1 John Dalton put forward a theory about atoms in 1808.

Atoms are very small. There are about 10^{16} atoms of carbon in the full stop at the end of this sentence. To see atoms, a special type of microscope called an electron microscope is used.

24.2 Particles inside atoms

Scientists have found that there are tiny particles inside an atom. These particles are called **subatomic particles**. The word *subatomic* means inside the atom. There are three types of subatomic particle.

- The **proton** has a positive charge on it. It is located in the centre of the atom. The centre of the atom is called the **nucleus**.
- The **electron** has a negative charge on it. It is located outside the nucleus of the atom in a region called the electron cloud.
- The **neutron** has no charge on it (neutral). It is located in the nucleus.

The properties of protons, neutrons and electrons are summarised in Table 24.1.

Name of particle	Location in the atom	Relative mass	Relative charge
Proton	Nucleus	1 unit	+1 unit
Neutron	Nucleus	1 unit	0
Electron	Outside the nucleus	$\frac{1}{1840}$ unit	-1 unit

▶ Table 24.1 Summary of the properties of the subatomic particles

The electron is the lightest of the subatomic particles. The mass of the electron is only $\frac{1}{1840}$ of the mass of the proton, Figure 24.2.

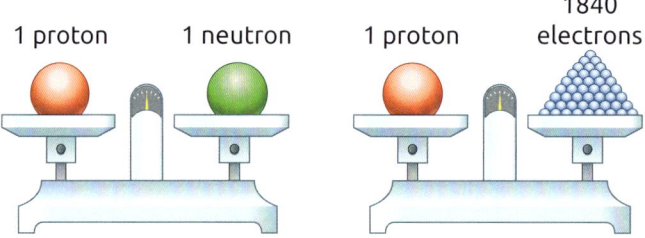

▶ Figure 24.2 Protons and neutrons have the same mass. The electron is a very light particle compared to the proton and neutron.

24.3 Atomic structure of some elements

A Danish scientist called Niels Bohr proposed that the electrons move around the nucleus in fixed paths called **orbits**, Figure 24.3. These orbits are also called **shells**.

- Bohr's model is often called the planetary model.
- The electrons revolve around the nucleus just like the planets move around the Sun, Figure 24.4.

▶ Figure 24.3 Niels Bohr proposed that electrons orbit the nucleus. He received the Nobel prize for physics for his work on the structure of the atom.

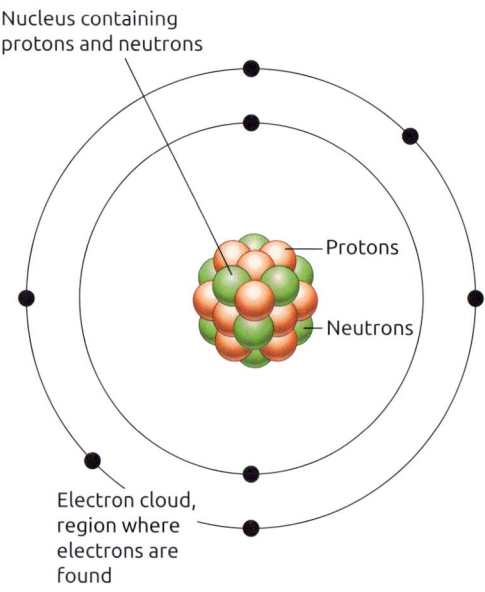

▶ Figure 24.4 The protons and neutrons are in the nucleus of the atom. The electrons revolve around the nucleus in orbits.

The common image for an atom shows the electrons in orbit around the nucleus, Figure 24.5.

- All atoms are neutral. Therefore, the number of protons (positive) must be equal to the number of electrons (negative).

The **atomic number** of an atom is the number of protons in the nucleus of that atom.

- The **mass number** gives us information about the mass of an atom.

Mass Number = Number of Protons + Number of Neutrons

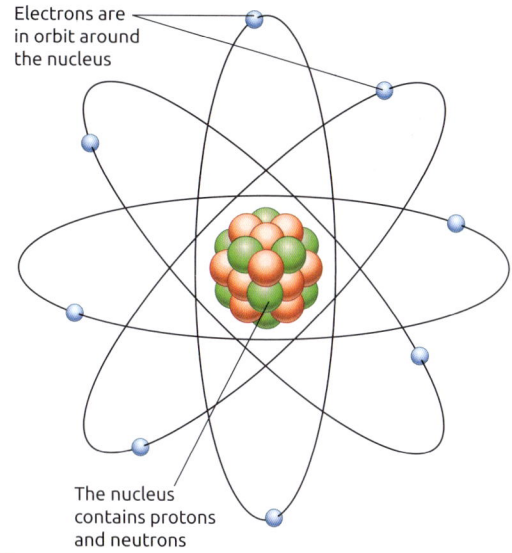

▶ Figure 24.5 This type of image is commonly used to represent atoms. It shows the electrons in orbit around the nucleus.

- The atomic number and the mass number are often written with the symbol of the element, as shown for aluminium in Figure 24.6.
- This shorthand method of showing the atomic number and the mass number of an atom is called the **nuclear formula**.

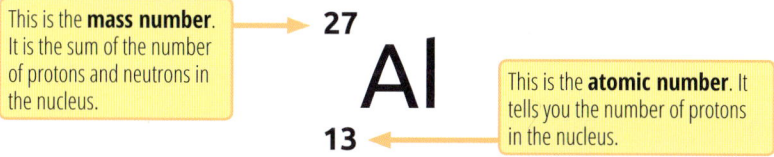

▶ Figure 24.6 Writing the nuclear formula for an atom gives us information about its structure.

Studying Figure 24.6 gives us the following information.
- Atomic number of aluminium = 13. This means that an atom of aluminium contains 13 protons and 13 electrons.
- Mass number of aluminium = 27. This means that the sum of the protons and neutrons = 27.
- Since the atomic number is 13, this means that aluminium is the thirteenth element in the Periodic Table.
- We know that the mass of the atom is 27. We know there are 13 protons in the atom. Therefore, there must be 14 neutrons with the protons so that the sum will be 27. Number of neutrons = 27 − 13 = 14.

Number of neutrons = mass number − atomic number

The structures of the atoms of the first 20 elements are given in Table 24.2. Study this table carefully. Note that hydrogen is the only element that has no neutrons in its nucleus.

Element	Atomic number	Number of protons	Number of electrons	Mass number	Number of neutrons (= mass no. – atomic no.)
$^{1}_{1}H$	1	1	1	1	1–1 = 0
$^{4}_{2}He$	2	2	2	4	4–2 = 2
$^{7}_{3}Li$	3	3	3	7	7–3 = 4
$^{9}_{4}Be$	4	4	4	9	9–4 = 5
$^{11}_{5}B$	5	5	5	11	11–5 = 6
$^{12}_{6}C$	6	6	6	12	12–6 = 6
$^{14}_{7}N$	7	7	7	14	14–7 = 7
$^{16}_{8}O$	8	8	8	16	16–8 = 8
$^{19}_{9}F$	9	9	9	19	19–9 = 10
$^{20}_{10}Ne$	10	10	10	20	20–10 = 10
$^{23}_{11}Na$	11	11	11	23	23–11 = 12
$^{24}_{12}Mg$	12	12	12	24	24–12 = 12
$^{27}_{13}Al$	13	13	13	27	27–13 = 14
$^{28}_{14}Si$	14	14	14	28	28–14 = 14
$^{31}_{15}P$	15	15	15	31	31–15 = 16
$^{32}_{16}S$	16	16	16	32	32–16 = 16
$^{35}_{17}Cl$	17	17	17	35	35–17 = 18
$^{40}_{18}Ar$	18	18	18	40	40–18 = 22
$^{39}_{19}K$	19	19	19	39	39–19 = 20
$^{40}_{20}Ca$	20	20	20	40	40–20 = 20

▶ Table 24.2 The structures of the atoms of the first 20 elements

▶▶ Science Self-Assessment

Now I am able to:	🟢	🟠	🔴
Explain the term *atom*			
Describe the structure of the atom			
Explain the terms *atomic number* and *mass number*			
Write the numbers of protons, neutrons and electrons in the atoms of the first 20 elements			

25
The Periodic Table

The Chemical World strand

▶▶ **Main topics in this chapter:**
- Structure of the Periodic Table
- Drawing Bohr structures of atoms
- Using the Periodic Table to predict ratios of atoms in compounds

25.1 What is the Periodic Table?

- The word *periodic* means at regular intervals.
- The properties of the elements repeat at regular intervals in the Periodic Table. For example, the properties of lithium (element number 3) are repeated in sodium (element number 11) and also in potassium (element number 19), Figure 25.1.

> The **Periodic Table** is an arrangement of elements in order of increasing atomic number.

																		0 18
	I	II			Name	1 H HYDROGEN 1.008	Atomic number Symbol Relative atomic mass					III	IV	V	VI	VII		2 He HELIUM 4.003
n = 1 period	1	2										13	14	15	16	17		
n = 2 period	3 Li LITHIUM 6.941	4 Be BERYLLIUM 9.012										5 B BORON 10.81	6 C CARBON 12.01	7 N NITROGEN 14.01	8 O OXYGEN 16.00	9 F FLUORINE 19.00		10 Ne NEON 20.18
n = 3 period	11 Na SODIUM 22.99	12 Mg MAGNESIUM 24.31	3	4	5	6	7	8	9	10	11	12	13 Al ALUMINIUM 26.98	14 Si SILICON 28.09	15 P PHOSPHORUS 30.97	16 S SULFUR 32.07	17 Cl CHLORINE 35.45	18 Ar ARGON 39.95
n = 4 period	19 K POTASSIUM 39.10	20 Ca CALCIUM 40.08	21 Sc SCANDIUM 44.96	22 Ti TITANIUM 47.87	23 V VANADIUM 50.94	24 Cr CHROMIUM 52.00	25 Mn MANGANESE 54.94	26 Fe IRON 55.85	27 Co COBALT 58.93	28 Ni NICKEL 58.69	29 Cu COPPER 63.55	30 Zn ZINC 65.41	31 Ga GALLIUM 69.72	32 Ge GERMANIUM 72.64	33 As ARSENIC 74.92	34 Se SELENIUM 78.96	35 Br BROMINE 79.90	36 Kr KRYPTON 83.80
n = 5 period	37 Rb RUBIDIUM 85.47	38 Sr STRONTIUM 87.62	39 Y YTTRIUM 88.91	40 Zr ZIRCONIUM 91.22	41 Nb NIOBIUM 92.91	42 Mo MOLYBDENUM 95.94	43 Tc TECHNETIUM (97.91)	44 Ru RUTHENIUM 101.1	45 Rh RHODIUM 102.9	46 Pd PALLADIUM 106.4	47 Ag SILVER 107.9	48 Cd CADMIUM 112.4	49 In INDIUM 114.8	50 Sn TIN 118.7	51 Sb ANTIMONY 121.8	52 Te TELLURIUM 127.6	53 I IODINE 126.9	54 Xe XENON 131.3
n = 6 period	55 Cs CAESIUM 132.9	56 Ba BARIUM 137.3	57 ● La LANTHANUM 138.9	72 Hf HAFNIUM 178.5	73 Ta TANTALUM 180.9	74 W TUNGSTEN 183.8	75 Re RHENIUM 186.2	76 Os OSMIUM 190.2	77 Ir IRIDIUM 192.2	78 Pt PLATINUM 195.1	79 Au GOLD 197.0	80 Hg MERCURY 200.6	81 Tl THALLIUM (204.4)	82 Pb LEAD (207.2)	83 Bi BISMUTH (208.98)	84 Po POLONIUM (209.0)	85 At ASTATINE (210.0)	86 Rn RADON (222.0)
n = 7 period	87 Fr FRANCIUM (223.0)	88 Ra RADIUM (226.0)	89 ● Ac ACTINIUM (227.0)	104 Rf RUTHERFORDIUM (261.1)	105 Db DUBNIUM (262.1)	106 Sg SEABORGIUM (266.1)	107 Bh BOHRIUM (264.1)	108 Hs HASSIUM (277.0)	109 Mt MEITNERIUM (268.1)	110 Ds DARMSTADTIUM (271)	111 Rg ROENTGENIUM (272.2)	112 Cn COPERNICIUM (285)						

● 58 – 71 Lanthanoid series
● 90 – 103 Actinoid series

▶ Figure 25.1 The Periodic Table of the elements. For simplicity, elements 58–71 and 90–103 are not included.

This type of table was first drawn up in 1869 by a Russian chemist called Dmitri Mendeleev, Figure 25.2. A copy of the Periodic Table is on p.264 of this book. A Periodic Table is also available in the *Formulae and Tables* booklet for use in the state exams.

The following are important points about the Periodic Table:

- In the Periodic Table elements with similar properties are arranged under one another in vertical columns.
- The vertical columns are called **groups** or **families**, Figure 25.3.
- There are eight main groups in the Periodic Table. The groups are numbered using the roman numerals I, II, III, IV, V, VI, VII and VIII.
- For each of the Groups I – VII, the group number is also the number of electrons in the outer orbit of the elements in that group.
- A more modern numbering system labels the groups from 1–18, as also shown in Figure 25.3.

▶ Figure 25.2 In 1869 Dmitri Mendeleev arranged all the known elements in the form of a table.

	Alkali metals I / 1	Alkaline Earth metals II / 2					Transition metals							III / 13	IV / 14	V / 15	VI / 16	Halogens VII / 17	Noble (inert) gases 0 / 18
n=1 period	1 H HYDROGEN 1.008																		2 He HELIUM 4.003
n=2 period	3 Li LITHIUM 6.941	4 Be BERYLLIUM 9.012												5 B BORON 10.81	6 C CARBON 12.01	7 N NITROGEN 14.01	8 O OXYGEN 16.00	9 F FLUORINE 19.00	10 Ne NEON 20.18
n=3 period	11 Na SODIUM 22.99	12 Mg MAGNESIUM 24.31	3	4	5	6	7	8	9	10	11	12		13 Al ALUMINIUM 26.98	14 Si SILICON 28.09	15 P PHOSPHORUS 30.97	16 S SULFUR 32.07	17 Cl CHLORINE 35.45	18 Ar ARGON 39.95
n=4 period	19 K POTASSIUM 39.10	20 Ca CALCIUM 40.08	21 Sc SCANDIUM 44.96	22 Ti TITANIUM 47.87	23 V VANADIUM 50.94	24 Cr CHROMIUM 52.00	25 Mn MANGANESE 54.94	26 Fe IRON 55.85	27 Co COBALT 58.93	28 Ni NICKEL 58.69	29 Cu COPPER 63.55	30 Zn ZINC 65.41		31 Ga GALLIUM 69.72	32 Ge GERMANIUM 72.64	33 As ARSENIC 74.92	34 Se SELENIUM 78.96	35 Br BROMINE 79.90	36 Kr KRYPTON 83.80
n=5 period	37 Rb RUBIDIUM 85.47	38 Sr STRONTIUM 87.62	39 Y YTTRIUM 88.91	40 Zr ZIRCONIUM 91.22	41 Nb NIOBIUM 92.91	42 Mo MOLYBDENUM 95.94	43 Tc TECHNETIUM (97.91)	44 Ru RUTHENIUM 101.1	45 Rh RHODIUM 102.9	46 Pd PALLADIUM 106.4	47 Ag SILVER 107.9	48 Cd CADMIUM 112.4		49 In INDIUM 114.8	50 Sn TIN 118.7	51 Sb ANTIMONY 121.8	52 Te TELLURIUM 127.6	53 I IODINE 126.9	54 Xe XENON 131.3
n=6 period	55 Cs CAESIUM 132.9	56 Ba BARIUM 137.3	57 La LANTHANUM 138.9	72 Hf HAFNIUM 178.5	73 Ta TANTALUM 180.9	74 W TUNGSTEN 183.8	75 Re RHENIUM 186.2	76 Os OSMIUM 190.2	77 Ir IRIDIUM 192.2	78 Pt PLATINUM 195.1	79 Au GOLD 197.0	80 Hg MERCURY 200.6		81 Tl THALLIUM (204.4)	82 Pb LEAD (207.2)	83 Bi BISMUTH (208.98)	84 Po POLONIUM (209.0)	85 At ASTATINE (210.0)	86 Rn RADON (222.0)
n=7 period	87 Fr FRANCIUM (223.0)	88 Ra RADIUM (226.0)	89 Ac ACTINIUM (227.0)	104 Rf RUTHERFORDIUM (261.1)	105 Db DUBNIUM (262.1)	106 Sg SEABORGIUM (266.1)	107 Bh BOHRIUM (264.1)	108 Hs HASSIUM (277.0)	109 Mt MEITNERIUM (268.1)	110 Ds DARMSTADTIUM (271)	111 Rg ROENTGENIUM (272.2)	112 Cn COPERNICIUM (285)							

▶ Figure 25.3 Some groups in the Periodic Table are given special names.

> All elements in the same group of the Periodic Table have similar chemical properties.

This is because all the elements in the same group have the same number of electrons in their outer orbit (shell). It is the electrons in the outer orbit that determine the chemical properties of the elements.

25.2 Drawing Bohr structures of atoms

We can use the Periodic Table to draw the structure of atoms of the elements. To draw the Bohr structure of an atom, follow two steps:

(i) Use the Periodic Table to work out the number of protons and neutrons in the nucleus of the atom.

(ii) Use the Periodic Table to show the arrangement of electrons in the atom.

(i) Work out the number of protons and neutrons

- Find the element in the Periodic Table.
- Note the number above the element (atomic number). This is the number of protons, e.g. carbon is the sixth element in the Periodic Table. Therefore, its atomic number is 6, i.e. there are 6 protons in the nucleus.
- Note the number under the symbol in the Periodic Table. This is the mass number, e.g. the mass number of carbon is 12 since the number 12 appears in the box underneath the symbol for carbon, Figure 25.4 (a). (The number is actually the 'relative atomic mass' but rounding it off gives us the mass number.)
- To work out the number of neutrons in the atom, subtract the atomic number from the mass number, as shown in Chapter 24.

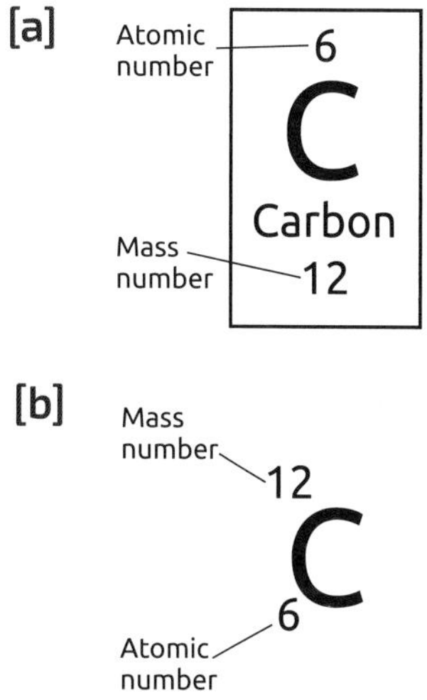

(ii) Show the arrangement of electrons in an atom

- The electron arrangement of the atoms of an element is the number of electrons in each orbit (shell).
- Another name for electron arrangement is **electron configuration**.
- The electron configuration of an element may easily be worked out from its position in the Periodic Table.

▶ Figure 25.4 (a) In the Periodic Table, the atomic number appears above the symbol and the mass number appears below the symbol. (b) The nuclear formula for an atom of carbon. Remember that the atomic number is always the **smaller** number.

The Bohr structures of the atoms of the first 20 elements in the Periodic Table are shown in Figure 25.5. For each element, carefully study the Bohr structure of its atoms. Note that, since atoms are neutral, the number of electrons is always equal to the number of protons.

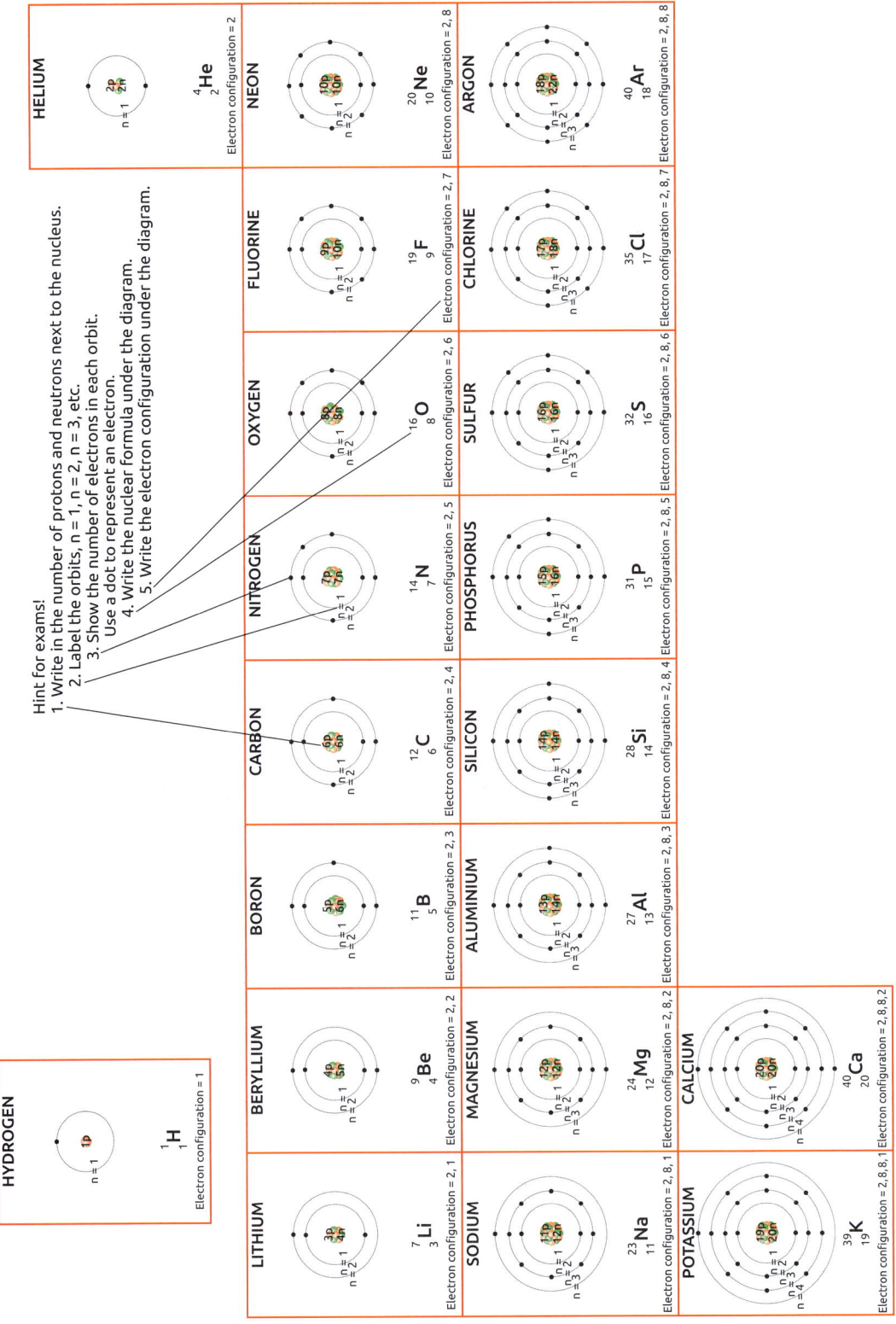

▶ Figure 25.5 Bohr structures of the atoms of the first 20 elements of the Periodic Table

25.3 Using the Periodic Table to predict ratios of atoms in compounds

We first study chemical reactions between elements on the extreme left and elements on the extreme right of the Periodic Table, Figure 25.6.

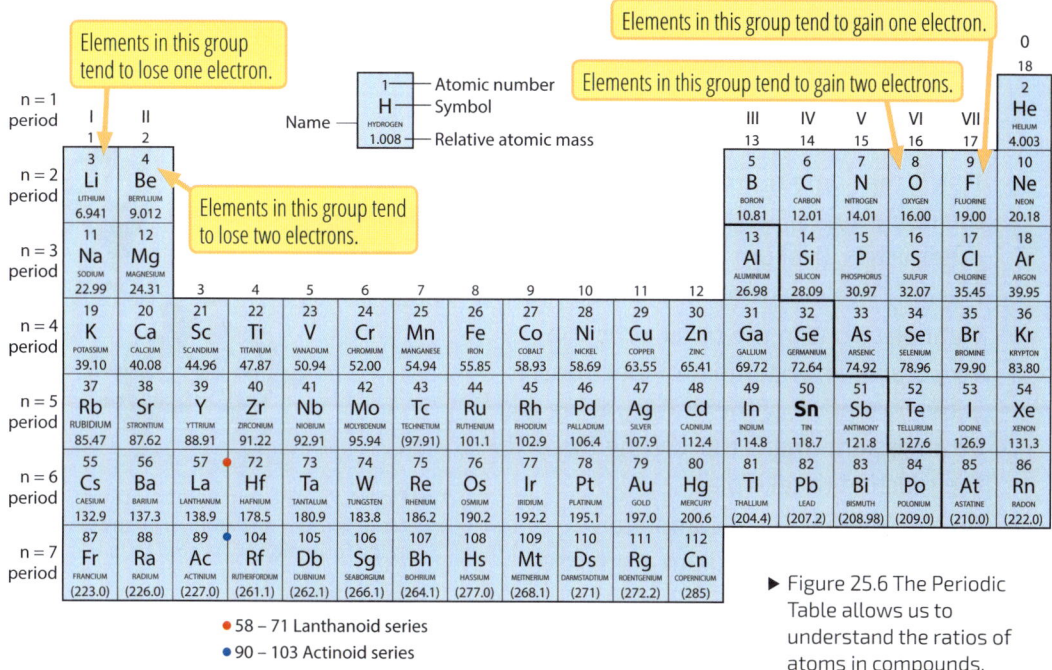

▶ Figure 25.6 The Periodic Table allows us to understand the ratios of atoms in compounds.

Formation of ionic bonds

If a piece of heated sodium metal is placed in a gas jar of chlorine, crystals of sodium chloride are immediately formed. Sodium chloride is common table salt.
The following reaction has occurred:

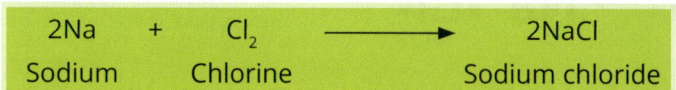

$$2Na + Cl_2 \longrightarrow 2NaCl$$
Sodium + Chlorine → Sodium chloride

- Sodium chloride is made up of charged atoms called ions.
- The sodium atoms have changed into positively-charged sodium ions: Na^+.
- The chlorine atoms have changed into negatively-charged chloride ions: Cl^-.

The following takes place when sodium reacts with chlorine:

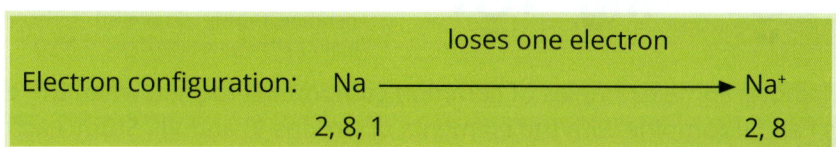

Electron configuration: Na $\xrightarrow{\text{loses one electron}}$ Na^+
2, 8, 1 → 2, 8

The sodium atom has lost an electron to form a positively-charged sodium ion. Each chlorine atom gains an electron to form a negatively-charged chloride ion:

Electron configuration:	Cl	gains one electron ⟶	Cl⁻
	2, 8, 7		2, 8, 8

- Both the Na⁺ ion and the Cl⁻ ion have **eight electrons** in their outer orbits.
- This is the same number of electrons as the noble gases (inert gases) have in their outer orbits. (Helium is an exception as it has only two electrons in its outer orbit.)
- Eight electrons in the outer orbit is a very stable arrangement of electrons. It is the formation of this stable, noble gas arrangement that is the 'driving force' for the reaction to take place.
- An electron has been completely transferred from a sodium atom to a chlorine atom, Figure 25.7.
- The force of attraction between the positive and negative charges binds the ions together in what is called an **ionic bond**. The formation of this ionic bond is shown in Figure 25.8.
- Since each sodium atom loses just one electron and each chlorine atom gains just one electron, the ratio Na : Cl is exactly 1 : 1. Therefore, the formula of sodium chloride may be written as Na⁺Cl⁻ or NaCl.

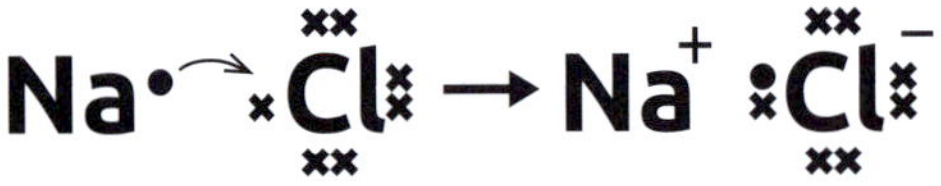

▶ Figure 25.7 The complete transfer of an electron from one atom to another results in the formation of Na⁺ and Cl⁻ ions.

Na• ⤳ ₓCl ₓ⁺ₓ → Na⁺ :Cl:⁻

▶ Figure 25.8 Each sodium atom loses just one electron and each chlorine atom gains just one electron. Therefore, the formula of sodium chloride is NaCl.

Similarly, the formation of the ionic bond in magnesium oxide is shown in Figure 25.9. Note that, since each magnesium atom loses exactly two electrons and each oxygen atom gains exactly two electrons, the ratio Mg : O is exactly 1 : 1. Therefore, the formula of magnesium oxide may be written as $Mg^{2+}O^{2-}$ or MgO.

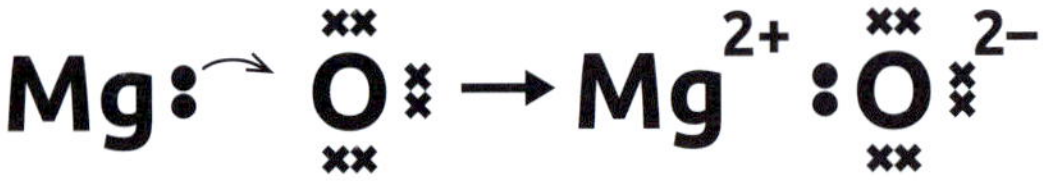

Mg: ⤳ :Ö: → Mg²⁺ :Ö:²⁻

▶ Figure 25.9 Each magnesium atom loses two electrons. Each oxygen atom gains two electrons. Therefore, the Mg : O ratio is 1 : 1. Therefore, the formula of magnesium oxide is MgO.

Table 25.1 shows some examples of common compounds formed when the elements of Groups I and II combine with the elements of Groups VI and VII. Study each example carefully and check that you understand how the formula of each compound is found.

Group I or Group II element	Group VI or Group VII element	Formula of compound formed	Name of compound
Li	Cl	LiCl	Lithium chloride
Na	F	NaF	Sodium fluoride
K	I	KI	Potassium iodide
Mg	F	MgF_2	Magnesium fluoride
Ca	Cl	$CaCl_2$	Calcium chloride
Li	O	Li_2O	Lithium oxide
Na	O	Na_2O	Sodium oxide
K	S	K_2S	Potassium sulfide
Mg	O	MgO	Magnesium oxide
Ca	S	CaS	Calcium sulfide

▶ Table 25.1 Some examples of compounds formed between the elements of Groups I and II and those of Groups VI and VII

Formation of covalent bonds

In Figure 25.10 we have indicated that a carbon atom combines with four atoms of hydrogen.

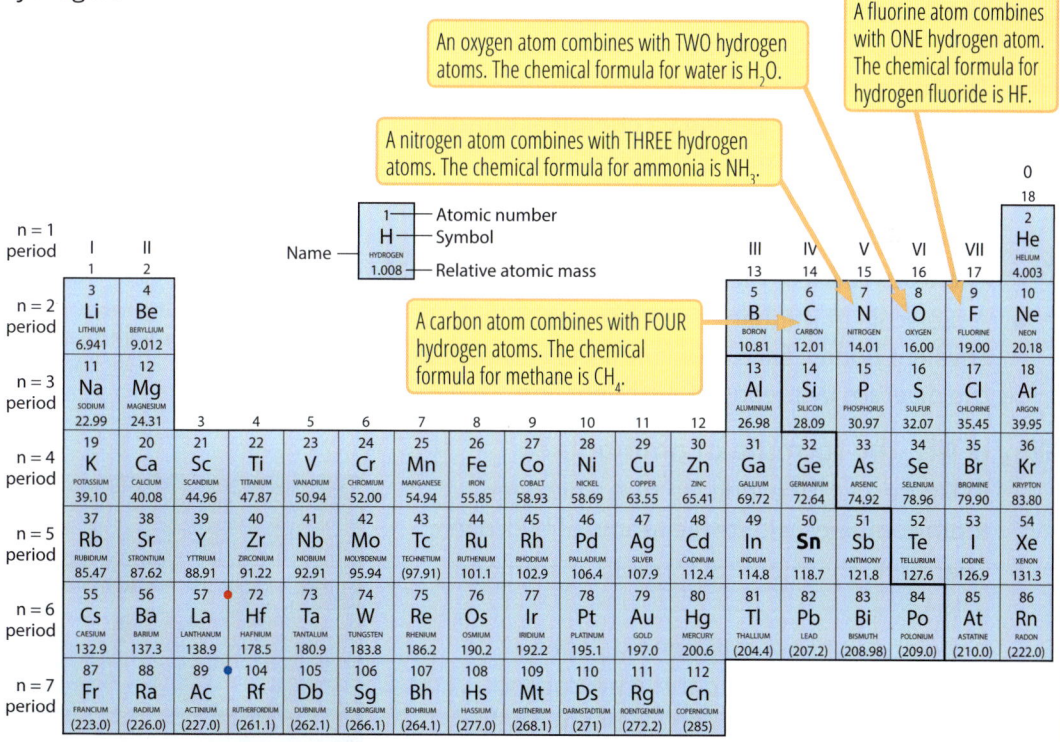

▶ Figure 25.10 The Periodic Table allows us to understand the ratios of atoms in compounds

Methane is commonly referred to as *natural gas*. This gas consists of tiny particles made up of one carbon atom joined to four hydrogen atoms, Figure 25.11. These tiny particles are called **molecules**.

> A **molecule** is a group of atoms joined together. It is the smallest particle of an element or compound that can exist independently.

Why is CH_4 the formula of methane?

- If you look back at Figure 25.5, you will see that there are four electrons in the outer orbit of a carbon atom.
- We can also see this from the fact that since carbon is in Group IV of the Periodic Table, it must have four electrons in its outer orbit.
- Chemists have found that atoms try to have eight electrons in the outer orbit.
- To get these eight electrons, the four electrons in the outer orbit of a carbon atom are shared with four atoms of hydrogen as shown in Figure 25.12.
- The carbon atom and the four hydrogen atoms are joined or **bonded** together.
- The force of attraction that holds a molecule of methane together is called a **chemical bond**. In methane, there are four chemical bonds.
- Since this type of chemical bond involves sharing of electrons we call it a **covalent bond**. The word *covalent* means 'sharing'.
- A molecule of methane is held together by four covalent bonds. Each covalent bond is shown in the diagram by means of a straight line.

▶ Figure 25.11 Methane consists of one carbon atom joined to four hydrogen atoms. Therefore, the formula of methane is CH_4.

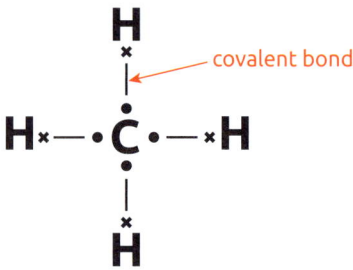

▶ Figure 25.12 In the methane molecule, a carbon atom is joined by covalent bonds to four hydrogen atoms.

Why is NH_3 the formula of ammonia?

- In Figure 25.10 we indicate that a nitrogen atom combines with three atoms of hydrogen.
- Therefore, the chemical formula of ammonia is NH_3.
- A molecule of ammonia consists of one nitrogen atom joined to three hydrogen atoms. A model of a molecule of ammonia is shown in Figure 25.13.
- If you look back at Figure 25.5, you will see that there are five electrons in the outer orbit of a nitrogen atom.

▶ Figure 25.13 Ammonia consists of one nitrogen atom joined to three hydrogen atoms. Therefore, the formula of ammonia is NH_3.

- We can also see that since nitrogen is in Group V of the Periodic Table, it must have five electrons in its outer orbit.
- To get eight electrons, three electrons in the outer orbit of a nitrogen atom are shared with three atoms of hydrogen.
- The three covalent bonds that are formed are shown in Figure 25.14.

▶ Figure 25.14 In the ammonia molecule, a nitrogen atom is joined by covalent bonds to three hydrogen atoms. The pair of electrons not involved in bonding is called a lone pair.

- Two electrons in the outer orbit of nitrogen are not involved in bonding. This pair of electrons is called a **lone pair**.

Why is H_2O the formula of water?

In Figure 25.10 we have indicated that an oxygen atom combines with two atoms of hydrogen. Therefore, the chemical formula of water is H_2O. A molecule of water consists of one oxygen atom joined to two hydrogen atoms. A model of a molecule of water is shown in Figure 25.15.

▶ Figure 25.15 A water molecule consists of one oxygen atom joined to two hydrogen atoms. Therefore, the formula of water is H_2O.

The bonding in the water molecule is shown in Figure 25.16.

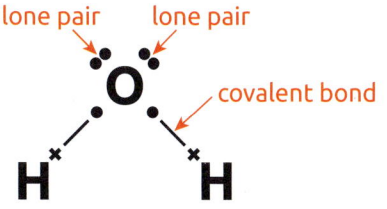

▶ Figure 25.16 In the water molecule, an oxygen atom is joined by covalent bonds to two hydrogen atoms. The four electrons of oxygen which are not involved in bonding are present as two lone pairs.

Why is HF the formula of hydrogen fluoride?

In Figure 25.10 we have indicated that a fluorine atom combines with one atom of hydrogen. Therefore, the chemical formula of hydrogen fluoride is HF. A molecule of hydrogen fluoride consists of one fluorine atom joined to one hydrogen atom. A model of a molecule of hydrogen fluoride is shown in Figure 25.17.

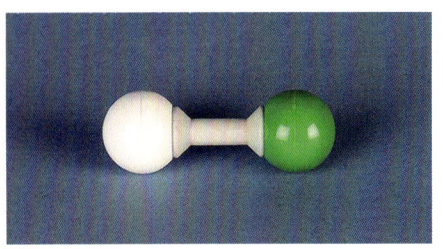

▶ Figure 25.17 Hydrogen fluoride consists of one fluorine atom joined to one hydrogen atom. Therefore, the formula of hydrogen fluoride is HF.

The bonding in the hydrogen fluoride molecule is shown in Figure 25.18.

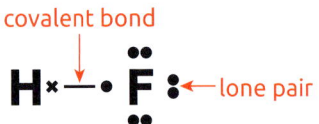

▶ Figure 25.18 In the hydrogen fluoride molecule, a fluorine atom is joined by a covalent bond to a hydrogen atom. Note that there are three lone pairs on the fluorine atom.

Since chlorine is in the same group of the Periodic Table as fluorine, the formula for hydrogen chloride is HCl.

▶▶ Science Self-Assessment

Now I am able to:	🟢	🟡	🔴
Describe the structure of the Periodic Table			
Draw Bohr structures of atoms			
Use the Periodic Table to predict the ratios of atoms in compounds			
Explain how ionic and covalent bonds are formed			

26 Metals and non-metals

The Chemical World strand

Main topics in this chapter:
- Metals in our everyday lives
- Properties of metals
- Properties of non-metals
- Alloys
- Rusting and its prevention

26.1 Introduction

Metals play an important role in our everyday lives.
- All the metals are on the left of the 'steps of stairs' of the Periodic Table, Figure 26.1.
- The elements on the right of the 'steps of stairs' are called non-metals.

▶ Figure 26.1 The elements of the Periodic Table may be divided into metals and non-metals by the 'steps of stairs' going from boron to astatine.

141

26.2 Properties of metals

The properties of metals may be summarised as follows:

- Many metals are shiny, e.g. gold and silver. Scientists use the word **lustrous** to describe this property of metals.
- Metals can be stretched and made into wires, e.g. copper wire. Since metals can be stretched, we say that they are **ductile**.
- Metals can be beaten into various shapes. For example, panel beaters have to beat the steel in a crashed car back into shape. Scientists use the word **malleable** to describe the property of metals which allows them to be beaten into various shapes.
- Metals are **good conductors of heat**, i.e. they allow heat to pass through them easily. This means that metals are very useful for making pots and pans.
- Metals are **good conductors of electricity**, i.e. they allow electricity to pass through them easily. Therefore, metals are very useful as wiring in electrical circuits.
- Many metals are **strong**. The fact that steel is so strong means that it can support a heavy load. Therefore, it can be used for building bridges and for supporting buildings.

▶ Figure 26.2 Metals have certain properties that make them very useful in our everyday lives.

Some uses of metals are summarised in Figure 26.2.

Many metals tend to lose electrons. For example, when sodium metal reacts with chlorine gas, each sodium atom loses an electron.

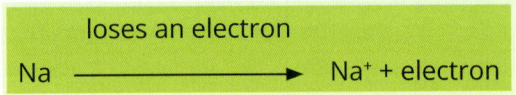

This property of metals is used to give a definition of the term *metal*.

A **metal** is an element that tends to form positive ions.

26.3 Properties of non-metals

Some examples of non-metals in our everyday lives are shown in Figure 26.3.

Some properties of **non-metals** may be summarised as follows:

- Many non-metals are gases.
- Non-metals are **not good conductors of heat**.
- Non-metals are **not good conductors of electricity**.
- Non-metals that are solids tend to be brittle, i.e. they cannot be hammered into different shapes but shatter instead.

Non-metals tend to gain electrons. For example, when sodium metal reacts with chlorine gas, each chlorine atom gains an electron.

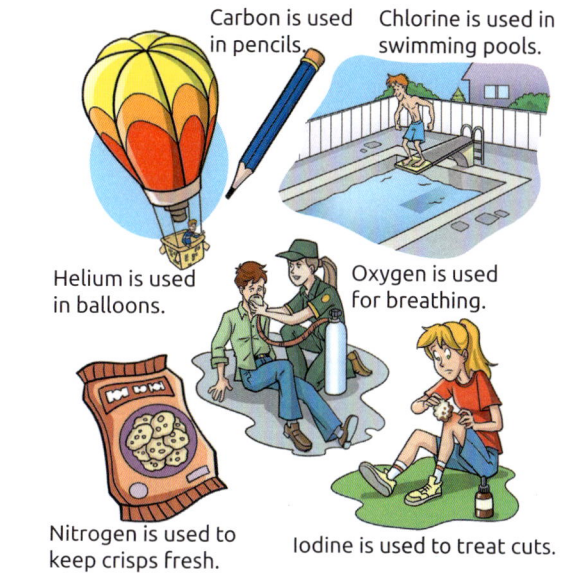

Figure 26.3 Some examples of non-metals

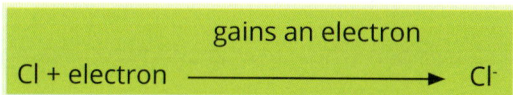

This property of non-metals is used to give a definition of the term *non-metal*.

A **non-metal** is an element that tends to form negative ions.

26.4 A metal or a non-metal?

To distinguish between a metal and a non-metal, we carry out an experiment to see if it conducts electricity, Figure 26.4. Metals conduct electricity. Non-metals do not conduct electricity.

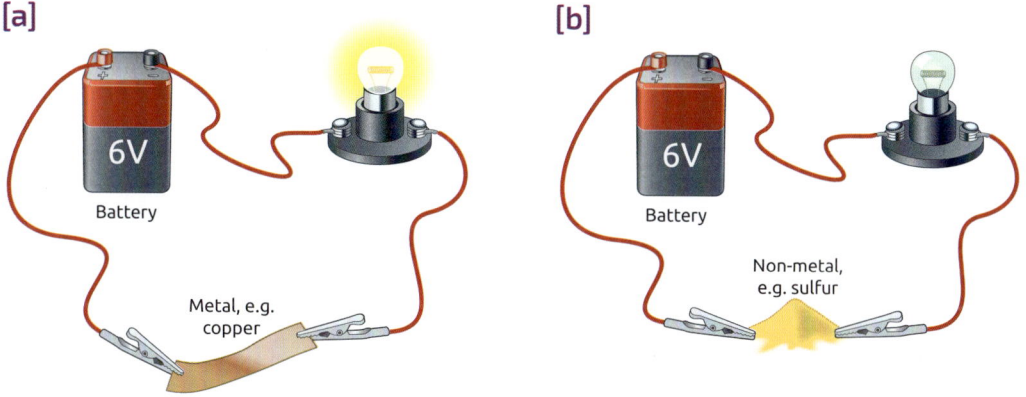

Figure 26.4 (a) Metals are good conductors of electricity: the bulb lights. (b) Non-metals do not conduct electricity: the bulb does not light.

26.5 Alloys

Some of the metallic substances that we meet in our everyday lives are not made of pure metals. The coins you use every day are mixtures of metals. Such mixtures of metals are called **alloys**.

An **alloy** is a mixture of metals.

Examples of alloys are:
- **Brass** is a mixture of copper and zinc.
- **Bronze** is a mixture of copper and tin.
- **Steel** is a mixture of iron and carbon.
- **Solder** is a mixture of lead and tin.

Some uses of each of the above alloys are shown in Figure 26.5.

▶ Figure 26.5 Some uses of the alloys brass, bronze, steel and solder

26.6 Corrosion of metals

The corrosion of iron and steel is called rusting.

Rusting is a chemical reaction in which iron is changed into a new substance (rust).

▶▶ Experiment 26.1

To investigate the conditions necessary for rusting to occur

The experiment to investigate the conditions necessary for rusting to occur is summarised in Figure 26.6.

- The only nail that rusts is the nail in contact with both air (oxygen) and water (test tube 1).
- We conclude that both air (oxygen) and water are necessary for rusting.

▶ Figure 26.6 This experiment proves that both air and water are necessary for rusting to occur. The only nail that rusts is the nail in the first test tube. Only this nail is in contact with both air and water.

 www.folensonline.ie/for-students

How is rusting prevented?

The three main ways of rust prevention are:

1. **Painting:** The paint forms a layer over the metal and prevents air and water coming into contact with the metal.
2. **Oiling or greasing:** The oil or grease forms a layer over the surface of the metal and prevents air and water coming into contact with the metal.
3. **Galvanising:** The object is coated with zinc to prevent the metal coming into contact with air or water. Iron coated with zinc is called **galvanised** iron.

▶▶ Science Self-Assessment

Now I am able to:	🟢	🟠	🔴
Discuss the role played by metals and non-metals in our everyday lives			
State some properties of metals and non-metals			
Carry out an experiment to distinguish between a metal and a non-metal			
Name some examples of alloys and give some examples of alloys in our everyday lives			
Investigate the conditions necessary for rusting to occur			
Explain three methods of rust prevention			

27 Sustainability

The Chemical World strand

Main topics in this chapter:
- The meaning of sustainability and sustainable development
- The three pillars of sustainability
- Sustainability and population growth
- Sustainability and fossil fuels
- Disposal and recycling of materials
- How we as individuals contribute to sustainability

27.1 What is sustainability?

The word *sustainable* means 'able to be maintained or held at a certain level and kept going into the future'.

Sustainability is the conservation of balance in the world's ecology indefinitely.

- Sustainability means that the Earth will continue to provide fresh air, food and clean water, and ensure a good quality of life for ourselves and for all future generations, Figure 27.1.
- We must try to avoid damage to the environment and also to maintain our natural resources at a certain level so that they do not become completely used up.

Sustainable development is development that meets the needs of the present without compromising the ability of future generations to meet their own needs.

▶ Figure 27.1 The study of sustainability helps to provide us with 'care instructions' for our planet.

27.2 The three pillars of sustainability

Sustainability may be explained in terms of three pillars, Figure 27.2.

Environmental pillar: This includes the area of environmental protection, such as addressing climate change, protection of resources and protection of biodiversity.

Economic pillar: This involves planning economic development, e.g. setting up new industries to provide employment and developing the agricultural industry.

Social pillar: This involves social sustainability in the areas of international and national laws, careful planning for future developments in cities and towns and planning transport systems.

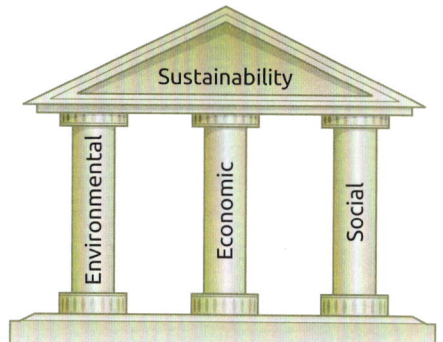

▶ Figure 27.2 To solve the overall challenges of sustainability, we must address environmental sustainability, economic sustainability and social sustainability.

27.3 Sustainability and population growth

- The growth in population increases the demand for clean air, clean water and food.
- An increased population puts greater pressure on land and raw materials. More land is needed for building new houses and for increasing the sizes of towns and cities.
- An increase in population also means an increase in the consumption of natural resources.

27.4 Sustainability and fossil fuels

Any substance that burns in oxygen (or air) to produce heat is called a **fuel**.

> A **fuel** is any substance that burns in oxygen to produce heat.

- The most commonly used fuels in the world are coal, oil and natural gas.
- Coal, oil and natural gas are commonly called **fossil fuels**.

> **Fossil fuels** are fuels that were formed from the remains of plants and animals that lived millions of years ago.

Although the three types of fossil fuel look completely different, they all consist of the same sort of compounds. These compounds are called **hydrocarbons**.

> **Hydrocarbons** are compounds consisting of hydrogen and carbon only.

- When hydrocarbons are burned, carbon dioxide and water are formed.
- Since fossil fuels contain hydrocarbons, when these fuels are burned, carbon dioxide and water are always formed.

fossil fuel	+	oxygen	→	carbon dioxide	+	water
e.g. methane	+	oxygen	→	carbon dioxide	+	water
(natural gas)						
CH_4	+	$2O_2$	→	CO_2	+	$2H_2O$

- As more fossil fuels are burned, increased levels of carbon dioxide gas are building up in the atmosphere, Figure 27.3.
- Carbon dioxide is one of the main 'greenhouse gases'. Without these greenhouse gases, heat would be lost from the Earth and life on Earth could not exist.
- This natural trapping of the Sun's energy by the atmosphere is called the **greenhouse effect**.
- Scientists are concerned that increasing concentrations of carbon dioxide are causing the Earth to get warmer. This is called the **enhanced greenhouse effect**. The extra warming that results from the enhanced greenhouse effect is called **global warming**.
- There is concern that the supply of fossil fuels on Earth is running out.
- This type of fuel is said to be a **non-renewable** fuel, i.e. once the fossil fuels are used up, there will be no more left.
- In order to have sustainable development we must reduce our dependence on fossil fuels. Scientists are now developing biofuels.
- **Biofuels** are fuels made from plants, e.g. rapeseed oil and sunflower oil.

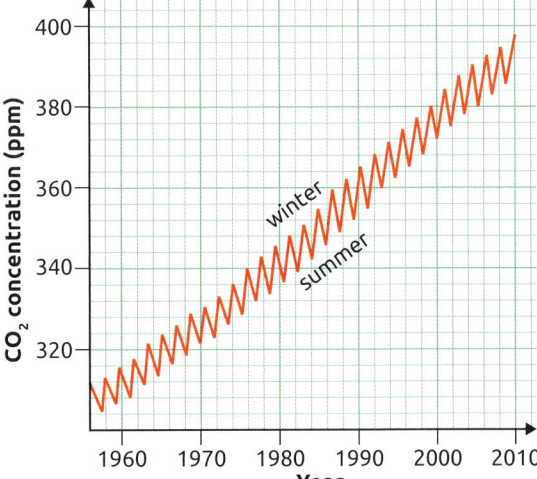

▶ Figure 27.3 The rising levels of carbon dioxide in the atmosphere are causing concern as it is thought that this increase is contributing to global warming.

27.5 Extraction and use of materials – implications for sustainability

Many raw materials are obtained from the Earth. These raw materials are employed in the making of many useful products. Examples of these raw materials are:

- **Crude oil**. This is extracted from the ground. When the crude oil is refined, many useful products are obtained from it, e.g. petrol, diesel and central heating oil. The crude oil is heated and various parts (or 'fractions') are separated from it by distillation. Therefore, the process is called fractional distillation.
- **Timber**. Efforts are being made to develop sustainable forests. This means that no more timber is being cut than can be regrown.

27.6 Disposal and recycling of materials – implications for sustainability

Pollution is the addition of harmful substances to the environment in quantities greater than can be dealt with efficiently by the environment itself.

- Examples of pollutants are sewage, excessive amounts of fertilisers and toxic substances.
- Air pollution commonly arises from the burning of fossil fuels, which causes acid rain.
- For sustainability to be achieved, the amount of material that ends up in landfill needs to be kept to a minimum.

Recycling of plastics is important for a number of reasons:

- It saves one of our most important natural resources – crude oil, which is the raw material for the manufacture of plastics.
- It helps keep the cost of plastics low when oil becomes too costly to be used as a raw material.
- It keeps down the cost of waste disposal. Plastic materials make up about 20 per cent by volume of domestic refuse.
- It helps reduce litter. Since most plastics are non-biodegradable, discarded plastics are among the worst forms of litter.
- It helps create employment for workers with a wide variety of skills.

Therefore, it is necessary to sort the plastics into their individual types, Figure 27.4.

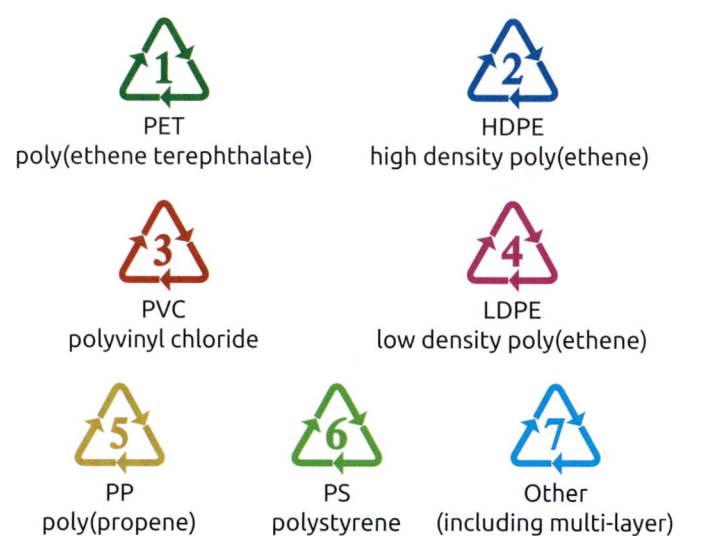

▶ Figure 27.4 The coding system used to help separate plastics for recycling

27.7 How can we as individuals contribute to sustainability?

Some examples of ways that we can contribute to sustainability are illustrated in Figure 27.5 and summarised in Table 17.1.

▶ Figure 27.5 Some examples of ways that we can contribute to sustainability

Area of our lives	Examples of contributions to sustainability
Travel and leisure	When possible, walk or cycle rather than drive. Use public transport wherever possible. Take holidays nearer home to reduce demand for air travel.
At home	Insulate your home to conserve heat energy. Turn off lights and other appliances when not needed. Use low-energy bulbs. Recycle as many materials as possible.
Purchasing goods	Reuse shopping bags rather than getting new ones. Purchase products that are made locally. Complain to manufacturers when goods are supplied with excessive packaging. Repair rather than replace items where possible.
At school and at work	Treat your consumption of water, heat and electricity as if you were paying for them yourself. Encourage the authorities at school and at work to implement initiatives that encourage sustainability.

▶▶ Science Self-Assessment

Now I am able to:	🟢	🟠	🔴
Explain the terms *sustainability* and *sustainable development*			
Discuss the three pillars of sustainability			
Discuss how the burning of fossil fuels affects sustainability			
Explain how the extraction, use, disposal and recycling of materials affects sustainability			
Give examples of how individuals can contribute to sustainability			

28

Measuring length, area, volume, time, mass and temperature

The Physical World strand

Main topics in this chapter:
- Selecting the most suitable instruments to measure length, area, volume, time, mass and temperature
- The units used to measure length, area, volume, time, mass and temperature

28.1 Measuring

In order to measure a quantity, we need a suitable **instrument** and a **unit** of measurement that others will understand.

28.2 Length

- The unit of length is the metre.
- A number of instruments can be used to measure length, Figure 28.1. Different instruments are needed for different situations. Table 28.1 summarises these instruments and their uses.

[a]

[b]
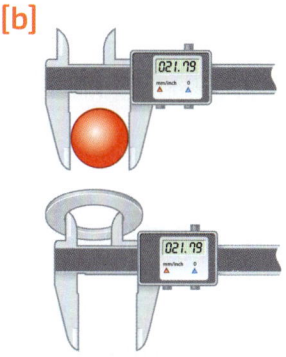

[c]

▶ Figure 28.1 (a) Trundle wheel (b) Digital callipers (c) Opisometer

151

Instrument	Use
Trundle wheel	Measuring large distances such as the length of a field
Metre stick	Measuring lengths up to 1 metre
Digital callipers	Measuring small distances accurately Measuring the diameter of a circular object
Opisometer	Measuring the length of a curved line

▶ Table 28.1 Different instruments for measuring length

28.3 Area

You will have learned how to calculate the **area** of various shapes in your Maths course. For example, the area of a rectangle is calculated by the formula: **Area = Length × Width**

> The **area** of an object is the amount of surface enclosed within its boundary.

- The area of an irregular shape can be estimated using centimetre grid paper, Figure 28.2.

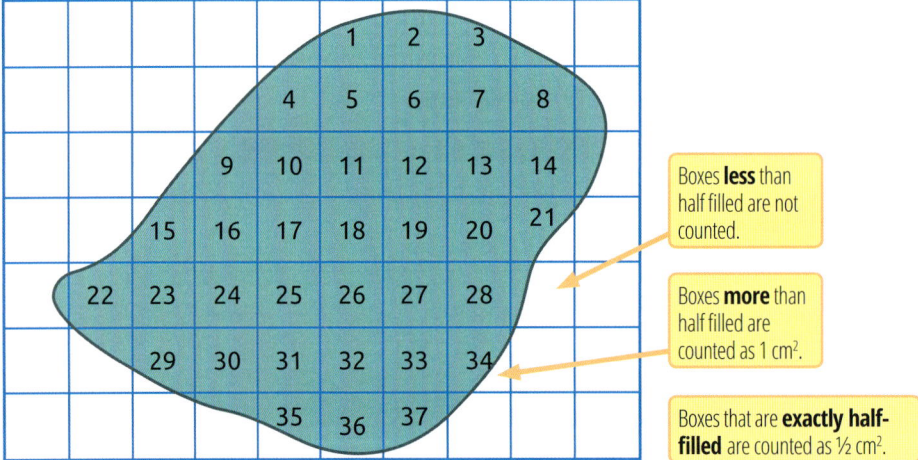

Boxes **less** than half filled are not counted.

Boxes **more** than half filled are counted as 1 cm².

Boxes that are **exactly half-filled** are counted as ½ cm².

▶ Figure 28.2 Estimating the area of an irregular shaped object using centimetre grid paper

28.4 Volume

> The **volume** of an object is the amount of space that the object takes up.

- The unit that we use most commonly in the laboratory is the centimetre cubed (cm³).
- In your Maths course, you will have learned how to **calculate** the volume of a number of regular shapes.
- For example, the volume of a cube or a rectangular object can be calculated by the formula: **Volume = Length × Width × Height**

> **Exam Tip!**
>
> If you are asked to give a use for the graduated cylinder, a vague answer such as 'to measure a liquid' will not gain full marks. The correct answer is 'to measure the **volume** of a liquid'.

- The volume of a liquid is found using a **graduated cylinder**.
- When using a graduated cylinder it is important to read the bottom of the meniscus at eye level, Figure 28.3 (b).
- In Chapter 22 you found out that a **pipette** and a **burette** can measure the volume of a liquid more accurately.
- The volume of an irregular shaped object can be found using an **overflow can with a graduated cylinder**. You will learn more about this in Chapter 29, Experiment 29.1.

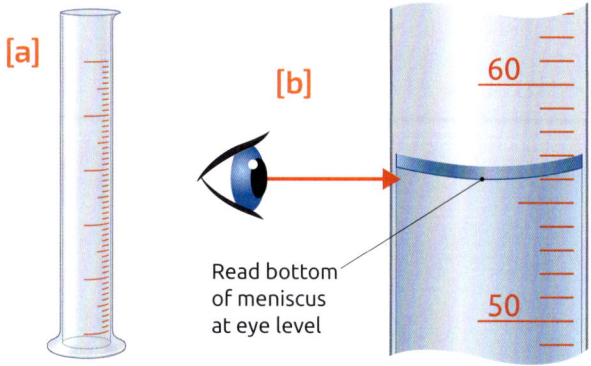

▶ Figure 28.3 (a) A graduated cylinder. (b) You should read the bottom of the meniscus at eye level.

28.5 Other measuring instruments

A variety of other measuring instruments are used to measure other quantities. You will use these instruments throughout your Physics course. Table 28.2 summarises information about these instruments.

Instrument	Used to measure	Unit
Thermometer	Temperature	Degree Celsius (°C)
Timer	Time	Second (s)
Electronic balance	Mass	Gram (g)
Motion sensor	Speed	Metre per second (m s^{-1})
Motion sensor	Acceleration	Metre per second per second (m s^{-2})
Newton meter	Force	Newton (N)
Joule meter	Electrical energy	Joules (J)
Voltmeter	Voltage	Volt (V)
Ammeter	Current	Ampere (A)
Ohmmeter	Resistance	Ohm (Ω)

▶ Table 28.2 Some instruments used to measure quantities in physics

▶▶ Science Self-Assessment

Now I am able to:	🟢	🟠	🔴
Choose, name and use the appropriate instruments to measure length, area, volume, time, mass and temperature			
Name the units of length, area, volume, time, mass and temperature			
Accurately measure (i) the length of a straight line, (ii) the length of a curved line, (iii) the diameter of a circular object			
Calculate the area of square and rectangular objects, and estimate the area of an irregular shape			
Describe how to find the volume of solids and liquids			

29 Density

The Physical World Strand

Main topics in this chapter:
- The meaning of density
- How to calculate the density of an object
- How density helps us to explain flotation
- The importance of density in our everyday lives

29.1 Density – definition and calculations

$$\text{Density} = \frac{\text{mass (g)}}{\text{volume (cm}^3\text{)}}$$

Density can also be defined as the mass of 1 cm³ of a substance.
The units of density are g/cm³.
The following example shows how density may be calculated.

▶▶ Worked Example 29.1

The mass of a stone is 60 g and its volume is 30 cm³. Calculate the density.

Answer

1. Write down the formula: $\text{Density} = \dfrac{\text{mass}}{\text{volume}}$

2. Fill in the mass in grams and the volume in cm³: $= \dfrac{60 \text{ g}}{30 \text{ cm}^3}$

3. Calculate the answer. Always include the correct units. $= 2 \text{ g/cm}^3$

Exam Tip!
If you use this step-by-step method in calculations and you make an error in the calculation, you may still get some marks for showing the correct method. If you take a shortcut and get the incorrect answer, you will not get any marks!

29.2 Measuring the density of an object

To measure the density of an object:

(i) Find the mass of the object in grams.

(ii) Measure the volume of the object in cm^3.

(iii) Divide the mass by the volume.

▶▶ Experiment 29.1

To measure the density of a stone

- Measure the mass of a dry stone using an electronic balance, Figure 29.1.
- Measure the volume of the stone using an overflow can and a graduated cylinder.
- Calculate the density as shown in Worked Example 29.1.

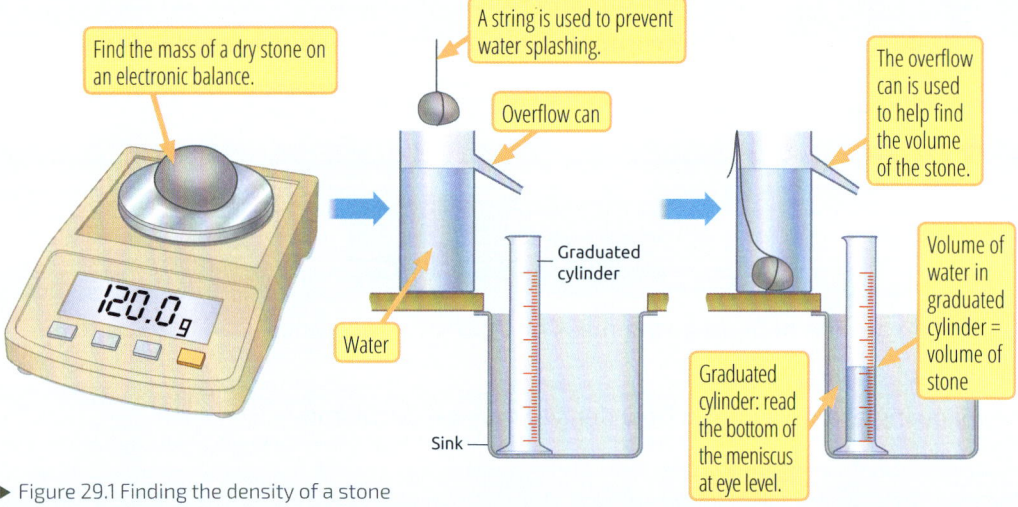

▶ Figure 29.1 Finding the density of a stone

Exam Tip!

When describing an experiment, a good-quality **labelled** diagram can help you organise your information and obtain more marks in an exam.

Note: In Chapter 28 a number of methods were used to find the volume of a substance:

- The volume of regular shapes can be calculated mathematically.
- The volume of liquids, small solid objects and substances that float in water can be measured with a graduated cylinder.
- In Chapter 22, a burette and a pipette are used as a more accurate method to measure the volume of liquids.

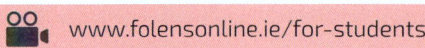 www.folensonline.ie/for-students

29.3 Why a knowledge of density is useful

Density and flotation

A substance will float on a liquid or gas if it has a lower density than that liquid or gas. Using a table of densities of substances we can predict if a substance will float or sink in another substance, Table 29.1.

The density of water is 1 g/cm³. We can say that oil will float on water as oil has a density (0.8 g/cm³) lower than water. However, aluminium will sink in water as it has a density (2.7 g/cm³) greater than water.

Substances with densities lower than water	
Substance	Density (g/cm³)
Polystyrene	0.02
Cork	0.3
Paraffin oil	0.8
Ice	0.9
(Water)	1.0

*Paraffin oil floats on water as it has a **lower** density than water.*

Substances with densities higher than water	
Substance	Density (g/cm³)
Brick	2.0
Aluminium	2.7
Lead	11.2
Mercury	13.6
Gold	19.3

*Aluminium sinks in water as it has a **higher** density than water.*

▶ Table 29.1 Densities of some common substances

Identifying a substance

Calculating the density of a substance can help to identify that substance.

The density of a block of metal is 19.3 g/cm³. Using Table 29.1, can you identify the metal?

Designing lightweight objects

Materials of low density are deliberately used to reduce the weight of objects such as suitcases, aeroplanes and cars.

▶▶ Science Self-Assessment

Now I am able to:	🟢	🟠	🔴
Define density			
Calculate the density of an object given its mass and volume			
Carry out an experiment to measure the density of a substance			
Predict if an object will sink or float in a liquid given information on densities			

30 Speed, displacement, velocity and acceleration

The Physical World strand

Main topics in this chapter:
- Calculate speed, displacement, velocity and acceleration
- Measure speed and acceleration in the laboratory
- Use distance–time graphs to analyse the motion of a body
- Use velocity–time graphs to analyse the motion of a body

30.1 Speed

- Speed is a measure of how much time it takes for a body to move from one place to another. In order to calculate speed you need to know the **distance** travelled (in metres) and the **time** taken to travel that distance (in seconds).

$$\text{Speed} = \frac{\text{Distance travelled (m)}}{\text{Time taken (s)}}$$

▶▶ Worked Example 30.1

Usain Bolt can run a distance of 200 m in 20 seconds. Calculate his average speed.

Answer

1. Write down the **formula**: $\text{Speed} = \dfrac{\text{distance}}{\text{time}}$

2. Fill in the **distance** in metres and the **time** in seconds: $= \dfrac{200 \text{ m}}{20 \text{ s}}$

3. **Calculate** the answer. Always include the correct **units**. $= 10 \text{ m/s}$

   Note that the unit for speed can also be written as 10 m s^{-1}.

30.2 Displacement

Displacement is distance in a given direction.

▶▶ Worked Example 30.2

A person walks along the orange lines from A to B, Figure 30.1.
(i) What is the total distance travelled?
(ii) What is the displacement of B from A?

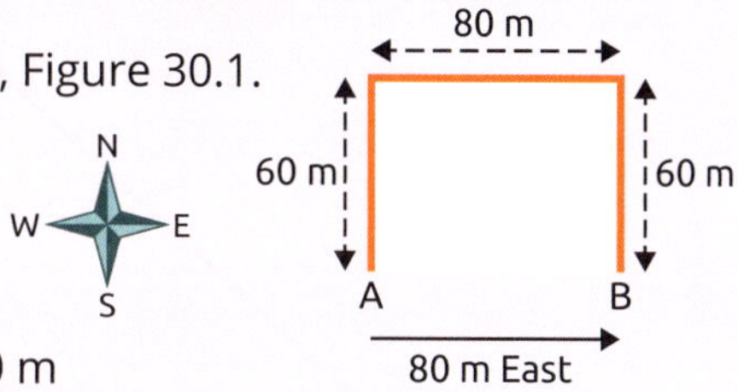

Answer
(i) Total distance travelled is 60 + 80 + 60 = 200 m
(ii) Standing at A, B has a displacement of **80 m East** from A.

▶ Figure 30.1

- Note that displacement depends only on the starting point and finishing point.
- It is the distance and direction 'as the crow flies' between these two points.

30.3 Velocity

Velocity is similar to speed, except that with velocity you will need to give the **direction** also.

$$\text{Velocity} = \frac{\text{Change in displacement}}{\text{Time taken}}$$

▶▶ Worked Example 30.3

An athlete ran 1 km south in 3 minutes. Calculate her average (i) speed (ii) velocity

Answer
(i) 1. Write down the **formula**: $\text{Speed} = \frac{\text{distance}}{\text{time}}$

2. Fill in the **distance** in metres and the **time** in seconds: $= \frac{1000 \text{ m}}{180 \text{ s}}$

3. Calculate the answer. Always include the correct **units**. $= 5.56 \text{ m s}^{-1}$

(ii) The velocity is the speed with the direction included. $= 5.56 \text{ m s}^{-1}$ **south**

30.4 Distance–time graph can be used to calculate speed

▶▶ Worked Example 30.4

Two joggers were asked to run a distance of 24 m. One was wearing a red bib and the other was wearing a green bib. Table 30.1 shows the distance that each had travelled after each second for 8 seconds. A graph was drawn to show the information, Figure 30.2.

▶ Table 30.1

Time	0	1	2	3	4	5	6	7	8
Distance red jogger	0	3	6	9	12	15	18	21	24
Distance green jogger	0	4	8	12	16	20	24	24	24

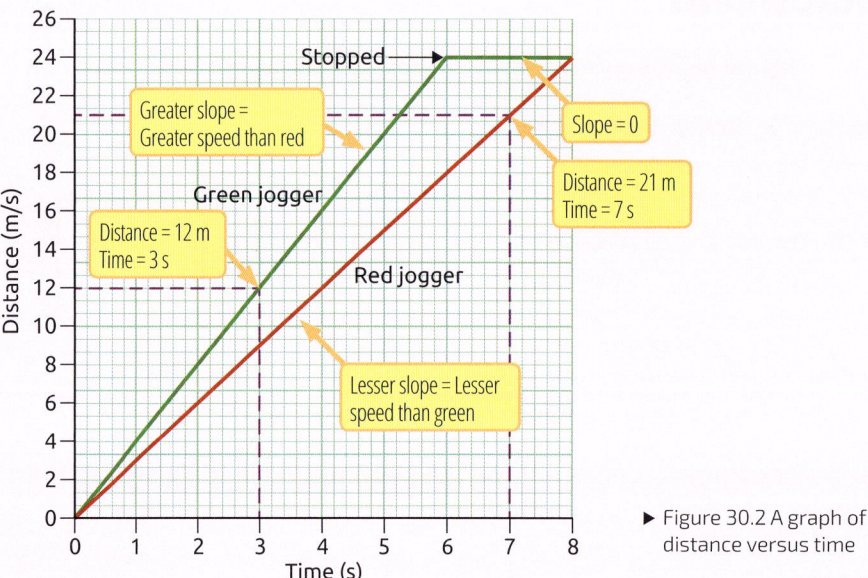

▶ Figure 30.2 A graph of distance versus time

(i) Describe the motion of both joggers during the jog.
(ii) Calculate the speed of (a) the red jogger (b) the green jogger while moving.

Answer

(i) The **red** jogger ran at a constant speed (graph has constant slope) for 8 seconds. The **green** jogger ran at a constant speed (graph has constant slope) for 6 seconds and then stopped (zero slope) for 2 seconds.

(ii) (a) The speed of the **red** jogger can be calculated by taking a point on the line, reading the distance and time at that point and finally using the speed formula. You can see on the graph that we have taken a point on the line at 7 seconds. The distance travelled at this point was 21 m.

1. Write down the **formula**: $\text{Speed} = \dfrac{\text{distance}}{\text{time}}$

2. Fill in the **distance** in metres and the **time** in seconds: $= \dfrac{21 \text{ m}}{7 \text{ s}}$

3. **Calculate** the answer. Always include the correct **units**. $= 3 \text{ m s}^{-1}$

(b) Similarly the speed of the **green** jogger can be calculated by taking a point on the green line. You can see on the graph that we have taken a point on the line at 3 seconds. The distance travelled at this point was 12 m.

1. Write down the **formula**: $\text{Speed} = \dfrac{\text{distance}}{\text{time}}$

2. Fill in the **distance** in metres and the **time** in seconds: $= \dfrac{12 \text{ m}}{3 \text{ s}}$

3. **Calculate** the answer. Always include the correct **units**. $= 4 \text{ m s}^{-1}$

30.5 Measuring speed in the laboratory

▶▶ Experiment 30.1

To find the speed of a trolley

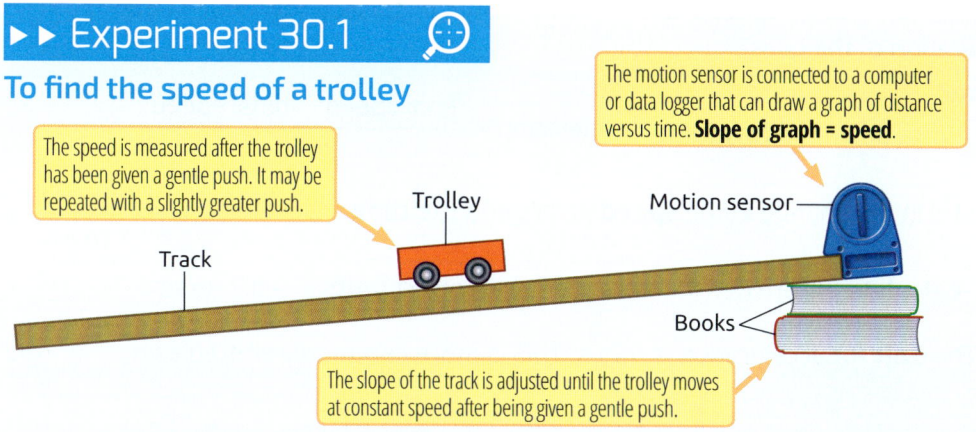

▶ Figure 30.3 The data logging software will produce a **graph of distance versus time**. The **slope** of the graph is the **speed**. The slope tool in the software will allow you to calculate the speed of the trolley.

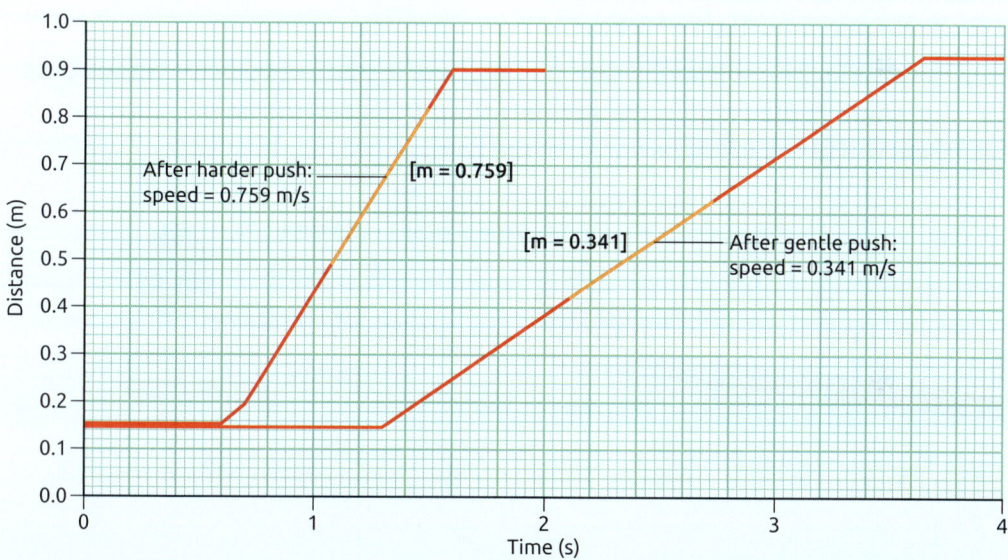

▶ Figure 30.4 A graph of distance versus time produced by a motion sensor. Note the slope tool allows you to find the slope at any place on the graph. The slope tells you the speed.

The slope of a distance versus time graph gives the speed of the object.

 www.folensonline.ie/for-students

30.6 Acceleration

The **acceleration** of an object is the change in velocity per second.

$$\text{Acceleration} = \frac{\text{Change in velocity}}{\text{Time taken}}$$

▸▸ Worked Example 30.5

The Luas can change speed from 3 m/s to 10 m/s in 10 seconds. What is the acceleration of the Luas?

Answer

1. Write down the **formula**: $\text{Acceleration} = \dfrac{\text{final speed} - \text{initial speed}}{\text{time}}$
2. Fill in the change in the **speed** in m/s and the **time** in seconds: $= \dfrac{10\text{ m/s} - 3\text{ m/s}}{10\text{ s}}$
3. **Calculate** the answer. Always include the correct **units**. $= 0.7$ m/s/s

Note: The **unit** for acceleration is m/s/s. This is more commonly written as m s^{-2} or m/s^2.

30.7 Measuring acceleration in the laboratory

▸▸ Experiment 30.2

To find the acceleration of a cart

- The data logging software is set up to produce a graph of **velocity versus time**.
- The **slope** of the graph is the **acceleration**. The slope tool in the software will allow you to calculate the speed of the cart.

The motion sensor is connected to a computer or data logger that can draw a graph of velocity versus time. Slope of graph = acceleration
Trolley
Motion sensor
Track
Books
The slope of the track is adjusted until the trolley speeds up when it travels down the track.

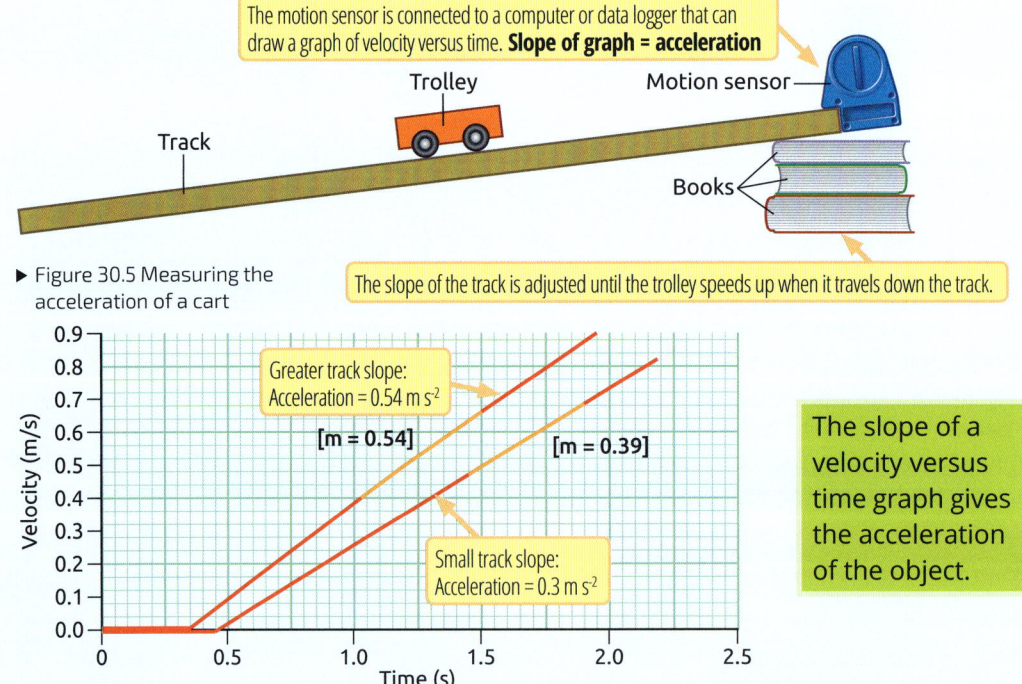

▸ Figure 30.5 Measuring the acceleration of a cart

Velocity (m/s)
Time (s)
Greater track slope:
Acceleration = 0.54 m s-2
[m = 0.54]
[m = 0.39]
Small track slope:
Acceleration = 0.3 m s-2
0.0 0.1 0.2 0.3 0.4 0.5 0.6 0.7 0.8 0.9
0 0.5 1.0 1.5 2.0 2.5

The slope of a velocity versus time graph gives the acceleration of the object.

▸ Figure 30.6 A graph of velocity versus time produced by a motion sensor. Note the slope tool allows you to find the slope at any place on the graph. The slope tells you the acceleration.

www.folensonline.ie/for-students

▶▶ Science Self-Assessment

Now I am able to:

	🟢	🟠	🔴
Calculate speed, displacement, velocity and acceleration			
Measure speed and acceleration in the laboratory			
Use distance–time graphs to analyse the motion of a body			
Use velocity–time graphs to analyse the motion of a body			

31 Forces

The Physical World strand

Main topics in this chapter:
- Forces: balanced and unbalanced
- Friction
- Weight and gravity
- Forces on elastic objects (Hooke's law)

31.1 What is a force?

You may have some idea that force is a push or pull. In physics, we need a more precise definition of what a force is:

A **force** is anything that causes a body to accelerate.

Two ways that force can be measured are shown in Figure 31.1.

31.2 Balanced and unbalanced forces

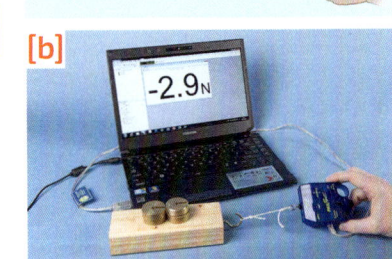

▶ Figure 31.1 Force can be measured using (a) a newton meter or (b) a force sensor.

- When a car is travelling at constant speed on the motorway, the engine is putting a force on the car. This causes the car to move forward.
As the car moves forward, it has to push the air in front of it out of the way. This air resistance and friction between the wheels and the road causes a force to push backwards against the car.
- At constant speed, the force that the engine is pushing forward on the car is equal to the forces pushing back on the car. We say that the forces are balanced.
- Since the forces are equal but opposite, they cancel each other out. There is **no net force** on the car.
- **Where forces are balanced, the car will not accelerate**. It will continue at a constant speed.

- In order to accelerate the car, more force is needed from the engine to push the car forward than the forces pushing back. This is achieved by using the accelerator pedal to make the engine push harder.
- Since there is now more force pushing forward than backwards, the forces are unbalanced, Figure 31.2.
- The speed of the car increases in the direction of the additional force.
- In order to get the car to stop, the force from the engine is stopped and the brakes put a force against the forward motion of the car.

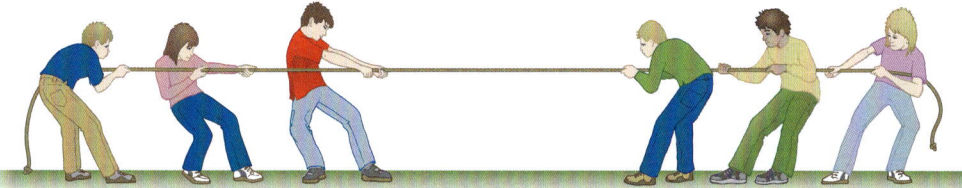

▶ Figure 31.2 If both teams in a tug-of-war pull with the same force, the forces on each side are balanced and the rope stays stationary. If one side pulls with a little more force than the other side, then the forces are unbalanced and the rope and team **accelerate** towards the side with the greater force.

- **Balanced forces** cause an object to stay stationary or move at a **constant velocity**.
- **Unbalanced forces** cause an object to **accelerate** (change velocity)

▶▶ Worked Example 31.1

Figure 31.3 (a) shows a car with forces acting on it.
 (i) Suggest what is causing the forward force.
 (ii) What could be causing the backward force?
 (iii) Are the forces balanced or unbalanced?
 (iv) The car is moving at a speed of 10 m/s. What effect, if any, will the forces have on the speed?

Figure 31.3 (b) shows the forces on a car as it moved onto the motorway.
 (v) Are the forces balanced or unbalanced?
 (vi) What effect will the force shown have on the motion of the car?

Figure 31.3 (c) shows the force acting on a car as it reaches its destination.
 (vii) What effect will the forces have on the motion of the car?

[a]   [b]   [c]

▶ Figure 31.3 Forces acting on a car at various stages of its journey

165

Answer

(i) The forward force is caused by the engine.

(ii) The backward force is caused by air resistance and friction between the wheels and the road.

(iii) Since the forward force is equal to the backward force, the forces are balanced.

(iv) The forward force by the engine is cancelled by the backward force on the engine. There is no net force on the car and its speed will stay constant.

(v) In Figure 31.3 (b) there is a greater forward force than backward force. The forces are unbalanced.

(vi) Since the forward force is greater than the backward force, the car will accelerate forward. The car's speed will increase.

(vii) In Figure 31.3 (c) there is no force pushing forwards and there is a force pushing backwards. The forces are unbalanced and the car will decelerate. The car will slow down.

31.3 Friction

Whenever one object slides over another object, friction tries to stop the movement. Friction always opposes the motion of an object. The rougher the two surfaces are, the greater the friction, Figure 31.4.

Friction is a force that opposes motion.

▶ Figure 31.4 Smooth surfaces look rough under a microscope.

Table 31.1 summarises some of the advantages and disadvantages of friction. If you would like to consider what the benefits of friction are, think of the difficulties you would face while travelling to school in icy conditions.

Advantages	Disadvantages
Allows moving bodies to travel over a surface without slipping	Slows down moving bodies and wastes energy
Enables brakes to work (e.g. bicycle)	Causes wearing of surfaces
Slows down hailstones that could cause damage	Can cause excessive heating and noise

▶ Table 31.1 Advantages and disadvantages of friction

- Friction can be reduced by (i) using oil between moving surfaces, (ii) designing objects moving through the air to be more aerodynamic (streamlining), Figure 31.5, (iii) smoothing surfaces and (iv) using ball bearings and wheels between surfaces.

▶ Figure 31.5 Streamlining reduces air friction.

31.4 Weight and gravity

- Heavy objects attract other heavy objects. This force is very small between lighter, everyday objects.
- However, because celestial bodies such as planets have huge mass, they attract other bodies with a significant force of attraction.
- The greater the mass of the planet and the closer you are to the centre of the planet, the greater the force of attraction. This force of attraction is called **gravity**.

▶ Figure 31.6 Gravity pulls objects towards the **centre** of the Earth.

Gravity is a measure of the force of attraction between two bodies with mass.

- Figure 31.6 shows what a person would look like on the North and South Poles if you could see them from outer space. Notice also that no matter where you are on Earth, an apple falls towards the centre of the Earth.
- It is the force of gravity that can pull comets and asteroids into the Earth's atmosphere. In addition, the force of gravity between the Earth and the Sun keeps the Earth in orbit (rotating around) the Sun.
- The mass of a body is a measure of the amount of matter in that body. If you move it into outer space, the amount of matter does not change.
- Weight is a measure of the force of gravity between two bodies. If a body is moved away from the centre of the Earth, the force of gravity gets less and less.

The **weight** of an object is a measure of the force of gravity on it.

- The weight of a body depends on (i) its mass, (ii) the mass of the planet it is on and (iii) the distance from the centre of the planet it is on.
- We can calculate the weight of a body on the surface of a planet by multiplying its mass by the 'g' value on the surface of that planet. (The 'g' value takes the mass of the planet and the distance from the centre into account.)

Weight = mass (kg) × g value in that location

Weight on surface of Earth = mass (kg) × 10

Planet	g value (m s^{-2})
Earth	9.8 ≈ 10
Jupiter	25
Mars	3.8

▶ Table 31.2 Some *g* values on different planets

Note: *g* is called the acceleration due to gravity. Its units are m s^{-2}.

▶▶ Worked Example 31.2

What is the weight of a 60 kg student (i) on Earth and (ii) on Jupiter? (g on Earth = 10 m s^{-2} and g on Jupiter = 25 m s^{-2}.)

Answer

(i) 1. Write equation: **Weight (N) = Mass (kg) × g**
    2. Fill it in: = 60 × 10
    3. Write the answer with the unit: = **600 N**

(ii) 1. Write equation: **Weight (N) = Mass (kg) × g**
    2. Fill it in: = 60 × 25
    3. Write the answer with the unit: = **1,500 N**

Exam Tip!

This section of the course will also be important in the Earth and Space strand (see Chapter 37).

My WEIGHT on Earth is around 560 N, my mass is 56 kg.

My WEIGHT on the moon is around 90 N, my mass is 56 kg.

My MASS is always 56 kg!!

▶ Figure 31.7 The weight of a body will change depending on location. The mass of the body is not affected by location.

31.5 Forces on elastic objects

- One of the other effects of a force is that it can affect the shape of certain objects. An object that can return to its original shape when a force is removed is called an **elastic** object. Such objects include rubber bands and springs.
- You may be aware that the more you stretch a rubber band, the more it pulls back against you to restore itself to its original shape. We will investigate this in Experiment 31.1.

▶▶ Experiment 31.1

To investigate the relationship between the extension of a spiral spring and the force applied to it

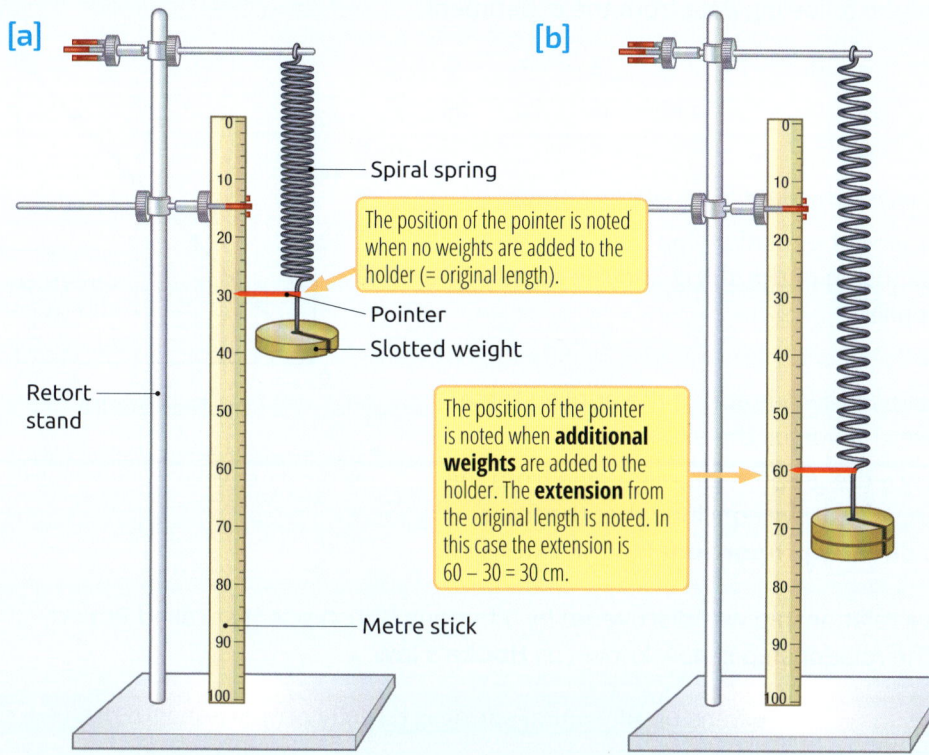

▶ Figure 31.8 To investigate the relationship between the extension of a spiral spring and the force applied to it.

- The position of the pointer when no weights are added is noted (the original length of the spring).
- The position of the pointer when additional **weights** are added is noted and the extension of the spring from its original length is noted. The total weight applied is also noted.
- A table of the applied weight (applied force) and the extension is drawn.
- A graph of extension versus applied force is drawn.

 www.folensonline.ie/for-students

▶▶ Worked Example 31.3

A student was asked to carry out an experiment to investigate how the extension of a spiral spring was affected by the force applied at the end of the spring. The student obtained the following data from the experiment.

Force (N)	0	1	2	3	4	5
Extension (cm)	0	5	10	15	20	25

(i) Analyse the data by drawing a graph.

(ii) What is the relationship between the extension of the string and the force applied?

Answer

(i) Let us draw a graph of the applied force (weight) versus the extension.

(ii) Since the graph is a straight line from the origin (0,0), we conclude that the force is **directly proportional** to the extension.

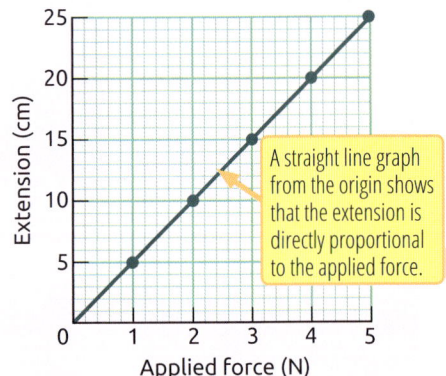

A straight line graph from the origin shows that the extension is directly proportional to the applied force.

▶ Figure 31.9 A graph of the applied force versus the extension for a spiral spring

The above relationship was discovered by a famous British scientist called Robert Hooke. The relationship is now known as **Hooke's law**.

> **Hooke's law:** The <u>extension</u> of a spiral spring is directly proportional to the applied force.

▶▶ Science Self-Assessment

Now I am able to:	🟢	🟡	🔴
Define and measure a force			
State what happens to a body when (i) balanced forces are applied to it (ii) unbalanced forces are applied to it			
Define *friction* and state advantages, disadvantages and methods to reduce friction			
Calculate the weight of an object given its mass and the g value			
State Hooke's law and describe an experiment to verify it			

32 Energy – sources of energy

The Physical World & Earth and Space strands

Main topics in this chapter:
- Energy and different forms of energy
- Energy conversions and the principle of conservation of energy
- Non-renewable and renewable sources of energy
- Efficient, sustainable and ethical electricity generation – thinking about the future
- Work and power
- Design an experiment to demonstrate an energy conversion and describe how to make the conversion more efficient

32.1 Different forms of energy

Energy is the ability to do work.

- If you arrive in school and you are tired, you probably will not do too much work. However, if you have energy you are likely to feel able to do a lot of work.

Some different forms of energy are summarised in Table 32.1 and Figure 32.1.

Energy form	Explanation
Kinetic	Due to movement, e.g. water flowing in a river
Potential	Due to position (height) or tension (spring), e.g. water in a dam
Chemical	Stored in chemicals, fuels or food, e.g. coal, oil, batteries
Nuclear	Energy stored in the nucleus of atom, e.g. nuclear power plant
Sound	Due to the vibration of an object, e.g. a loudspeaker
Light	Light from the Sun heats the Earth
Electrical	Electricity can be used to provide heat and light, produce sound and operate machines in our homes, schools and factories
Heat	Heat energy can be used to generate electricity in a power station

▶ Table 32.1. Some examples of different forms of energy

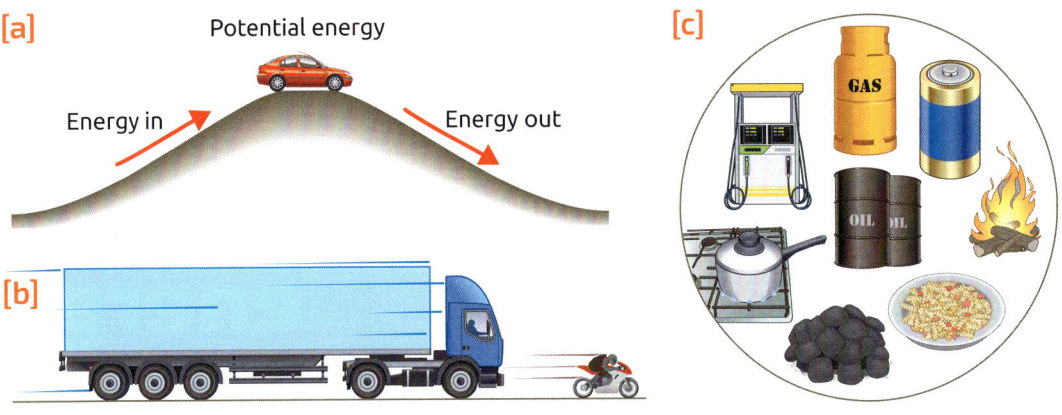

▶ Figure 32.1 (a) Potential energy due to height. (b) Kinetic energy due to movement. (c) Chemical energy in food, coal, oil, gas and batteries.

32.2 Energy conversions

- If you need energy in your home, you will probably need to buy it in the forms of electricity or fuel. You can then convert this energy into many other types of energy.
- Similarly, when you use an appliance the energy just does not disappear – it is converted into another form. For example, when you use your phone, the chemical energy of the battery is converted into sound, light, heat and even kinetic (vibration) energy. This fact is summarised in the principle of conservation of energy.

> **The principle of conservation of energy:**
> Energy cannot be created or destroyed but can only be changed from one form to another.

32.3 Non-renewable and renewable sources of energy

> A **non-renewable energy source** is one that will not be restored (regenerated) in our lifetime.

Some examples of non-renewable sources of energy are summarised in Table 32.2 and Figure 32.2.

Energy source	Advantage	Disadvantage
Fossil fuels, e.g. coal, oil, gas	Easy to store/transport	Causes global warming (CO_2)
Nuclear fuels, e.g. uranium	Does not produce CO_2	Nuclear accidents can contaminate the environment

▶ Table 32.2 Non-renewable sources of energy

- If we continue to use these sources of energy at today's rate, they will eventually run out. These sources of fuels are non-sustainable, Figure 32.2.

▶ Figure 32.2 Coal, oil, gas and turf are non-renewable sources of energy as they will not be regenerated in our lifetime. They will eventually run out.

A **renewable energy source** will never be used up.

Some examples of renewable sources of energy are summarised in Table 32.3 and Figure 32.3.

Energy source	Advantage	Disadvantage
Hydroelectric: A dam stores water to make electricity	Does not produce CO_2	Can permanently flood habitats after construction
Biomass: Fast-growing plants	Can get energy from waste (your compost bin)	Land once used for food is now used to grow energy crops
Wave energy: Waves can create electricity	Does not produce CO_2	Structures and machinery can be destroyed in storms
Tidal: Dam the tide and make electricity	Does not produce CO_2	Prevents ships and fish moving into certain areas
Geothermal: Hot water from deep in the Earth	Does not produce CO_2	Expensive to build
Wind energy: Wind turbines	Does not produce CO_2	Some people think they are unsightly
Solar energy: Solar panels	Does not produce CO_2	Cannot provide energy at night

▶ Table 32.3 Renewable sources of energy

[a]

[b]

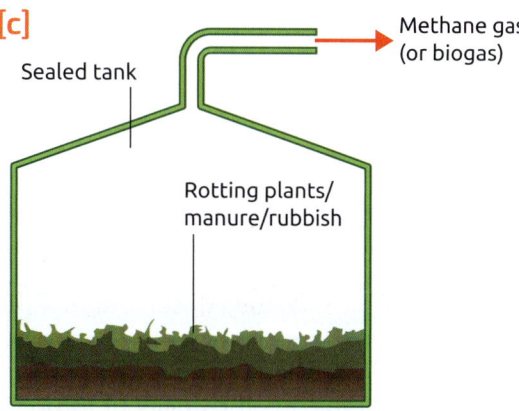

[c]

▶ Figure 32.3 Some examples of renewable sources of energy: (a) Solar panels. (b) Wind turbines. (c) Biomass. The source of this energy will never run out.

32.4 Energy efficiency and sustainability

- When you supply energy to a light bulb, only some of the energy is converted to light. The greater the amount of energy converted to light, the greater the efficiency of the bulb.
- The greater the energy efficiency of the appliances you buy, the less energy will be wasted in other forms, Figure 32.4.

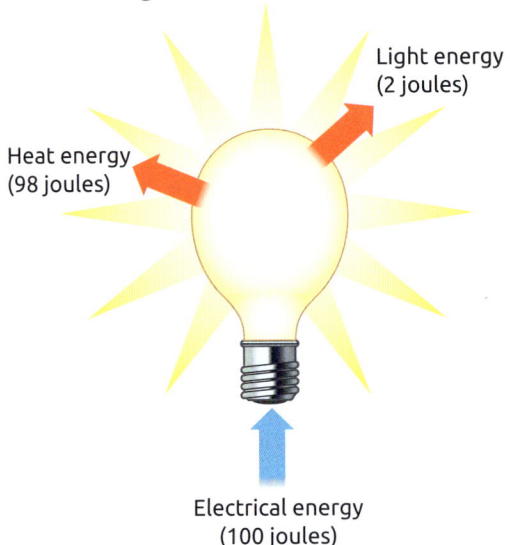

▶ Figure 32.4 Of the 100 joules of energy, only 2 joules are converted to light. The rest is wasted as heat. This bulb is only 2 per cent efficient.

- An LED bulb is much more efficient than a traditional light bulb and should be used where possible.
- You can become more energy efficient by:
  ▸ Walking, cycling or using public transport instead of a car
  ▸ Insulating your home
  ▸ Choosing energy efficient appliances such as boilers, bulbs and dryers
  ▸ Having a shower instead of a bath
  ▸ Not overheating your house, especially when there is nobody at home.
  ▸ Installing solar panels at home as a source of some of the energy needed by the house.
- The more energy efficient you become, the more sustainable your energy use will be. Sustainability is studied in more detail in Chapter 27.

Sustainability is the conservation of balance in the world's ecology indefinitely.

- In sustainable energy usage, we should be able to meet the needs of the present without affecting the ability of future generations to meet their own needs.
- In addition to society **becoming more energy efficient**, the government should encourage renewable **energy sources** and more **recycling** in the future.

32.5 Sustainable and ethical electricity generation

- We are becoming more and more reliant on electricity in our homes and cars. This means that we need to generate more electricity in the future.
- The population of planet Earth is increasing at a huge rate. This is putting greater demands on the environment.
- In the past, the majority of energy was generated by burning fossil fuels. This is not sustainable because:
    (i) Fossil fuels will eventually run out.
    (ii) They create carbon dioxide, which is damaging the environment by contributing to global warming.
    (iii) They can create acid rain, which kills fish and trees.
- We can become more **environmentally sustainable** by ensuring that the energy sources we choose in the future will not damage the environment.
- We can become more **economically sustainable** by having more government incentives, e.g. grants to install sources of the renewable energy available in Ireland.
- We should not rely on imports of fossil fuels that will become more scarce and expensive over time. In addition, we will become more energy independent, since wars abroad may limit our ability to import fossil fuels (as has happened in the past).
- We can become more **socially sustainable** by educating citizens on the importance of energy efficiency, Figure 32.5, by having national policies and laws that favour the building of renewable energy sources for the country.

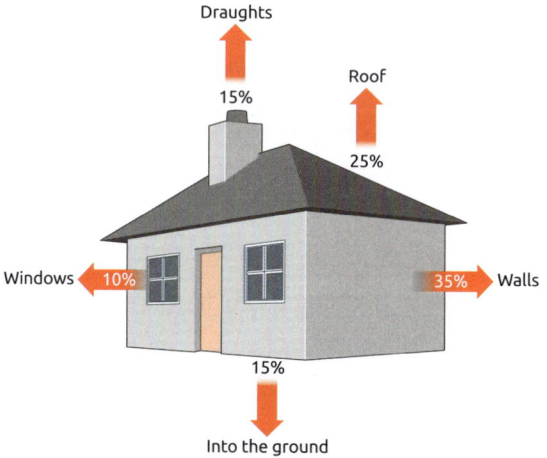

▶ Figure 32.5 Energy losses from a house

- In addition, we need to consider **ethical issues** when choosing methods for generating electricity, such as not damaging the environment with dams, not producing acid rain, not contributing to global warming, and minimising harm from radioactive substances in nuclear power stations.

32.6 Calculating energy usage

- Energy is the ability to do work. The unit of both energy and work is the **joule (J)**. The amount of work carried out can be calculated from the following formula:

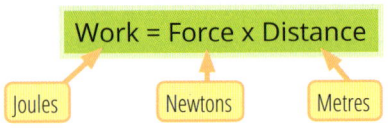

Work = Force × Distance
(Joules) (Newtons) (Metres)

▶▶ Worked Example 32.1

A builder pushes a box with a force of 200 N a distance of 5 metres. How much work is done?

Answer

1. Write down the formula: **Work (J) = Force (N) × Distance (m)**
2. Fill it in with force in newton and distance in metres: = 200 × 5
3. Write the answer with the correct unit: = 1,000 joule

32.7 Calculating power

- In the previous example, we did not take into account how long it took to move the box. A powerful machine can complete a lot of work in a short amount of time.
- When buying a kettle, the higher the power rating, the faster it will boil the kettle. The unit of power is the **watt**.
- The units of work must be in joules and the units of time must be in seconds.

$$\text{Power} = \frac{\text{Work done (in joules)}}{\text{Time taken (in seconds)}} \quad \text{or} \quad P = \frac{W}{t}$$

(Watt) (Joule / Second)

▶▶ Worked Example 32.2

A builder does 1,000 J of work in pushing a box in a time of 10 seconds. What is the power of the builder in doing this task?

Answer

1. Write down the formula: $\text{Power (W)} = \dfrac{\text{Work done}}{\text{Time taken}}$
2. Fill it in with work in joules and time in seconds: $= \dfrac{1{,}000 \text{ J}}{10 \text{ s}}$
3. Write the answer with the correct unit: = 100 W

- In Chapter 34 you will use a different formula to measure **electrical** power.

▶▶ Experiment 32.1

To build and test a device that transforms energy from one form to another in order to perform a function; to describe the energy changes and ways of improving efficiency

This experiment is summarised in Figure 32.6.

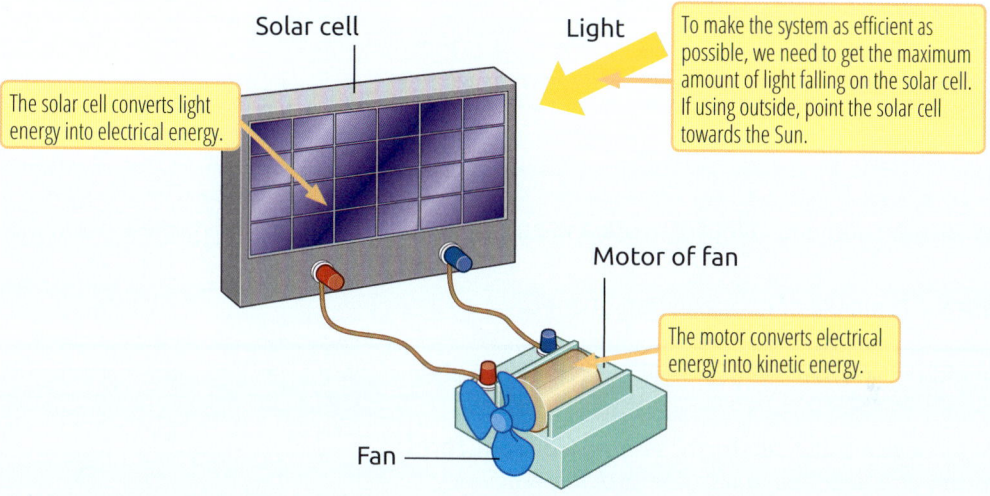

▶ Figure 32.6 A solar panel converts light energy into electrical energy. The motor converts electrical energy to kinetic energy.

- The efficiency of the system is measured by the speed of rotation of the fan.
- If using the solar cell in the open air, it is most efficient if the solar cell faces towards the Sun.
- If using the solar cell inside a building, efficiency can be increased by:
   (a) Moving the solar cell closer to an electrical bulb
   (b) Tilting the panel until it is at right angles to the direction of the light and
   (c) Exposing the maximum area of the panel to light (not blocking the light with your hand while holding the panel)
- **Note:** Not all of the light energy falling on the solar panel is converted into electricity. Some is converted into heat energy in the solar panel.

 www.folensonline.ie/for-students

▶▶ Science Self-Assessment

Now I am able to:	🟢	🟠	🔴
Describe eight different forms of energy			
Identify various energy conversions			
Identify non-renewable and renewable energy sources			
Define energy, work and power			
Perform calculations involving work and power			
State the principle of conservation of energy			
Discuss how to generate electricity in a sustainable and ethical way			
Build a device that transforms energy from one form to another and describe ways of improving efficiency			

33 Heat, energy and energy transfer

The Physical World strand

Main topics in this chapter:
- The meaning of heat
- The effects of adding heat energy to a substance
- Expansion and contraction of solids liquids and gases
- Movement of heat energy via conduction, convection and radiation

33.1 What is heat?

Heat is a form of energy. It is measured in joules.

It is important not to get confused between heat and temperature. Adding heat to a body usually causes the temperature (in °C) to rise. It may help you if you use the phrase *heat energy* instead of the term *heat*.

33.2 Effects of adding heat energy

Adding heat energy to a material can have three main effects.
- It can cause the temperature of a substance to increase.
- It can cause the material to expand.
- It can change the state of a substance from solid to liquid or from liquid to gas.

Removing heat energy has the opposite effects.

▶▶ Experiment 33.1

To show that solids expand when heat energy is added and that they contract when heat energy is removed

This experiment is summarised in Figure 33.1.

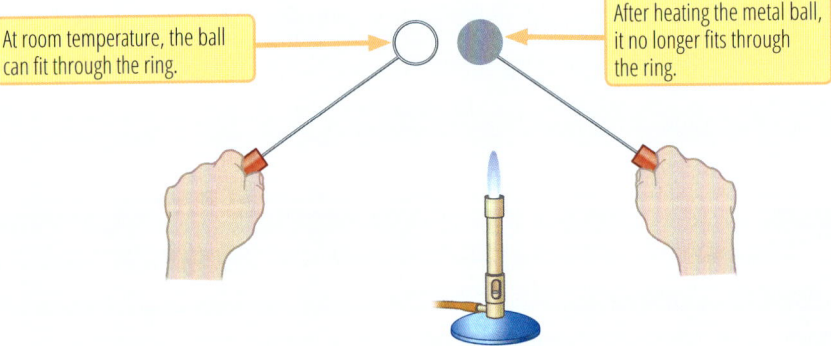

▶ Figure 33.1 Investigating expansion and contraction of solids

- At room temperature, the ball can fit through the ring.
- After heating the ball, it can no longer fit through the ring: it has expanded.
- After cooling the ball (by placing it in cold water), it can again fit through the ring: it has contracted.

▶▶ Experiment 33.2

To show that liquids expand when heat energy is added and that they contract when heat energy is removed

This experiment is summarised in Figure 33.2.

- As the liquid is heated, the level of the liquid in the narrow glass tube rises (because the liquid has expanded).
- As the liquid is allowed to cool, the level of the liquid in the tube falls (because the liquid has contracted).

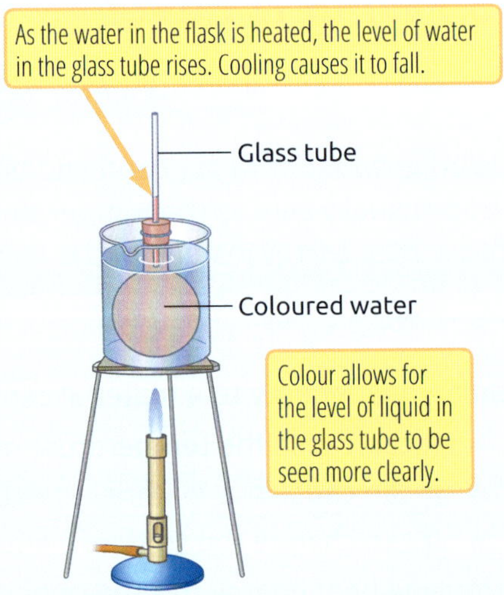

▶ Figure 33.2 Investigating expansion and contraction of liquids

- The above principle is used in alcohol and mercury thermometers. Placing the thermometer in warm substances causes the alcohol or mercury to expand up the tube.
- Water behaves in an unusual way when heated. As it freezes it expands, causing water pipes to burst.

▶▶ Experiment 33.3

To show that gases expand when heat energy is added and that gases contract when heat energy is removed

This experiment is summarised in Figure 33.3.

- As the gas (air) inside the flask is heated, bubbles of air are observed coming out of the tube (because the gas inside the flask has expanded).
- As the gas is allowed to cool, water is sucked back into the tube (because the gas inside the flask has contracted).

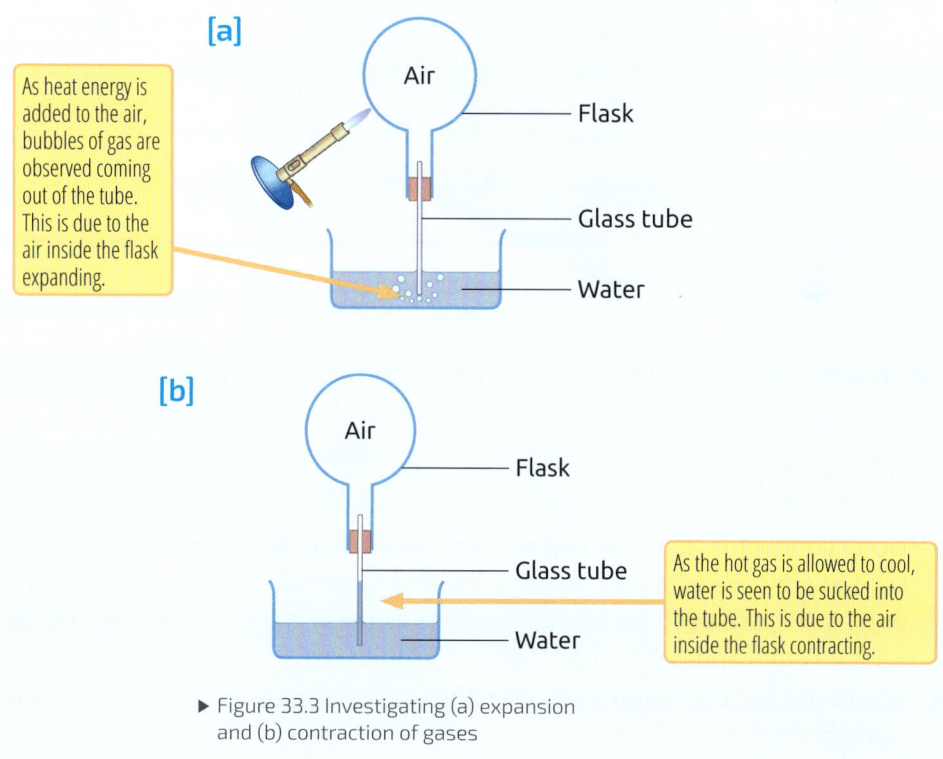

▶ Figure 33.3 Investigating (a) expansion and (b) contraction of gases

33.3 Movement of heat energy

Heat energy moves from a warm place to a cool place. There are three principal methods by which heat energy moves from a warm place to a cooler place.

(i) Conduction

- As particles gain heat energy, they vibrate more. This energy is passed from particle to particle.
- This is the main method of heat transfer through solids.
- Liquids and gases are usually not good conductors of heat.

Conduction is the movement of heat energy through a substance without any overall movement of the substance itself.

▶▶ Experiment 33.4

To investigate the rate of conduction through various materials

The experiment is set up as shown in Figure 33.4.

- After hot water is added to the tank, the time taken for the tack to fall off the bar of material is noted.

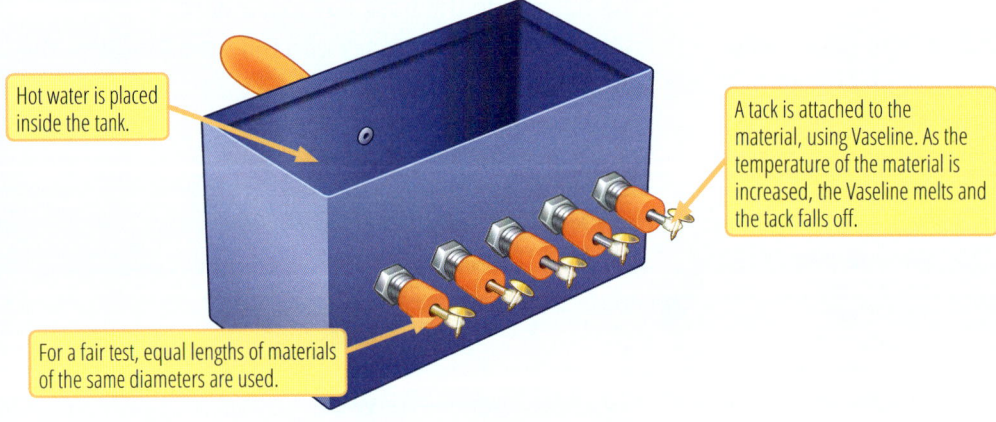

▶ Figure 33.4 Investigating the rate of conduction in various materials

- The tack will first fall off the best conductor of heat, copper.
- A bad conductor is called an **insulator**.

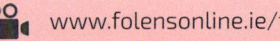 www.folensonline.ie/for-students

- Good conductors (such as copper) are used in saucepans and frying pans where heat energy needs to pass easily through a material. Insulators (such as wood and plastic) are used for making handles as these will not allow much heat to pass through and will protect the user from burns.
- Insulators such as polystyrene and fibreglass are used to insulate the walls of our homes.

(ii) Convection

- When particles of liquids or gases are heated, they rise. Cooler particles may fall to take their place. This is known as **convection**.
- Since the particles of a solid are stuck together, they are not free to move and convection does not happen in solids.

Convection is the movement of heat energy through liquids and gases due to the motion of the substance itself.

▶▶ Experiment 33.5

To investigate convection in liquids

This experiment is summarised in Figure 33.5.

- As the water is heated, it begins to rise. The crystals of dye colour the water as it moves.
- The heated water moves up and cooler water sinks to replace it. This is known as a **convection current**.

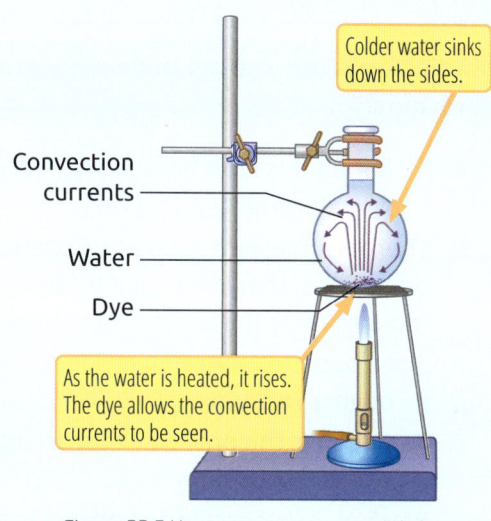

▶ Figure 33.5 Heat energy moves mainly by convection in liquids.

 www.folensonline.ie/for-students

- Convection currents in the sea cause the North Atlantic Drift, which moves warm seawater near Ireland and keeps our winters from becoming too cold. Global warming could move this current away from Ireland and cause colder winters (climate change).
- Convection in the air causes the wind. If the air around the Earth is warmed further as a result of global warming, it will produce more violent storms (climate change).

▶▶ Experiment 33.6

To investigate convection in gases

This experiment is summarised in Figure 33.6.

- The candle heats the air around the flame.
- The hot air rises and moves out of the box via the chimney on the right-hand side of the box.
- The warm air is replaced by colder air which comes down the chimney on the left-hand side of the box.
- Smoke (from a smouldering piece of paper or string) is used to help see the convection currents.

▶ Figure 33.6 Heat energy moves through gases via convection.

 www.folensonline.ie/for-students

(iii) Radiation

Radiation is the transfer of heat energy via radiation waves that can travel through a vacuum.

- All hot bodies emit heat energy via radiation. Your body emits a type of light known as infrared radiation.
- Thermal imaging cameras can detect warm objects. In search-and-rescue operations, thermal imaging cameras are used to find people lost in the mountains or the surface of the sea.
- Since particles are not needed for radiation to occur, heat energy can travel through a vacuum.
- Radiation is the only way that energy travels from the Sun to the Earth, through the vacuum of space.
- Black objects are good at absorbing heat energy but they also lose energy more quickly.
- White or silvered objects are not as good at absorbing and releasing heat energy as black objects.
- If more snow and glaciers on Earth melt because of global warming, more heat will be absorbed by the Earth from the Sun which, in turn, will cause further global warming.

▶▶ Experiment 33.7

To investigate heat transfer by radiation

This experiment is summarised in Figure 33.7.

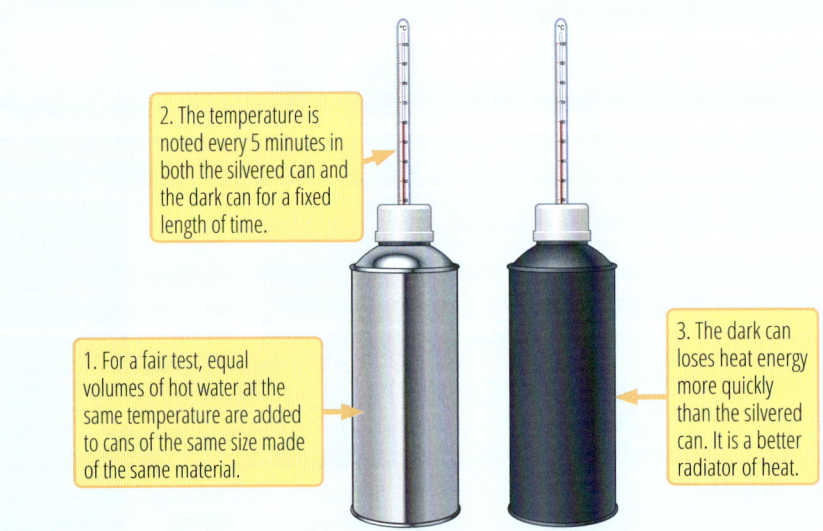

2. The temperature is noted every 5 minutes in both the silvered can and the dark can for a fixed length of time.

1. For a fair test, equal volumes of hot water at the same temperature are added to cans of the same size made of the same material.

3. The dark can loses heat energy more quickly than the silvered can. It is a better radiator of heat.

▶ Figure 33.7 Comparing the amount of heat lost by radiation

 www.folensonline.ie/for-students

The main points about conduction, convection and radiation are summarised in Table 33.1.

Heat transfer mode	Substance	Explanation
Conduction	Solids	Vibrating particles pass on this energy to other particles
Convection	Liquids and gases	Warm particles rise; cooler particles fall to take their place
Radiation	All substances	All warm objects release energy as rays of infrared light

▶ Table 33.1 Comparison of conduction, convection and radiation

▶▶ Science Self-Assessment

Now I am able to:	🟢	🟠	🔴
Explain what is meant by heat			
State three changes that can be made by adding heat energy to a substance			
Describe experiments to show that solids, liquids and gases expand when heat energy is added to them			
Investigate the movement of heat energy by conduction, convection and radiation			

34 Current electricity: constructing some simple circuits

The Physical World strand

Main topics in this chapter:
- What is current electricity?
- Construction of some simple electric circuits
- Conductors and insulators
- Measuring and calculating voltages (potential difference) and currents in simple circuits
- Measuring and calculating the resistance of electronic components
- Investigating the relationship between current, voltage and resistance
- Calculating electrical power

34.1 What is current electricity?

- In order for electricity to flow, a continuous loop (usually made of metal) is needed for the electrons to flow. This is called a **circuit**.
- The amount of 'force' with which the battery can push electrons is called the **voltage** of the battery. Voltage is also called **potential difference**. The battery pushes electrons from its negative side, around the circuit and accepts electrons back into its positive side.

Current: The flow of electrons in a wire.

- Some components in the circuit may try to slow down the flow of current. This is known as **resistance**. Whenever a current flows through a resistor, electrical energy is converted into **heat** energy, Figure 34.1.

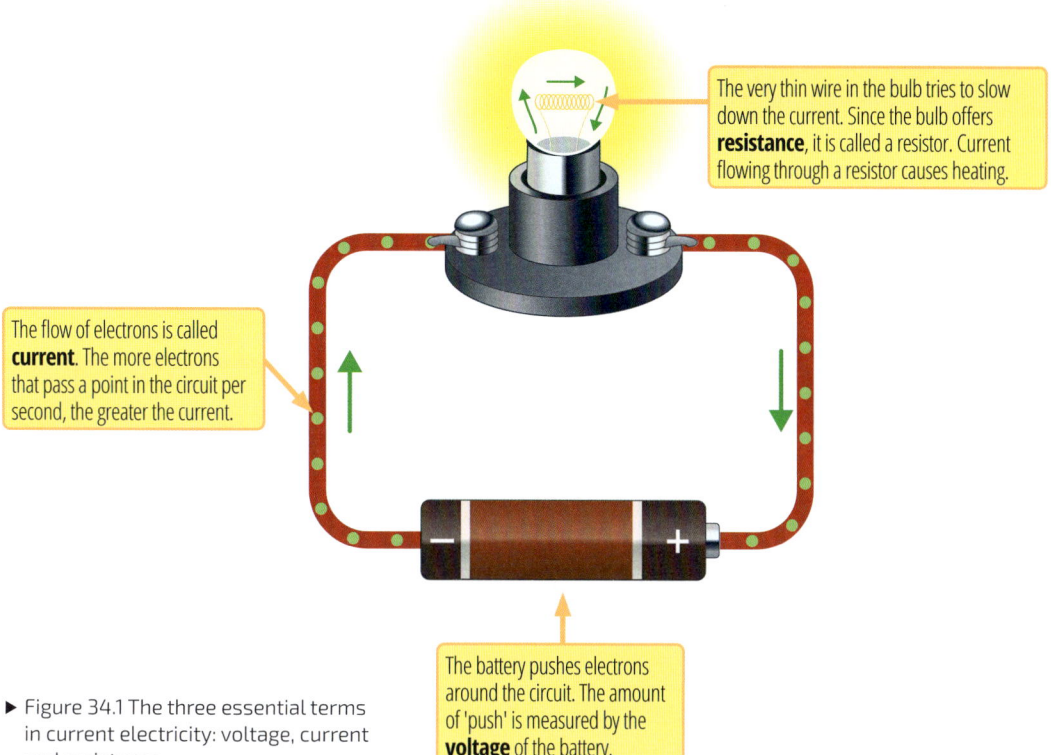

▶ Figure 34.1 The three essential terms in current electricity: voltage, current and resistance

34.2 Circuit symbols

- In order to make the drawing of electrical circuits simpler, there is an internationally agreed set of symbols for the different components in a circuit.
- You can find this on p.73 of the *Formulae and Tables* booklet available to you in the state exams. Some basic symbols are shown in Table 34.1.

Component	Symbol	Component	Symbol
Wire	———	Switch (off and on)	—o/o— —o o—
Lamp (bulb)	—⊗— —○—	Voltmeter (to measure voltage)	—(V)—
Battery (cell)	—┤├┤├— —┤├—	Resistor (slows down current flow)	—▭—
Ammeter (to measure current)	—(A)—	Ohmmeter (measures electrical resistance)	—(Ω)—

▶ Table 34.1 Some circuit symbols

34.3 Series and parallel circuits

- If two bulbs are connected in **series**, all the current that flows through one bulb **also** has to flow through the other. If one bulb fails (blows), the other bulb will not remain lighting, Figure 34.2 (a).
- If two bulbs are connected in **parallel**, the current flowing in the circuit is **split** between both bulbs. The advantage of this is that if one bulb fails (blows), then the other remains lighting. This is the case with car headlights and lights in a room, Figure 34.2 (b).

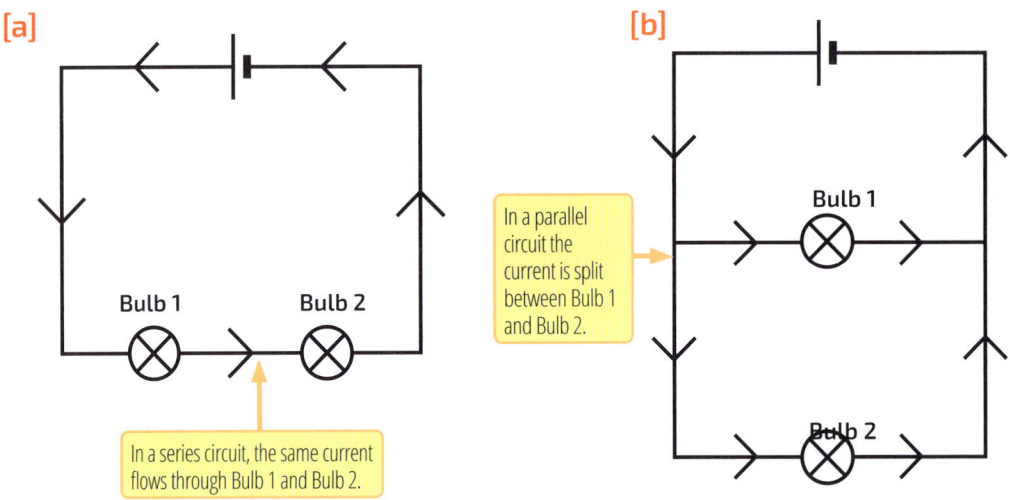

▶ Figure 34.2 The difference between series and parallel circuits

- When electric current was first discovered, scientists thought it flowed from the positive side to the negative side of a battery. It was only when the electron was discovered that it became clear that an electric current is a flow of electrons from the negative side to the positive side of a battery. However, rather than change all the writings about electric current, scientists decided to keep describing electric current as flowing from the positive side to the negative side of the battery.

34.4 Conductors and insulators

Some substances such as metals allow current to flow through themselves. These substances are called **conductors**.

Some substances such as plastics do not allow current to flow through themselves. These substances are called **insulators**.

- Conductors allow electricity to flow through themselves.
- Insulators do not allow electricity to flow through themselves.

▶▶ Experiment 34.1

To classify materials as electrical conductors or insulators

This experiment is summarised in Figure 34.3.

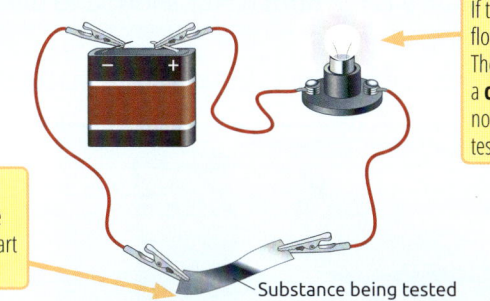

If the bulb lights then current is flowing through the substance. The substance being tested is a **conductor**. If the bulb does not light, the substance being tested is an **insulator**.

Different materials are connected between the crocodile clips in this part of the circuit.

Substance being tested

▶ Figure 34.3 If the bulb lights, the material is a conductor. If the bulb does not light, then the substance is an insulator.

 www.folensonline.ie/for-students

34.5 Measuring the size of an electric current

- In order to measure the size of an electric current in a circuit, Figure 34.4 (a), it is necessary to break the circuit and insert a 'counting device' that counts the number of electrons passing through the device each second.
- This device is called an **ammeter**, Figure 34.4 (b). The ammeter is connected in series in the circuit. The unit for current is the **amp**. The symbol for current used in mathematical equations is ***I***.

34.6 Measuring voltage (potential difference)

- To measure the voltage across a component in a circuit, a **voltmeter** is connected on either side of the component (in parallel), Figure 34.4 (c).
- Another term used to describe voltage is **potential difference**.
- You may like to think of it as a device measuring the pressure drop between both sides of the component. The unit of voltage is the **Volt** and the symbol in a mathematical equation is ***V***.

[a]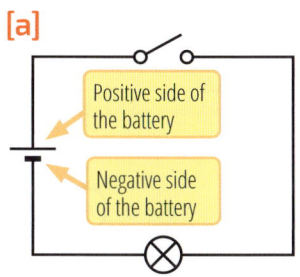

Positive side of the battery

Negative side of the battery

[b]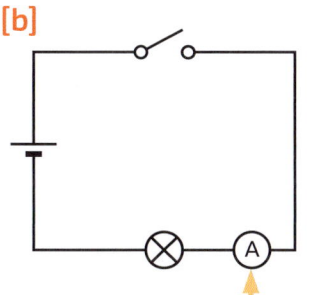

To measure the current flowing through the bulb, the circuit is broken at any point and an ammeter is added in series.

[c]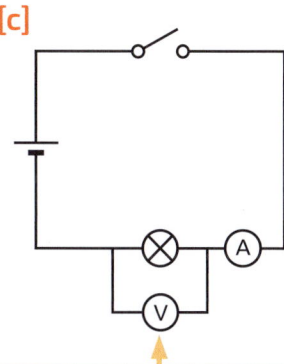

To measure the voltage across the bulb, a voltmeter is placed in parallel with the bulb.

▶ Figure 34.4 (a) A bulb in a circuit. (b) An ammeter is used to measure the current flowing in the circuit. (c) To measure the voltage across a bulb, a voltmeter is placed in parallel with the bulb.

34.7 Measuring resistance

- The resistance of an object can be measured using an **ohmmeter**, Figure 34.5. The ohmmeter is connected across both sides of the resistor and the resistance is read. The unit of resistance is the **ohm** (Ω for short) and the symbol in a mathematical equation is **R**.
- The resistance of an object can also be calculated by a mathematical equation.

▶ Figure 34.5 This ohmmeter is measuring the resistance of the resistor.

34.8 How voltage, current and resistance are related

- The relationship between voltage (V) current (I) and resistance (R) can be summarised by the equation:

$$\text{Voltage} = \text{Current} \times \text{Resistance}$$
$$V = I \times R$$

- Unit of voltage (V) = volt (V)
- Unit of current (I) = amp (A)
- Unit of resistance (R) = ohm (Ω)
- This relationship is called the Ohm's law equation.
- Worked Example 34.1 shows how this equation can be used.

▶▶ Worked Example 34.1

A motor of resistance 20 Ω has a current of 0.5 amps flowing through it. What is the voltage of the battery connected to the motor?

1. Write the equation: $V = I \times R$
2. Fill in the values: $= 0.5 \times 20$
3. Write the answer with the unit: $= 10$ V

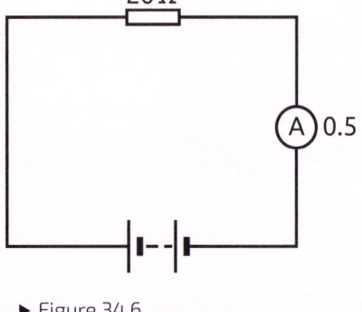

▶ Figure 34.6

34.9 To investigate how the voltage across a conductor affects the current flowing in the conductor

In this experiment, you will measure the voltage across a conductor. You will also measure the current flowing through the conductor. You will then investigate how voltage and current are related.

▶▶ Experiment 34.2

To investigate how the voltage across a conductor affects the current flowing in the conductor

- The circuit is set up as shown, Figure 34.7.
- The current flowing in the circuit is noted from the ammeter.
- The voltage across the coiled wire is noted from the voltmeter.
- Using the variable resistor, the voltage across the wire is changed. The new voltage and current are recorded. This step is repeated at least five times.
- A graph of voltage versus current is drawn.
- Some sample data are given in Worked Example 34.2.

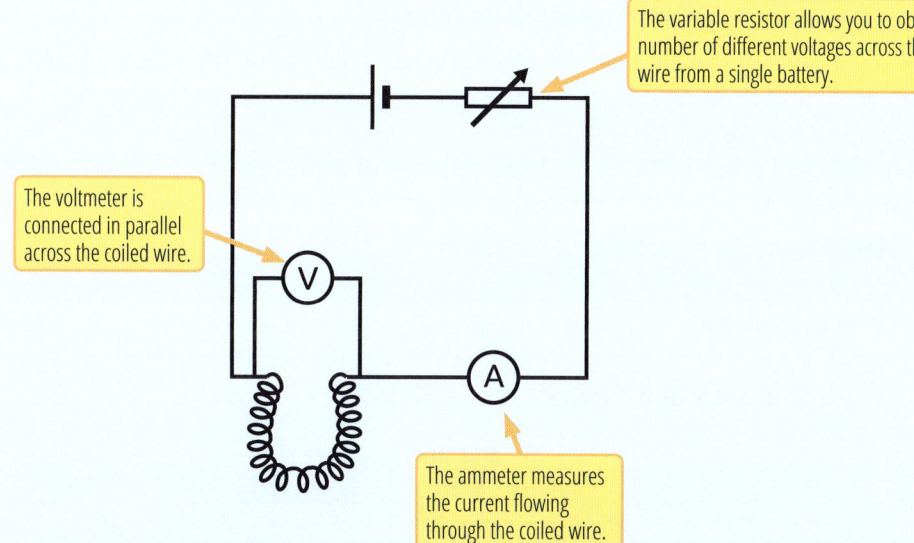

▶ Figure 34.7 Investigating how voltage affects current in a circuit

Exam Tip!

It is very important that you can draw this diagram accurately.

All the components are placed in series **except** the voltmeter. Make sure you draw the voltmeter in the diagram **across** the resistor (coiled wire).

www.folensonline.ie/for-students

▶▶ Worked Example 34.2

In an experiment to investigate how the voltage across a wire affects the current flowing in a wire, the data shown in Table 34.2 were obtained:

Voltage (V)	0	0.5	1.0	1.5	2.0	2.5
Current (A)	0	0.1	0.2	0.3	0.4	0.5

▶ Table 34.2

(i) Draw a graph of the data.
(ii) What does your graph tell you about the relationship between the voltage and current?
(iii) Calculate the resistance of the wire, using data from Table 34.2.
(iv) Using your graph, predict the voltage needed to cause a current of 0.35 A to flow through the wire.
(v) Using your graph, predict the current that will flow if the voltage applied is 2.25 V.

Solution

(i) See Figure 34.8 (a) below.
(ii) Since the graph is a straight line from the origin (0, 0), this tells us that the current is **directly proportional** to the voltage.
(iii) The resistance of the wire can be found by using any value of voltage (other than zero) and dividing it by the corresponding current. (Rearranging the equation $V = IR$ we get $R = \frac{V}{I}$.)
From the data given in Table 34.2, we see that at a voltage of 2.5 V the current flowing is 0.5 A.

1. Write down the equation: $\quad R = \dfrac{V}{I}$

2. Fill in the values: $\quad R = \dfrac{2.5}{0.5}$

3. Write the answer and the unit $\quad = 5\,\Omega$

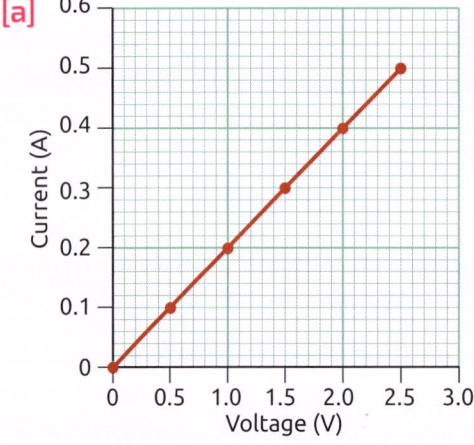

▶ Figure 34.8 (a) and (b)

(iv) Go to 0.35 A on the y-axis (current) axis. Draw a line horizontally from this point over to the graph line and then vertically down from this point to find the corresponding voltage = 1.75 V, Figure 34.8 (b).

(v) Go to 2.25 V on the voltage axis. Draw a line up from this point to the graph line and then across to the current axis, Figure 34.8 (b), to find the corresponding current = 0.45 A.

The result of the above experiment leads to a very important law in physics called Ohm's law.

Ohm's law: For a metallic conductor at constant temperature the current is directly proportional to the voltage.

34.10 Some electronic components

In the Junior Cycle Science course, you are expected to design and build simple electronic circuits. Table 34.3 shows the symbols of some basic electronic components.

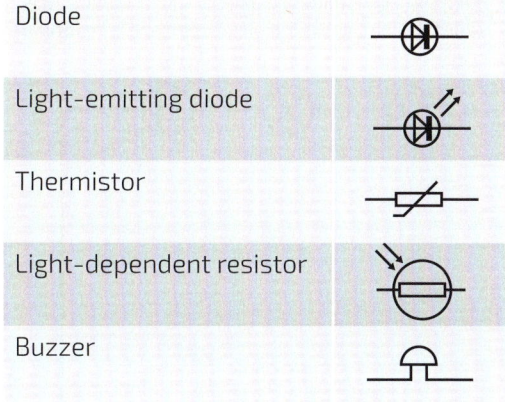

▶ Table 34.3 Some basic electronic components

The diode

- A diode is a device that allows current to flow in one direction only, Figure 34.9.
- A diode can only allow small currents to flow or it will become damaged. Diodes are protected from large current by placing a resistor in series with them.

A **diode** is a device that allows current to flow through it in one direction only.

Exam Tip!

It is important that you can identify the negative and positive side of a diode so that you can connect it up properly in a circuit. (The + and − on Figure 34.9 will not appear on the symbol if used in a circuit diagram in a state exam.)

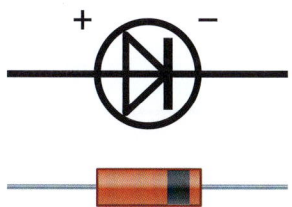

▶ Figure 34.9 The symbol for a diode and an illustration of a diode

- A Light Emitting Diode, or LED, is a special type of diode, Figure 34.10. These diodes emit light when current flows through them. LEDs are much more efficient (use less electricity) than regular bulbs and do not need to be replaced as often.

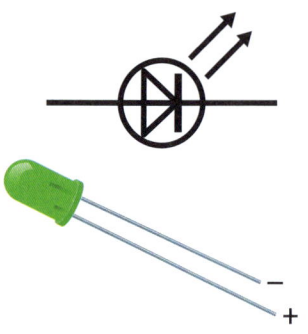

▶ Figure 34.10 The symbol for a light-emitting diode and an illustration of a light-emitting diode

▶▶ Experiment 34.3

To investigate the operation of a diode

This experiment is summarised in Figure 34.11.

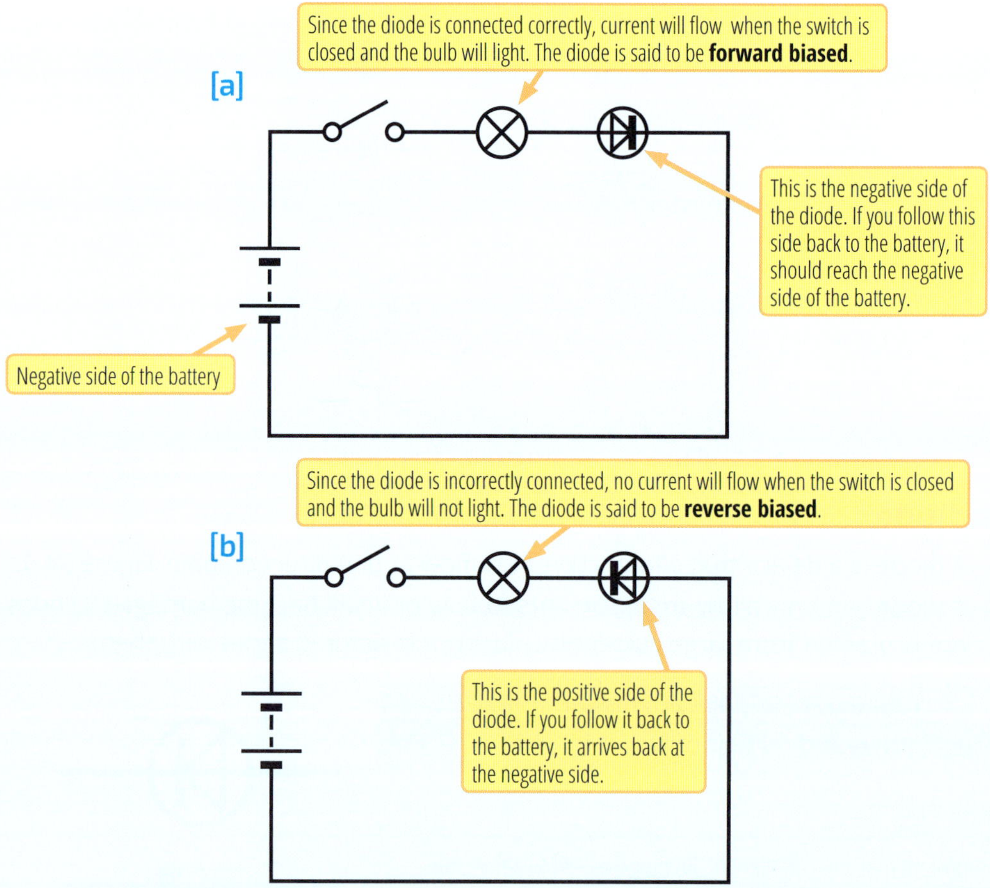

[a] Since the diode is connected correctly, current will flow when the switch is closed and the bulb will light. The diode is said to be **forward biased**.

This is the negative side of the diode. If you follow this side back to the battery, it should reach the negative side of the battery.

Negative side of the battery

[b] Since the diode is incorrectly connected, no current will flow when the switch is closed and the bulb will not light. The diode is said to be **reverse biased**.

This is the positive side of the diode. If you follow it back to the battery, it arrives back at the negative side.

▶ Figure 34.11 (a) Diode circuit in forward bias (current will flow). (b) Diode circuit in reverse bias (current will not flow).

►► Experiment 34.4

To investigate the operation of a light emitting diode (LED)

This experiment is summarised in Figure 34.12.

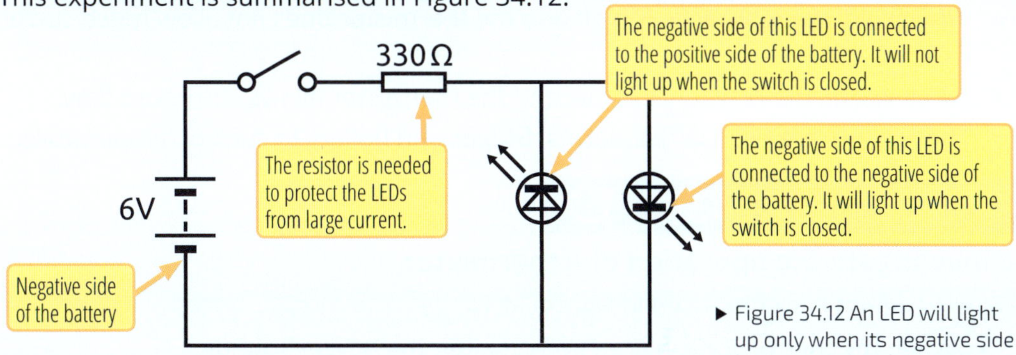

▶ Figure 34.12 An LED will light up only when its negative side is connected to the negative side of the battery.

www.folensonline.ie/for-students

The light-dependent resistor (LDR)

- As the name suggests, the LDR changes resistance with the amount of light falling on it.
- At low light levels its resistance is high and it will not allow much current to flow.
- At higher light levels its resistance is low and it allows more current to flow.
- LDRs are used to switch on street lights and in light meters in cameras.

►► Experiment 34.5

To investigate the operation of a light-dependent resistor

This experiment is summarised in Figure 34.13.

- When a bright light is brought close to the LDR, the buzzer sounds.
- When the light is moved away from the LDR, the buzzer volume decreases and eventually stops.

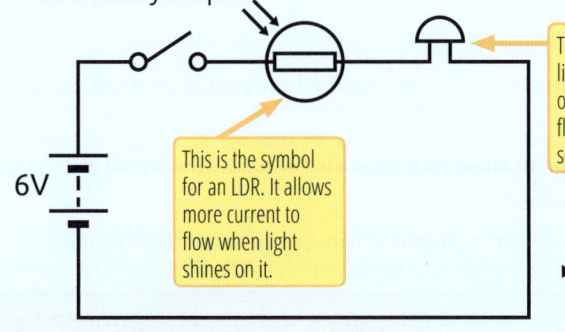

▶ Figure 34.13 Circuit to investigate the operation of a light-dependent resistor

www.folensonline.ie/for-students

- LDRs can control current flow in a circuit. The flow is high when light is brought close to the LDRs and the current is much less when the light is moved away.

The thermistor

- A thermistor is a resistor whose resistance can be changed by changing its temperature.
- When cold, the resistance is high and the thermistor does not allow much current to flow.
- When warm, the resistance is low and the thermistor allows current to flow.
- Thermistors are used in fire alarms, fridges and boilers to control temperature.

▶▶ Experiment 34.6

To investigate the operation of a thermistor

This experiment is summarised in Figure 34.14.

- When the thermistor is placed in hot water, the buzzer sounds.
- When the thermistor is placed in cold water, the buzzer becomes silent.
- Thermistors allow more current to flow when hot than when cold.

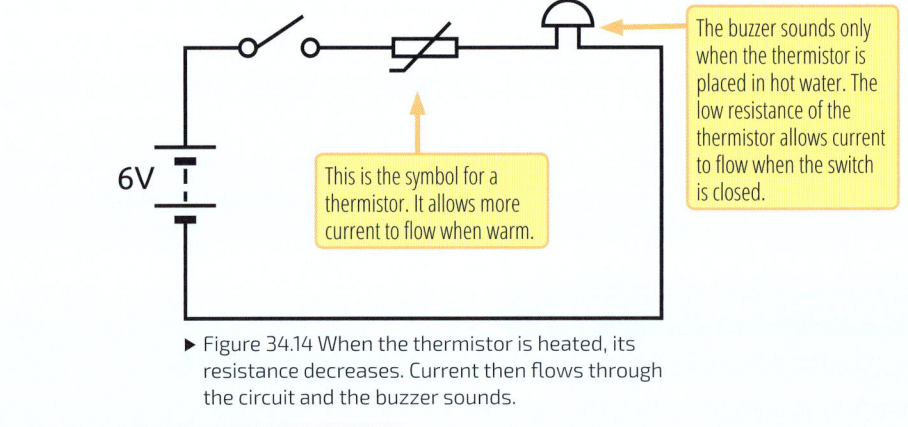

▶ Figure 34.14 When the thermistor is heated, its resistance decreases. Current then flows through the circuit and the buzzer sounds.

 www.folensonline.ie/for-students

34.11 Electrical power

- The power of an electrical appliance is the amount of electrical energy converted to other forms in one second.
- A powerful kettle will boil the same quantity of water more quickly when compared to a less powerful kettle.
- The unit of power is the Watt and the symbol of power in a mathematical equation is **P**.
- The power of an appliance can be measured using a wattmeter, Figure 34.15.

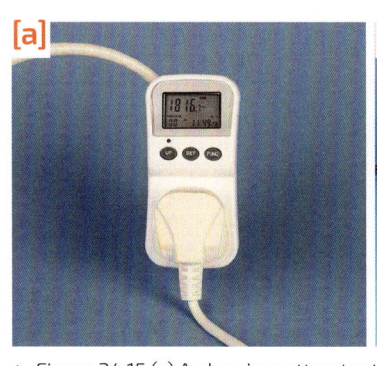 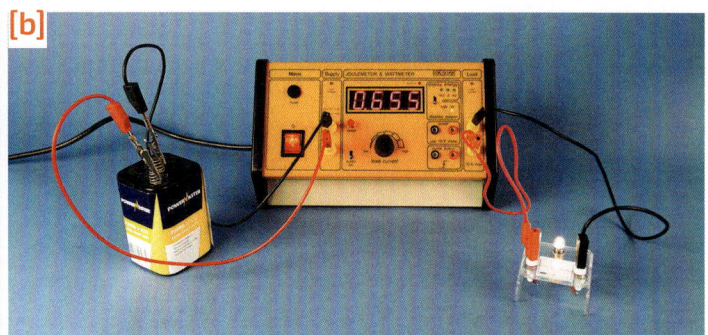

▶ Figure 34.15 (a) A plug-in wattmeter that you can use at home. (b) A laboratory wattmeter.

- Power can be calculated from the following equation:

> Power = voltage × current
>
> $P = V \times I$

P = power measured in watts (W)
V = voltage measured in volts (V)
I = current measured in amps (A)

▶▶ Worked Example 34.3

A heater is connected to the 230 V mains power supply in a house. If the heater draws a current of 13 A, calculate the power of the heater.

1. Write the equation: $P = V \times I$
2. Fill the values: $= 230 \times 13$
3. Write the answer and the unit: $= 2990$ W

▶▶ Science Self-Assessment

Now I am able to:	🟢	🟡	🔴
Construct simple circuits using wires, bulbs, variable resistors, LEDs, LDRs, thermistors and diodes			
Investigate if a substance is a conductor or an insulator			
Measure and calculate current, voltage (potential difference), resistance and electrical power			
Investigate the relationship between voltage and current for a fixed resistor and hence calculate the resistance of the resistor			
State and apply Ohm's law			

35 A technological application of physics

The Physical World strand

Main topics in this chapter:
- The discovery of radioactivity
- The scientific, social and environmental impacts of nuclear fission

Case Study: Nuclear fission

The discovery of radioactivity

- In 1896 Henri Becquerel was studying the radiation emitted from uranium salts when exposed to sunlight, Figure 35.1.
- During a dull period, he placed the uranium salts in a drawer with some photographic film. When he later went to use the film, he found that it had been exposed (blackened) even though the film had not been exposed to light.
- He deduced that something had come from the uranium, which had made the film black. He later called this spontaneous release of radiation **radioactivity**.
- Otto Hahn, Lise Meitner and Fritz Strassmann began performing experiments on uranium in Berlin in 1938. It was discovered that when a neutron was fired at a uranium nucleus, two smaller nuclei were produced. It appeared that the uranium nucleus had been split in two by the neutron. This is called **nuclear fission**, Figure 35.2.

▶ Figure 35.1 Becquerel discovered radioactivity in 1896.

Nuclear fission is the splitting of a large nucleus into two smaller nuclei with the release of a large amount of energy.

- Further experiments on fission showed that fission produces neutrons. These neutrons could cause further nuclei to split by fission, Figure 35.3.
- One occurrence of fission could cause many other nuclei to undergo fission, releasing vast amounts of energy in a process called a chain reaction.

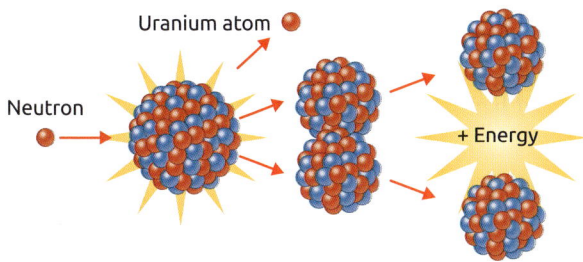

▶ Figure 35.2 Nuclear fission is the breakdown of a large nucleus into two smaller nuclei with the release of a large amount of energy.

One neutron causes one nucleus to undergo fission, but also releases another three neutrons, which cause further fission of nearby nuclei, producing more neutrons and causing more fission. This is called a **chain reaction**, Figure 35.3. The chain reaction ensures that once a reaction has started, more and more energy is released, as in an atomic bomb.

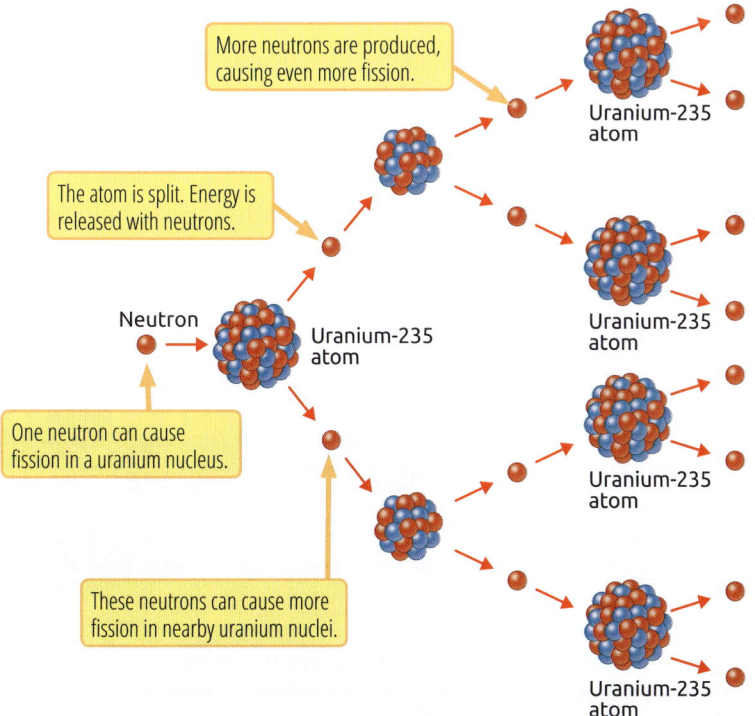

▶ Figure 35.3 Fission is an example of a chain reaction.

- Today nuclear power plants use a controlled chain reaction to produce steam to generate electricity.

199

- Many scientists realised that this reaction could be used to make an atomic bomb.
- In 1943 the USA developed the Manhattan Project to build the world's first atomic bomb. Before World War II, Germany had some of the world's finest nuclear scientists. However, many scientists – including Albert Einstein – emigrated from Germany, as they were Jewish.
- The USA invested heavily in the project in case the Nazis were planning their own atomic bomb.
- In July 1945 the first atomic bomb, named 'Trinity', was tested in the New Mexico desert. It was a plutonium bomb. In August 1945 two more atomic bombs were used against the Japanese cities of Hiroshima and Nagasaki, Figure 35.4. This brought a sudden end to World War II.

▶ Figure 35.4 An atomic bomb exploding over Hiroshima in 1945

Scientific impact of fission

- Scientists are still very interested in nuclear research and radioactivity. Nuclear fission was found to be a huge source of energy. It was used in nuclear bombs and is still used in a controlled way to make electricity.
- Other uses are in the manufacture of smoke alarms, medical treatment, sterilisation of materials and food, and in radiotherapy to help fight cancer.
- One of the drawbacks is that fission can produce highly radioactive cancer-causing products.

Social impact of fission

- The discovery of the atomic bomb brought World War II to a quick end in Japan in 1945. However, over 150,000 innocent people were killed in Hiroshima and Nagasaki, mostly from the heat and explosion and not from radioactivity, Figure 35.5.

▶ Figure 35.5 Hiroshima after the atomic bomb exploded

- After World War II there was a race between the USA and Russia to build more and more nuclear weapons. This led to the Cold War, which heightened secrecy and tensions between Russia and the USA. Tensions were so great that nuclear war almost broke out between the USA and Russia in the 1960s.
- Eventually there was agreement between Russia and the USA that this arms race had to stop and that missiles on both sides would be destroyed.

▶ Figure 35.6 A nuclear fission power station: it does not release carbon dioxide into the atmosphere but accidents can happen, which would release cancer-causing radioactivity into the environment.

- However, some countries still want to create their own nuclear weapons. The United Nations regulates the production of nuclear weapons and tries to discourage other countries from creating them.
- Society has benefited from the huge amounts of energy that nuclear reactors can create for electricity production, Figure 35.6.

Environmental impact of fission

- Fission reactions do not produce carbon dioxide. This means that they do not make a great impact on global warming and climate change.
- Fission reactors produce toxic nuclear waste that can be dangerous for thousands of years. This waste has to be stored safely.
- There have been leaks of radioactivity from Chernobyl in Russia, Fukushima in Japan and Three Mile Island in the USA. Each leak has contaminated farm land, food and water supplies. This radioactivity can cause cancer and other illnesses in animals and humans.

▶▶ Science Self-Assessment

Now I am able to:	🟢	🟠	🔴
Outline a technological application of physics			
Explain the terms *nuclear fission* and *chain reaction*			
Discuss the scientific, social and environmental impacts of nuclear fission			

36 Space, celestial objects and the origin of the universe

The Earth and Space strand

Main topics in this chapter:
- Introduction to astronomy
- Celestial bodies – stars, planets, moons, asteroids, comets, planetary systems and galaxies
- Our solar system
- The Big Bang and the formation of the universe

36.1 What is astronomy?

For thousands of years, humans have studied the night sky. The universe consists of all the matter and energy that exists. The study of the universe outside the Earth's atmosphere is called **astronomy**. Famous astronomers include Ptolemy, who proposed that the Earth was at the centre of the universe; Copernicus, who proposed that the Sun is at the centre of the universe; and Galileo, who proved that the Sun was at the centre of the universe, using observations made with a telescope.

> **Astronomy** is the study of the universe beyond the Earth's atmosphere.

36.2 Celestial bodies

As scientists studied the night sky with telescopes, they noticed that objects in space could be sorted into different classes. The name for any naturally made object outside the Earth's atmosphere is a celestial body. Some celestial bodies are shown in Figure 36.1.

> A **celestial body** is a naturally made object outside the Earth's atmosphere.

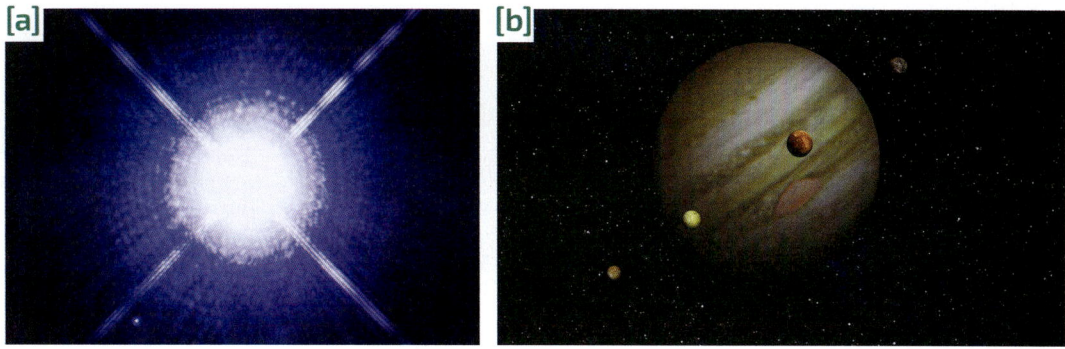

▶ Figure 36.1 (a) A star creates its own light and heat. (b) The planet Jupiter with some of its moons in orbit.

Table 36.1 summarises some information about the celestial bodies on your Junior Cycle course.

Celestial Body	Definition	Additional information
Star	A star is a celestial body that generates its own **light and heat**. It consists of a mass of gas held together by its own gravity, Figure 36.1 (a).	Our Sun is an example of a star. Because of the great heat and gravity, atoms join together and release a vast amount of energy (nuclear fusion).
Planet	A planet is a celestial body that is **in orbit around a star**, Figure 36.1 (b).	Planets have an almost spherical shape and should have enough gravity to pull objects into their pathway as they orbit a star. They are by far the largest object within their own orbit.
Moon	A moon is a **natural satellite of a planet**, Figure 36.1 (b). (A satellite is a body which is in orbit around another larger body.)	Many of the planets have moons orbiting them. Saturn and Jupiter have more than 60 moons each.
Asteroid	An asteroid is a small **rocky** body orbiting the Sun.	It is thought that an asteroid that hit the Earth caused the extinction of the dinosaurs millions of years ago.
Comet	A comet is a made from **ice and dust** and orbits the Sun, Figure 36.2 (a).	When comets are near the Sun, their **tails** of gas and dust can be seen pointing away from the Sun, which makes them visible.
Planetary systems (Solar System)	A planetary system (solar system) is a **group of planets, asteroids, comets and other celestial bodies** that are in orbit around a star and held together by the star's gravity.	Our solar system is only one of many millions of planetary systems in the universe.
Galaxy	A galaxy is a **very large system of stars** held together by gravity and isolated from similar systems by vast regions of space, Figure 36.2 (b).	Our solar system is a part of the Milky Way galaxy. It is one of millions of galaxies in the universe.

▶ Table 36.1 Celestial bodies in our universe

▶ Figure 36.2 (a) A comet is a dusty snowball that may have a tail. (b) A galaxy is a group made up of millions of stars and their planets.

36.3 Our solar system

- Our Sun is a **star** at the centre of our solar system. The size of our solar system is controlled by how far out its gravity can control objects.
- The Earth is one of eight **planets**. The eight planets in order of distance from the Sun are Mercury, Venus, Earth, Mars, Jupiter, Saturn, Uranus and Neptune. Use the following mnemonic to learn the order: **M**y **V**ery **E**ducated **M**other **J**ust **S**erved **U**s **N**oodles.
- Each planet takes a different amount of time to orbit the Sun. The time taken for a planet to make one complete revolution around the Sun is called a **year**. The Earth takes 365·25 days to go around the Sun. The length of a year in other planets is different. On Mercury it is 88 Earth days and on Mars it is 687 Earth days.
- Many of the planets have **moons**. Our Moon is visible because it reflects light from the Sun. You will revise the phases of the Moon in Chapter 37.
- Most of the **asteroids** in our solar system stay in a region called the asteroid belt, between Mars and Jupiter. From time to time, an asteroid can escape from this region. It is in danger of colliding with another celestial body such as the Earth.
- Most of the **comets** in our solar system are found in a region of gas clouds called the Kuiper belt, just outside the orbit of Neptune, Figure 36.3. Some comets have escaped from this region and their orbits are not circular. Sometimes they are close to the Sun. Sometimes they can move very far away in the outer reaches of our solar system. When comets are near the Sun, their **tails** of gas and dust can be seen pointing away from the Sun, which makes them visible.

▶ Figure 36.3 Part of our solar system: note the planets in orbit around the Sun. The Kuiper belt is the source of comets. The asteroid belt contains most of the asteroids found in the solar system.

- **Halley's Comet** is visible from Earth approximately every 75 years. This allows us to predict when the comet will be visible from Earth in the future.
- Our solar system is a part of the **Milky Way galaxy**. It is one of millions of galaxies in the universe.
- Outer space, or simply **space**, is the empty volume that exists between galaxies. It is not completely empty, but consists of a vacuum containing low-density particles, mostly hydrogen and helium, as well as dust and radiation.

> **Exam Tip!**
> In the exam, you may be presented with tables of data such as the radius of a planet's orbit from the Sun, the years when a comet was visible from Earth, the size of planets, etc. Make sure that you get plenty of practice in interpreting data.

▶▶ Worked Example 36.1

Data about some planets are summarised in Table 36.2. Use this table to answer the questions given.

Planet	Mass (compared with the Earth)	Distance from the Sun (astronomical units)*	Diameter (compared with the Earth)	Density kg/m³
Mercury	0.06	0.39	0.38	5427
Venus	0.81	0.72	0.95	5243
Earth	1	1	1	5514
Mars	0.11	1.52	0.53	3933
Jupiter	316.33	5.19	11.21	1326

▶ Table 36.2 Summary of data about some planets

*An astronomical unit is the distance between the Sun and the Earth.

(i) Are the data in each column of the table listed in order of mass, in order of distance from the Sun, in order of diameter or in order of density?

(ii) List the order of the planets in order of increasing distance from the Sun, starting with the one closest to the Sun.

(iii) One of the planets is mostly made of gas. Using the table, predict which one of the planets this is likely to be. Justify your answer.

(iv) A certain comet has been observed from Earth in the years 1835, 1910 and 1985. Estimate when it is likely to be seen from Earth again.

Answer

(i) The data are listed in order of increasing distance from the Sun.

(ii) The data in the table (Distance from the Sun column) tells me that the order of the planets from the Sun is Mercury, Venus, Earth, Mars and Jupiter.

(iii) Since Jupiter has the least density of all the planets, it is most likely to be made of gas. Gases have lower density than solids or liquids.

(iv) The time from 1835 to 1910 is 75 years. The time from 1910 to 1985 is also 75 years. I would expect to see it again 75 years after the last sighting in 1985. This would be in the year 2060.

36.4 The Big Bang and the formation of the universe

> The **universe** consists of all the matter and energy that exists.

- The most commonly accepted theory for the formation of the universe is the Big Bang theory.
- The universe consists of all the galaxies, space and the energy within, which were created during the Big Bang.
- About 14 billion years ago, all the mass and energy of the universe existed in a tiny bubble less than the size of a pinhead that was extremely hot and dense.
- Suddenly it exploded (the Big Bang). This was the birth of the universe, Figure 36.4.
- Within minutes, the universe expanded from the size of a pinhead to the size of a galaxy.
- Over a period of time, protons, neutrons and electrons were made. Eventually these combined to form atoms of smaller elements, e.g. hydrogen and helium.
- After a billion years, these giant clouds of atoms were pulled together by gravity to make the first stars and galaxies.
- After five billion years, these first stars died. They exploded (supernova) and forced new heavier elements into space. These gathered together and formed new stars, planets, planetary systems and galaxies.

▶ Figure 36.4 The Big Bang and the formation of the universe

Evidence for the Big Bang theory

1. Edwin Hubble and Vesto Slipher discovered that the **universe is continuously expanding**. They noticed that distant galaxies are moving away faster than nearby ones. This would suggest that all the galaxies started from one point. You can compare it to a race. Everybody starts at the same point. The faster runners will move further away from the starting position. This is the same for galaxies.

2. When we look at stars in the night sky, the light we see is from distant galaxies. It has taken millions of years to get here! **Looking at distant galaxies with telescopes is like looking back in time to what our galaxy was like a long time ago**, Figure 36.5. Scientists are able to look at the light coming from galaxies that are less than a billion years old. (They are the same age as our galaxy, but the light from what happened billions of years ago is only getting here now!) This gives us information about what happened in our galaxy billions of years ago.

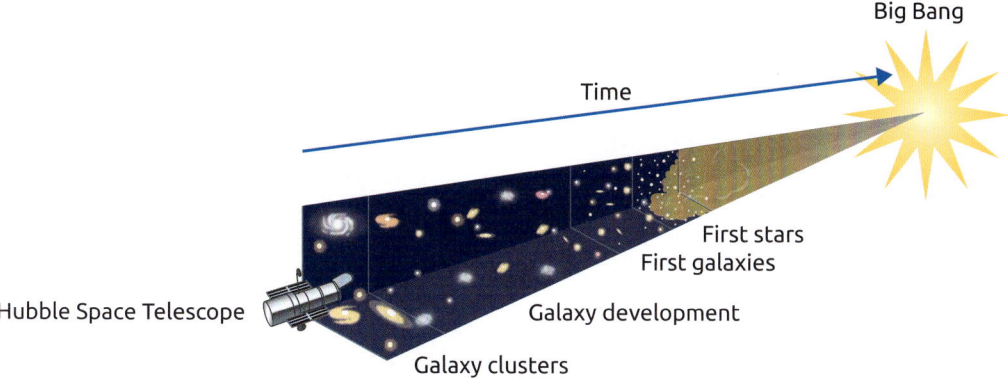

▶ Figure 36.5 Looking at distant galaxies is like looking back in time. This diagram summarises the areas being studied by the Hubble Space Telescope.

3. There is energy called **'cosmic background radiation'** remaining everywhere in space. Scientists predicted that this would be present if the Big Bang took place. Cosmic background radiation was detected in 1964, which strongly supports the theory.

▶▶ Worked Example 36.2

Answer the following questions by yourself. Then check your answers on p.208.

i. Which of the following is **not** a celestial body?
   (a) the Sun   (b) Pluto   (c) the International Space Station   (d) the Moon

ii. Which of the following is a list of celestial bodies in order of increasing size?
   (a) galaxy, planet, star, asteroid   (b) asteroid , planet, star, galaxy
   (c) planet, asteroid, star, galaxy   (d) asteroid, star, planet, galaxy

iii. Which of the following celestial bodies make their own heat and light?
   (a) moons   (b) stars   (c) both moons and stars   (d) asteroids

iv. Name the fifth planet from the Sun.
   (a) the Earth   (b) the Moon   (c) Mars   (d) Jupiter

v. Which of the following is **not** evidence for the Big Bang Theory?
   (a) Cosmic background radiation in the universe
   (b) The universe is continuously expanding.
   (c) Observations from telescopes allow us to look back in time.
   (d) The same comet is visible at regular intervals from Earth.

vi. Which of the following statements about the Sun is **incorrect**?
   (a) The Sun is the only star in our solar system.
   (b) The Sun is in orbit around the Earth.
   (c) The Sun creates its light and heat by nuclear fusion.
   (d) There are eight planets in orbit around the Sun.

vii. A certain celestial body was observed in a telescope at night from the Earth. It appeared to be bright and had a tail. It was no longer visible after a few months. Name this celestial body.

▶ Figure 36.6

(a) an asteroid   (b) a moon of another planet   (c) a comet   (d) a star

viii. Name the most widely accepted scientific theory of how the universe was created.

(a) the Steady State theory   (b) astronomy theory

(c) the Big Bang theory   (d) chaos theory

ix. In 2004 a celestial body named Apophis was discovered approaching Earth and there was concern that it would hit the Earth. The body has a radius of 185 m, is made of rock and does not have a tail. What type of celestial body is this?

(a) a comet   (b) a star   (c) an asteroid   (d) a UFO

x. Which of the following statements about our solar system is **incorrect**?

(a) The Sun's gravity keeps celestial bodies in the solar system.

(b) There are just ten celestial bodies in our solar system.

(c) The Sun is the only star in our solar system.

(d) The Sun is at the centre of our solar system.

Answers

i. (c)   **ii.** (b)   **iii.** (b)   **iv.** (d)   **v.** (d)   **vi.** (b)   **vii.** (c)   **viii.** (c)   **ix.** (c)   **x.** (b)

▶▶ Worked Example 36.3

Table 36.3 shows some data about some celestial bodies that are in orbit around our Sun. The values given are relative to the Earth (e.g. Saturn is 9.58 times further from the Sun than the Earth).

Body	Relative density	Relative diameter	Relative distance from the Sun	Number of moons
Mercury	0.984	0.383	0.387	0
Earth	1	1	1	1
Neptune	0.297	3.88	30	14
Saturn	0.125	9.45	9.58	62

▶ Table 36.3

Carefully study the data in each column and answer the following questions.

(i) Is the table in order of relative density, relative diameter or relative distance from the Sun?
(ii) Which of the celestial bodies is the largest? Justify your answer.
(iii) Which of the celestial bodies is closest to the Sun?
(iv) Which of the celestial bodies is in orbit around the Sun and has an orbit that is greater than that of Saturn?
(v) Which of the planets Mercury or Saturn is most likely to be made of gas?
(vi) Which of the celestial bodies is likely to be the coldest?
(vii) Each of the celestial bodies has at least one moon. What is a moon?

Answers

(i) The table is in order of increasing relative diameter.
(ii) Saturn is the largest body as it has the largest relative diameter.
(iii) Mercury is closest to the Sun since it has the smallest relative distance from the Sun.
(iv) Neptune has a greater relative distance from the Sun than Saturn. Neptune's orbit must be outside the orbit of Saturn.
(v) Saturn has a lower relative density than Mercury and is therefore more likely to be made up of gas.
(vi) Neptune is most likely to be the coldest as it is farthest from the Sun.
(vii) A moon is a natural satellite of a planet.

▶▶ Worked Example 36.4

Table 36.4 shows some data about some planets in our Solar System. The data on mass, diameter and distance from the Sun is relative to the Earth (e.g. Neptune is 30 times further from the Sun than the Earth). Use this table to help you answer the questions below.

	Mercury	Earth	Jupiter	Saturn	Neptune
Relative diameter	0.383	1	11.2	9.5	3.9
Relative distance from the Sun	0.387	1	5.2	9.6	30
Surface composition	Rocky	Rocky	Gas	Gas	Gas
Mean temperature (°C)	167	15	−110	−140	−200
Relative mass	0.055	1	318	95.2	17.1

▶ Table 36.4

(i) Name **(a)** the largest planet by size, **(b)** the smallest planet listed in the table.

(ii) Are the planets in the table listed in order of relative mass, in order of relative distance from the Sun or in order of relative diameter?

(iii) Compare the planet Neptune with planet Earth for **(a)** size, **(b)** distance from the Sun, **(c)** mean temperature, **(d)** mass.

(iv) Is there a relationship (trend) between distance from the Sun and the surface temperature of a planet? What is this relationship (trend)?

(v) If water existed on the surface of Jupiter, predict if you would expect to find it as a solid, liquid or gas?

(vi) The NASA Voyager space programme uses space probes that travel at very high speeds to research the outer solar system. When designing the Voyager space probes, scientists favoured the use of a small nuclear reactor, especially when the probes moved further from the Sun. Why would this be the case?

Answers

(i) The largest planet by size is Jupiter and the smallest is Mercury. (This is obtained from the data on relative diameter.)

(ii) The objects are ordered by relative distance from the Sun. (The distance from the Sun increases as you go across the table.)

(iii) Neptune is:

   (a) Larger than Earth (greater relative diameter)

   (b) Further from the Sun than Earth (greater relative distance from the Sun)

   (c) Much colder average temperature than Earth (lower mean temperature)

   (d) Of a greater mass than Earth (greater relative mass)

(iv) Yes. The table shows that planets closer to the Sun have a high mean temperature. Planets further away from the Sun have a low mean temperature. As the distance from the Sun increases, the mean temperature decreases.

(v) If water existed on Jupiter it would exist as ice, since the mean surface temperature of Jupiter is much lower than 0°C.

(vi) As you move further from the Sun, the amount of energy from the Sun falling on the solar panels gets less and less. The power output of the panels decreases with distance from the Sun and may not be sufficient to power the probes equipment. A nuclear reactor would be a more reliable source of energy. Also, the large area of solar panels could be damaged by the collision with small objects as it moves at great speeds through the solar system.

▶▶ Worked Example 36.5

(i) The Sun is the star in the centre of our solar system. Name one planet that is closer to the Sun than the Earth and one planet that is further away from the Sun.

(ii) Stars release vast amounts of heat and light and other forms of energy. What is the source of this energy?

(iii) Name a natural satellite of the Earth, Figure 36.7.

(iv) The Solar System is part of the Milky Way galaxy. If we could look at the Milky Way from a very great distance, it would resemble the spiral galaxy in the photograph, Figure 36.8. The Milky Way is part of a still larger system known as the universe. Explain clearly the underlined terms.

(v) This photograph, of the planet Jupiter, was taken using the Hubble Space Telescope. Jupiter has sixteen known moons. Explain the underlined terms.

▶ Figure 36.7

▶ Figure 36.8

▶ Figure 36.9

Answers

(i) One planet closer: Any one of Mercury or Venus
One planet further away: Any one of Mars, Jupiter, Saturn, Uranus or Neptune.

(ii) The source of a star's heat and light is nuclear fusion.

(iii) The only natural satellite of the Earth is the Moon.

(iv) A solar system is group of planets, asteroids, comets and other celestial bodies that are in orbit around a star and held together by the star's gravity.
A galaxy is a very large system of stars.
The universe consists of all the matter and energy that exists.

(v) A planet is a celestial body that is in orbit around a star.
A moon is a natural satellite of a planet.

▶▶ Science Self-Assessment

Now I am able to:	🟢	🟠	🔴
Explain the terms *star, planet, moon, asteroid, comet, planetary system (solar system)* and *galaxy*			
Discuss how celestial objects are related to each other			
Interpret data about some planets			
Describe the formation of the universe during the Big Bang and outline evidence to support the theory			

37 The Earth, Sun and Moon

The Earth and Space strand

▶▶ Main topics in this chapter:
- Gravity: the glue of the universe
- Factors that affect the surface gravity on a celestial body
- The relationship between the Sun, Earth and Moon
- What causes the seasons?
- What causes the phases of the Moon?
- What causes lunar and solar eclipses?
- Benefits, hazards and the future of space exploration

37.1 Gravity

- Gravity is known as the 'glue of the universe'. It is responsible for holding planets and moons in position. Let us revise what we learned in Chapter 31 about gravity, Figure 37.1.
- If any two masses are placed near each other, they will be attracted to each other by the force of gravity.
- If the masses are small, the force of attraction is very small – too small to take into account.
- If one of the masses is very large (e.g. a moon, a planet or a star), the force of gravity is much larger.

My WEIGHT on Earth is around 560 N, my mass is 56 kg.

My WEIGHT on the moon is around 90 N, my mass is 56 kg.

My MASS is always 56 kg!!

▶ Figure 37.1 The weight of a body will change depending on location. The mass will not change just by moving it. The amount of the substance present is still the same.

- The force of gravity is also affected by distance. The smaller the distance between the centres of the masses, the greater the force of attraction.
- The weight of an object is a measure of the force of gravity on that body. Different planets have different surface gravity. Table 37.1 gives information on the relative surface gravity on different celestial objects.
- In Table 37.1 you can see that the surface gravity on Jupiter is 2.5 times greater than the surface gravity on Earth. This means that a body weighs 2.5 times more on Jupiter than Earth. As you move away from a celestial body, the force of gravity becomes less and less. As a rocket moves further away from the surface of the Earth, it feels less pull-back to the Earth and becomes easier to accelerate.
- Planets can be composed of rock (the Earth) or mostly gas (Jupiter). Planets of greater density are likely to be made of rock. Planets of lesser density are likely to be made mostly of gas.

▶▶ Worked Example 37.1

Table 37.1 shows some data on a few celestial bodies. The mass, radius, and surface gravity of each are compared with the Earth, i.e. Jupiter has 318 times the mass of the Earth.

Body	Relative mass	Relative radius	Surface gravity
Sun	333000	110	28
Jupiter	318	11	2.5
Earth	1	1	1
Mars	0.1	0.53	0.38
Ganymede	0.025	0.04	0.15
Titan	0.023	0.04	0.14
Body NK1	0.023	0.02	0.56

▶ Table 37.1 Data on some celestial bodies

(i) Suggest a reason why Jupiter has a greater surface gravity than Earth.
(ii) Why is the surface gravity on Body NK1 greater than the surface gravity on Titan?
(iii) Why does Ganymede have a slightly greater surface gravity than Titan?
(iv) How do you think the weight of a spaceship would change if moved from the surface of Mars to the surface of the Earth? (Ignore the loss of fuel, rockets, etc.)
(v) Would the surface gravity on Mars make any difference to how easy it would be to launch the spacecraft, in comparison to the surface gravity on Earth?
(vi) The company SpaceX plans to bring tourists on trips around the Moon. If you were on this trip, how would **(a)** your weight and **(b)** your mass change as you moved further from the surface of the Earth at constant velocity?

Solution:

(i) Jupiter has greater surface gravity than the Earth as Jupiter has a **greater mass** than Earth.

(ii) The surface gravity of NK1 is greater than that of Titan as NK1 has a **smaller radius than Titan**.

(iii) The surface gravity of Ganymede is slightly greater than that of Titan as Ganymede has a **greater mass** than Titan.

(iv) The weight of the spacecraft would be **less** on the surface of Mars than the surface of Earth (only 0.38 times the weight on Earth) due to lower surface gravity on Mars.

(v) As there is less surface gravity on Mars, the rockets would not need to be as powerful and would not need as much fuel to launch from the surface of Mars compared with the surface of Earth. It would be **easier** to launch from the surface of Mars than Earth.

(vi) As you would move further from the surface of the Earth, the force of gravity would lessen and I would expect my **weight to decrease**. Assuming that I did not eat, drink or excrete anything, I would expect my **mass to remain the same**.

37.2 The Sun, the Earth and the Moon

- The Earth orbits the Sun every 365.25 days. This causes the seasons, Figure 37.2.
- The Earth rotates on its own axis every 24 hours. This causes day and night.
- The Moon orbits the Earth approximately every 28 days. This causes the phases of the Moon.

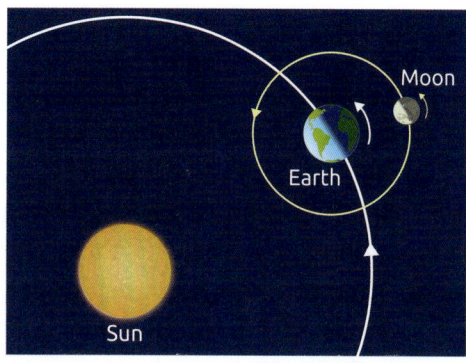

▶ Figure 37.2 The Earth is in orbit around the Sun and the Moon is in orbit around the Earth.

37.3 Seasons

- The Sun is the primary source of energy for the Earth. It provides the energy for photosynthesis that makes food and oxygen. It also heats the Earth.
- Different parts of the planet receive different amounts of light energy during the year. This causes the seasons.
- If we look at Figure 37.3, we can see that the Earth is tilted on its axis of rotation. In summer time in the northern hemisphere, we are tilted towards the Sun. The amount of energy falling on the northern hemisphere is increased because:
  - The length of daytime when we receive energy from the Sun is increased.
  - The rays of the Sun hit the Earth at almost right angles and their energy is spread over a smaller area.

- In winter the opposite is true: the northern hemisphere of the Earth is tilted away from the Sun. The amount of energy falling on the northern hemisphere is decreased because:
    - The length of daytime when energy is received from the Sun is decreased.
    - The rays from the Sun hit the Earth at oblique angles and have to spread the same energy over a larger area.
- Note that the Earth is always tilted at the same angle but, because of its rotation around the Sun, different parts get different exposure to the Sun during the year.
- Note from Figure 37.3 that when the northern hemisphere is tilted away from the Sun, the southern hemisphere is tilted towards the Sun. When we are in deep winter in Ireland it is high summer in Australia!

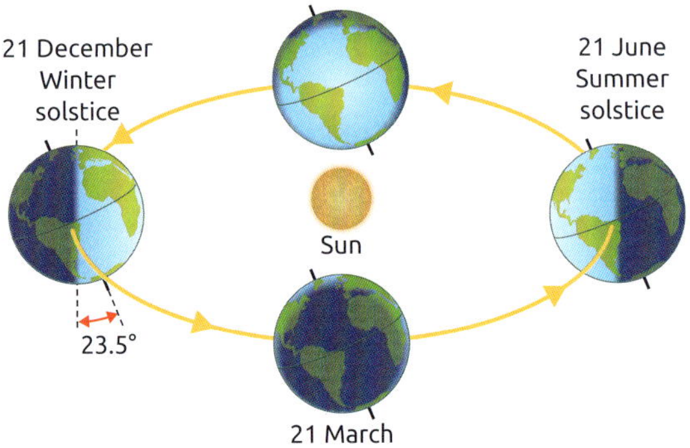

▶ Figure 37.3 The seasons are caused by the axis of the Earth being tilted. The northern hemisphere tilts towards the Sun during our summer and away during our winter.

37.4 The phases of the Moon

- The Moon does not create its own light (as the Sun does). We see the Moon because it **reflects** light from the Sun.
- Half the moon is always lit up (except during lunar eclipses). The parts of the Moon that are visible to us change during the month because the Moon is in orbit around the Earth. This takes about 28 days.
- The changing appearance of the Moon as it orbits the Earth is referred to as 'the phases of the Moon'. The phases of the Moon are summarised in Figure 37.4.
- In Figure 37.4 you should be able to figure out that **our view of the Moon from the Earth** changes as the Moon orbits the Earth. We are always looking at the same face of the Moon, but different parts are lit up.
- The lunar (Moon) phases begin on day 1 and can be broken into stages:
    - Day 1: **New Moon**. From Earth we cannot see any Moon because the sunlit part of the Moon is facing away from the Earth.
    - Day 7: **First quarter**. We see half of the lit side of the Moon.
    - Day 14: **Full Moon**. We see all of the illuminated (lit) part of the Moon.
    - Day 21: **Third quarter**. We see half of the lit side of the Moon.
    - Day 28: We have a **new Moon** and the cycle begins again.

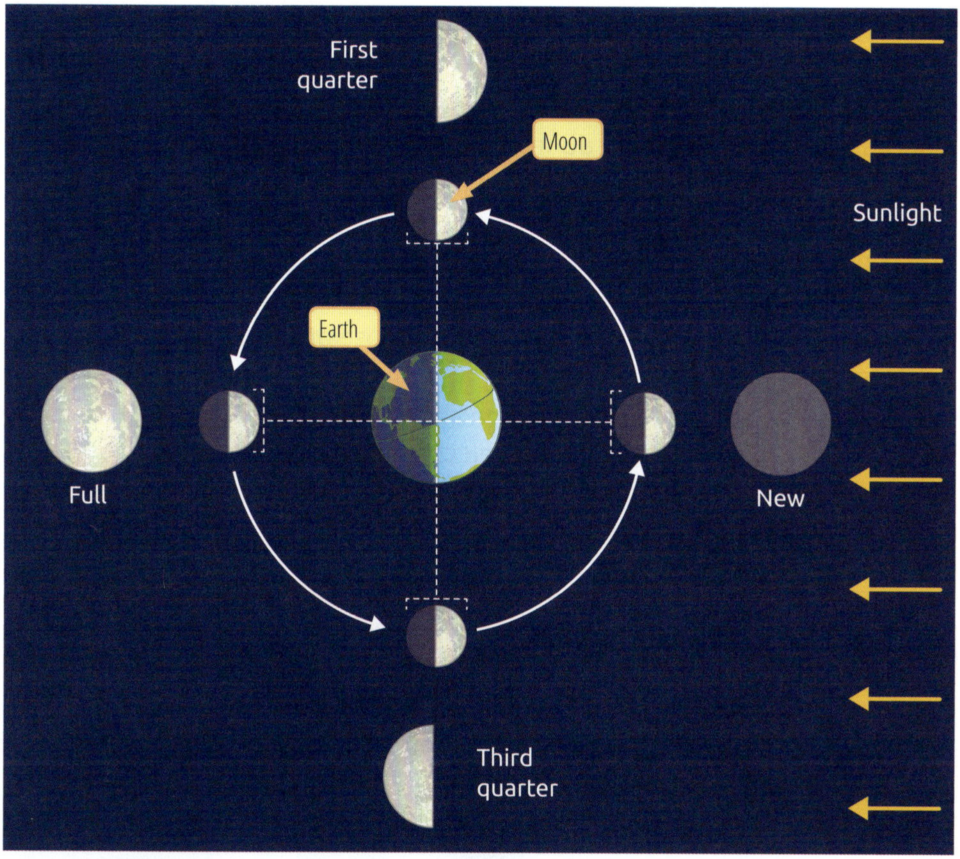

▶ Figure 37.4 A model of the lunar cycle. The inner circle represents the Moon as it orbits the Earth. The outer drawings represent the appearance of the Moon as seen from the Earth.

37.5 Eclipses

- The word *eclipse* means to obscure. An eclipse occurs when a celestial body gets in the way of the sunlight illuminating another celestial body. There are two main types of eclipse: a lunar eclipse and a solar eclipse.
- A **lunar eclipse** happens when **the Earth comes between the Sun and the Moon**. A lunar eclipse happens only during a full Moon and only if the Moon passes part of the Earth's shadow. This is indicated in Figure 37.5 (a).
- A **solar eclipse** occurs when the Moon comes between the Sun and the Earth. A solar eclipse can only happen during a new Moon and only if the Earth passes through the shadow of the Moon. This is indicated in Figure 37.5 (b).

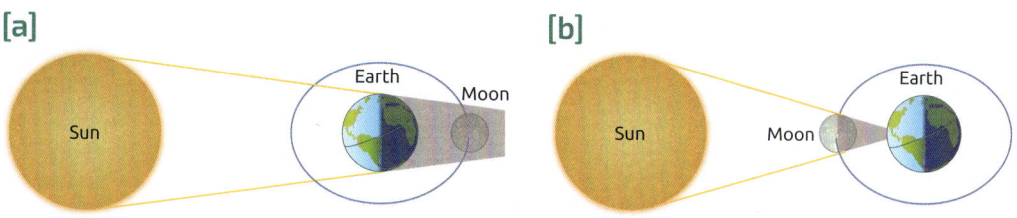

▶ Figure 37.5 (a) A lunar eclipse. (b) A solar eclipse.

37.6 Benefits of space exploration

Many improvements to everyday technologies came about because of the needs of space exploration. The following are some examples of **technologies** that were developed because of a need for them during space exploration.

- **Satellites:** With the development of artificial satellites around the Earth, scientists have come up with many uses for them on Earth. Global Positioning System (**GPS**) is used for aviation, shipping and personal satnav devices. **Weather satellites** give us information to carry out detailed weather forecasts. **Television signals, the internet** and some telephones make use of satellite technology to relay information (e.g. Sky TV).
- **Efficient solar panels:** Space stations such as the International Space Station require efficient solar panels to generate electricity to power the many systems necessary for the survival of humans, Figure 37.6. This technology is used today on Earth as a sustainable source of electricity.
- **Battery technology:** The International Space Station relies on efficient battery technology to keep its systems working while in the dark. Advanced battery technology is needed today on Earth to store electricity generated by solar panels and for electric cars.
- **New materials:** Materials such as memory foam, scratch-proof glass and Teflon-coated fibreglass were originally developed for use in space. We have a wide number of uses for these on Earth today.

▶ Figure 37.6 More efficient solar panels and battery technology were developed to power the International Space Station.

37.7 Some hazards of space exploration

- The life of an astronaut is a hazardous one in many ways, either when travelling or while in space itself.
- When travelling from Earth into space, the rockets can explode or go out of control, as happened in *Apollo 1* and *Challenger*, which resulted in the deaths of astronauts, Figure 37.7.
- When returning to Earth (re-entry), the outside of the spacecraft becomes extremely hot because of friction with the air. If the outside has become damaged, the spacecraft can burn up. This happened with *Columbia* and killed all the astronauts on board the spacecraft.

▶ Figure 37.7 In 1986 the Space Shuttle *Challenger* exploded soon after take-off.

- When in space, you are dependent on technology to make water and oxygen. If these technologies fail, human life is in danger.

37.8 The future of space exploration

- Over the past 20 years most space missions have taken place using spacecraft without crews on board. It is likely that most missions in the future will also take place in this way, with remotely controlled technology such as satellites and robots to carry out investigations.
- It is **unethical** to send astronauts on a hazardous one-way journey to Mars without access to hospital care or any prospect of returning to their families.
- Space exploration is **expensive** and it may be difficult to justify spending public money on such research while people at home die from poverty and lack of appropriate healthcare.

Planet Earth supports life because it is not too hot, not too cold and has liquid water. Scientists hope to one day **find a planet with similar conditions that may also be home to living organisms**. If anything was to destroy life on planet Earth, the human race could be wiped out (as happened with the dinosaurs) unless we travel into space.

▶▶ Worked Example 37.2

Answer the following questions by yourself. Then check your answers on p.220.

i. The seasons are caused by:
   (a) the change in distance between the Earth and the Sun
   (b) the tilting of the Earth towards the Sun in summer and away from the Sun in the winter
   (c) the rotation of the Earth on its own axis
   (d) the changing temperature of the Sun

ii. Figure 37.8 shows the Earth in orbit around the Sun. Which of the following statements is **incorrect**?
   (a) Diagram C represents the position of the Earth when it is summer in the northern hemisphere and winter in the southern hemisphere.
   (b) Diagram D represents the position of the Earth when it is autumn in the northern hemisphere.
   (c) It takes 365.25 days for the Earth to make one rotation around the Sun.
   (d) Diagram A represents winter in the southern hemisphere. 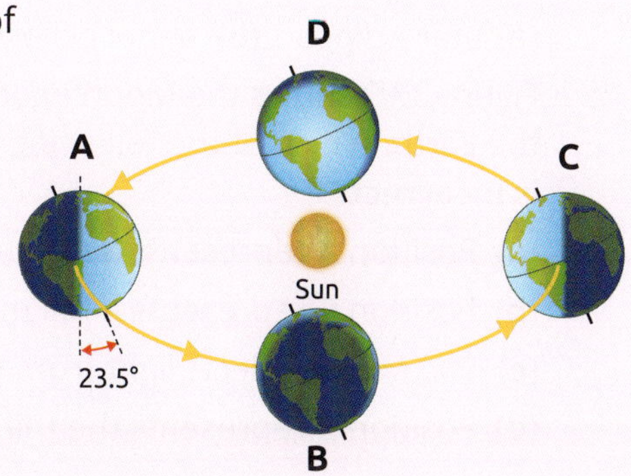

▶ Figure 37.8

iii. Which of the following statements is **correct**? In a lunar eclipse, the Moon:
   (a) casts a shadow on Earth   (b) is in the Earth's shadow
   (c) is between the Earth and the Sun   (d) blocks part of the Sun from view

iv. The Moon goes through a series of phases because of changes in one of the following:
   (a) the amount of the Moon's surface that is in the Earth's shadow
   (b) the amount of the illuminated side of the Moon that can be seen from Earth
   (c) the part of the Moon that faces the Earth as the moon rotates on its own axis
   (d) the tilt of the Moon on its axis

v. When the Moon appears completely illuminated it is called:
   (a) a new moon   (b) a full moon   (c) a blue moon   (d) a super moon

vi. Which statement about lunar eclipses is **correct**?
   (a) A lunar eclipse is caused because the Earth blocks the light travelling from the Sun to the Moon.
   (b) If a lunar eclipse happens by day, it causes part of the Earth to become dark.
   (c) Lunar eclipses only occur during a 'new moon'.
   (d) Lunar eclipses happen every 28 days.

vii. During the June solstice, the season south of the equator is:
   (a) summer   (b) winter   (c) spring   (d) autumn

viii. Which statement about a solar eclipse is **incorrect**? In a solar eclipse, the moon:
   (a) casts a shadow on Earth
   (b) is in Earth's shadow
   (c) is between the Earth and the Sun
   (d) blocks part of the Sun from view

ix. An eclipse that occurs when Earth passes between the Moon and the Sun is classified as a
   (a) star eclipse   (b) aerial eclipse   (c) lunar eclipse   (d) solar eclipse

x. Figure 37.9 shows the Moon in orbit around the Earth. Which of the following statements is **incorrect**?
   (a) Position A represents a new moon.
   (b) Position C represents a full moon.
   (c) The Moon reflects light from the Sun.
   (d) Position B represents the third quarter.

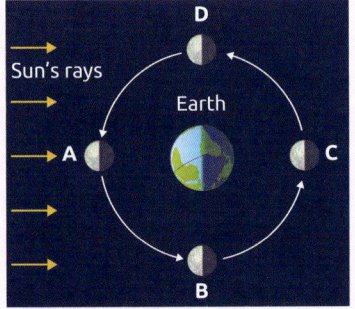

▶ Figure 37.9

Answers
i. (b)   **ii.** (d)   **iii.** (b)   **iv.** (b)   **v.** (b)   **vi.** (a)
vii. (b)   **viii.** (b)   **ix.** (c)   **x.** (d)

▶▶ Worked Example 37.3

Figure 37.10 picture shows a total solar eclipse. Describe how a solar eclipse happens. (9)

Exam Tip!

The maximum number of marks that can be awarded for a correct answer to this question is given in the brackets (9). Usually, 3 marks will be given for each point of information. Since the total is 9 marks here, the question is looking for (9 ÷ 3) = at least three key points of information.

▶ Figure 37.10

Note:

In a past exam, the 9 marks for this question on a solar eclipse were given for the following three points of information:

- Show in a diagram or state the words **Sun and Earth** (3 marks)
- Show in a diagram or state in words that the **Moon is between the Sun and the Earth** (3 marks)
- Show in a diagram or state in words either that the Moon's shadow is cast on the Earth **or** the **sunlight is blocked by the Moon** (3 marks)

Exam Tips!

1. To ensure maximum marks, draw a clearly labelled diagram, Figure 37.11, and write a short explanation.
2. Always attempt the question. If you explained a lunar eclipse by mistake, you would have been awarded at least three out of nine marks!

Solution:

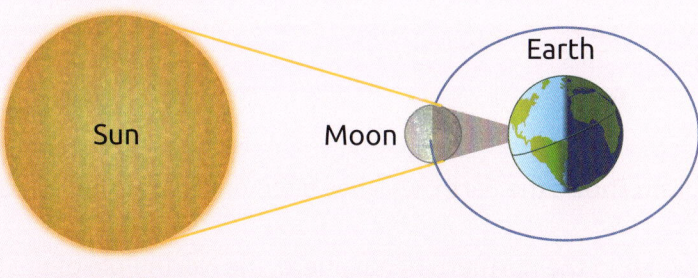

▶ Figure 37.11

- A solar eclipse happens when the Moon, the Sun and the Earth all line up.
- The Moon lies between the Earth and the Sun.
- Because the Moon is blocking some of the sunlight hitting the Earth, it casts a shadow on the Earth.

▶▶ Worked Example 37.4

Explain why we have seasons on Earth. (12)

Note:

In a past exam, the 12 marks for this question were given for the following information:

- Show in a diagram or state in words the **Earth is tilted on its axis** (3 marks)

and only **one** of the following points was required:

- Show in a diagram or state in words that when the **Earth's North Pole is tilted away from the Sun** (3 marks), causing **shorter days and less light to shine** on the surface during a day (3 marks), this causes **winter in the northern hemisphere** (3 marks)*

or

- Show in a diagram or state in words that when **the Earth's North Pole is tilted towards the Sun** (3 marks), **causing longer days and more light energy** shining on its surface during the day (3 marks), this **causes summer in the northern hemisphere** (3 marks)*

*Full marks for these points can be obtained if the correct information is given for the southern hemisphere.

Solution:

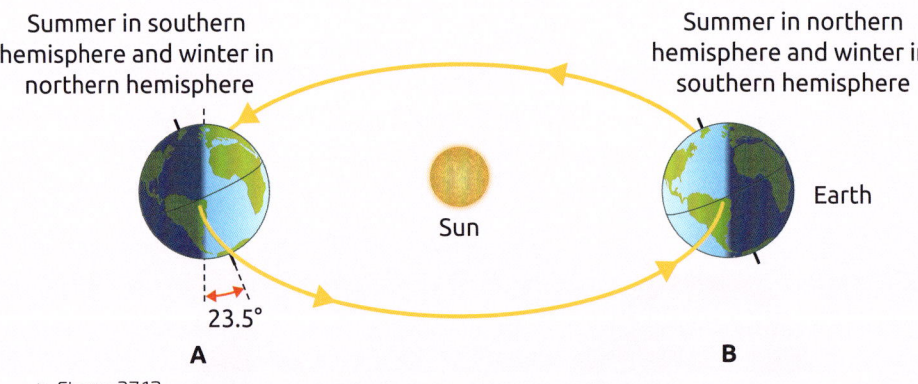

▶ Figure 37.12

- The diagram shows the Earth, which is tilted on its axis and is in orbit around the Sun.
- During winter in the northern hemisphere, the North Pole of the Earth is tilted away from the Sun, A in Figure 37.12. This causes shorter days and less light to fall on the northern hemisphere.
- Half a year later, during summer in the northern hemisphere, the North Pole of the Earth is tilted towards the Sun, causing longer days and more light to fall on the northern hemisphere every day, B in Figure 37.12.

▶▶ Worked Example 37.5

The Earth's Moon, viewed from Earth, changes in appearance in a monthly cycle called the phases of the Moon. Explain, using a labelled diagram, how the phases of the Moon arise. (12)

Note:

A total of 12 marks is given for the question. Therefore, the answer requires at least (12 ÷ 3) = four key pieces of information. In a past exam, the following points were essential:

- A diagram showing the **correct position of the Sun or Sun's rays** (i.e. the bright side of the Moon always faces the Sun) (3 marks)
- The **Moon orbits the Earth** either shown on the diagram or said (3 marks)
- **Any two phases shown** (named) correctly in the diagram (6 marks)

Solution:

- The Sun always lights up half of the Moon facing it.
- Since the Moon orbits the Earth, we see a different amount of the lit-up side of the Moon as it rotates.
- During the full moon, A in Figure 37.13, we can see the whole of the lit-up face of the Moon.
- 14 days later we cannot see any part of the lit-up face of the Moon, B in Figure 37.13.

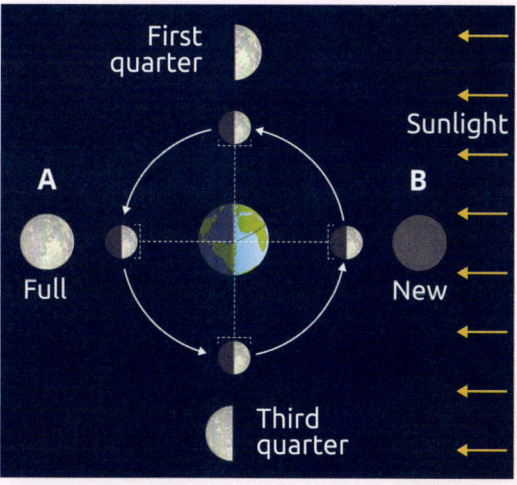

▶ Figure 37.13

Exam Tips!

Figure 37.13 above shows more information than is needed for the exam. In your exam, you should always include all the information you know, as the amount of information required to get full marks can change from year to year.

▶▶ Worked Example 37.6

Figure 37.14 shows the Moon's orbit around the Earth and the direction of light from the Sun.

(i) How long does it take the Earth to rotate once on its own axis? (3)
(ii) How long does it take the Moon to orbit the Earth once? (3)
(iii) Describe the appearance of the Moon, viewed from Earth, when it is in position C. (3)
(iv) Explain, using a labelled diagram, how a lunar eclipse occurs. (9)

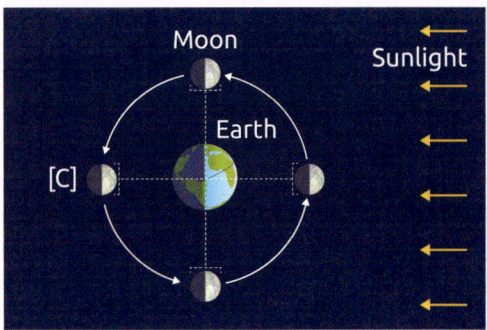

▶ Figure 37.14

Note: The number of marks tells us that we need (9 ÷ 3) = three main points to explain the lunar eclipse.
- Show in a diagram or state the words **Sun and Moon** (3 marks)
- Show in a diagram or state in words that the **Earth lies between the Sun and the Moon** (3 marks)
- Show in a diagram or state in words either that the Earth's shadow is cast on the Moon **or the sunlight hitting the Moon is blocked by the Earth** (3 marks)

Solution:
(i) It takes 24 hours for the Earth to rotate once on its own axis.
(ii) It takes approximately 28 days for the Moon to orbit the Earth once.
(iii) When the Moon is at position C, a full moon should be visible from Earth.

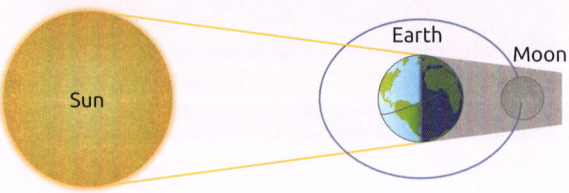

▶ Figure 37.15

(iv) A lunar eclipse is shown in Figure 37.15. It happens when the Sun, the Earth and the Moon all line up with each other. The Earth lies between the Sun and the Moon. Because the Earth is blocking the sunlight hitting the Moon, it casts a shadow on the Moon. From Earth, the Moon is observed to be partially or totally covered over.

▶▶ Science Self-Assessment

Now I am able to:	🟢	🟠	🔴
List two factors that affect the surface gravity on a celestial body			
Explain why the seasons occur			
Explain how the phases of the Moon occur			
Explain how lunar and solar eclipses occur			
Give reasons why space exploration is dangerous and explain how it has benefited society			
Discuss the future of space exploration			

38 The water cycle and the carbon cycle

The Earth and Space strand

Main topics in this chapter:
- The water cycle
- The carbon cycle
- Global warming and climate change

38.1 The water cycle

- Water is constantly moving from land to sea to sky, and back to land again. This is known as the water cycle, Figure 38.1. It is powered by the Sun.

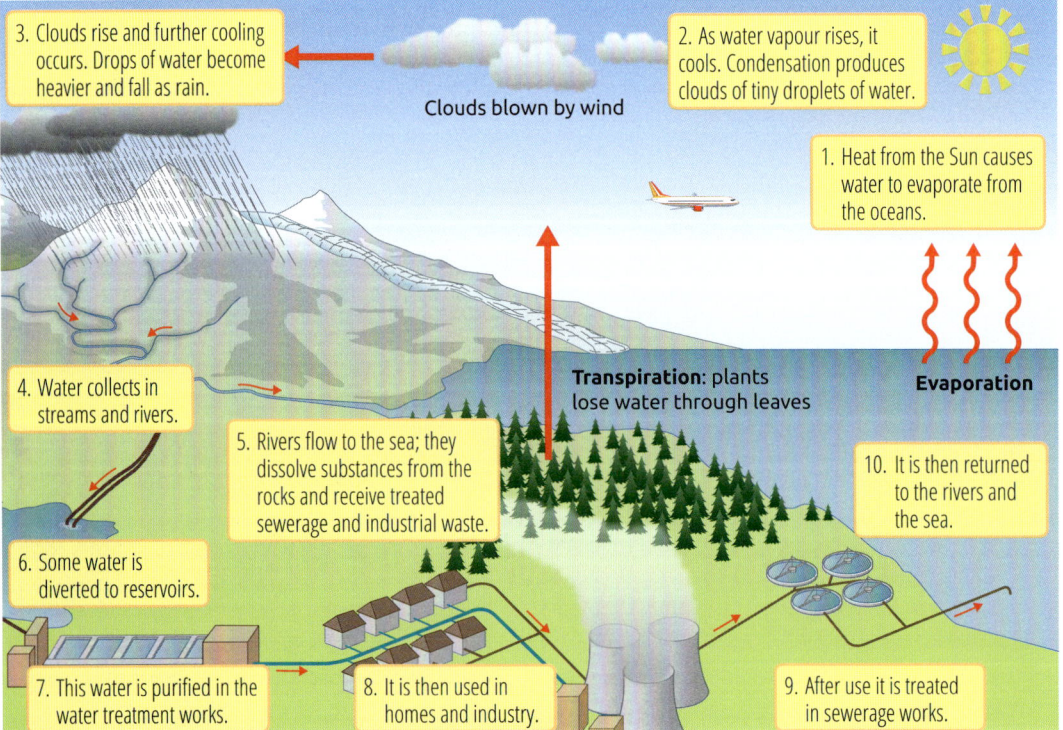

▶ Figure 38.1 The water cycle

- Water enters the atmosphere via **evaporation** from the land, seas and lakes.
- Water also enters the atmosphere from burning fossil fuels, from industry, and from evaporation from the surface of plants (transpiration).
- When the water vapour rises, it cools and **condenses** into clouds.
- Some of these clouds may be blown over land. If they travel over mountains, they may cool further and drop their water vapour in the form of rain, hail, sleet or snow. This is known as **precipitation**.
- If the precipitation falls on the ground in polar regions, it may stay on the ground for years and turn into a **glacier**. Water can be locked up in glaciers for thousands of years.
- If the precipitation falls as rain, some can soak deep into the Earth (infiltration) and can be stored there. It can come to the surface via springs or wells.
- Most rain collects in streams and rivers (**run-off**) and makes its way back to the sea.
- Some of this water can be dammed and produce a sustainable source of electricity.
- The water cycle is an advantage: it purifies the water during evaporation and supplies the energy for making hydroelectricity.

38.2 The carbon cycle

- Carbon compounds are found in our food, fuels, in the air and in rainwater and seas. Carbon can move between these forms via the carbon cycle, Figure 38.2.

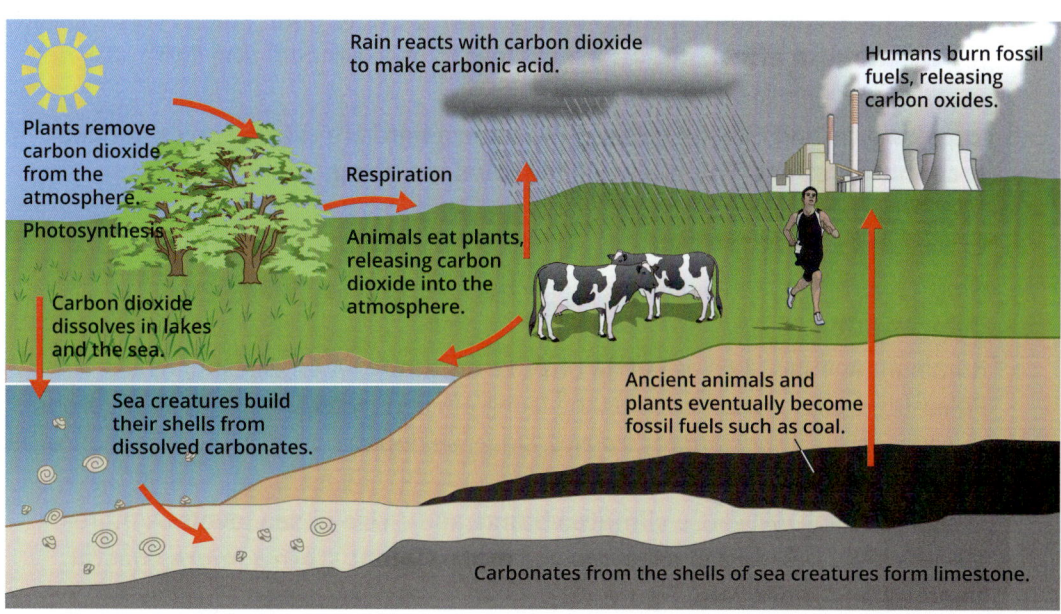

▶ Figure 38.2 The carbon cycle

- Carbon enters the atmosphere in the form of carbon dioxide via **respiration, burning of fossil fuels and other substances containing carbon** and **industrial processes** (e.g. making lime).

- Carbon dioxide is removed from the atmosphere via **photosynthesis** and **dissolving in rain and the sea**.
- Dissolved carbon dioxide is used by sea creatures to make their shells. After death, these shells can be turned into **limestone**. This limestone can be heated to make lime, which is widely used in construction. This releases carbon dioxide back into the atmosphere.
- Carbon can be **stored in the ground as turf, coal, oil and gas**. These are fossil fuels made from the bodies of plants and animals that lived millions of years ago. Burning these fuels will release stored carbon into the atmosphere as carbon dioxide, Chapter 27.
- Originally, plants took carbon dioxide from the atmosphere. Some died and turned into coal and oil. Other plants were eaten by animals.
- The carbon from these plants helped the animals to grow. When these animals died, their bodies decayed over millions of years and turned into **coal, oil and gas**.

38.3 What is the problem with the carbon cycle today?

- More carbon is being released into the atmosphere in the form of carbon dioxide than is being used up in photosynthesis or dissolving in rain and the sea. The concentration of carbon dioxide in the atmosphere is increasing.
- Gases in the atmosphere, such as water vapour and carbon dioxide, act as an insulator and slow down the loss of heat from Earth to outer space. This is called the **greenhouse effect**. It is very important to us – without it the Earth may not be warm enough to sustain life.
- Increasing carbon dioxide levels in the atmosphere are causing an **enhanced greenhouse effect**. This is leading to **global warming**.

38.4 Global warming

- Global warming is caused by excessive **burning of fossil fuels and deforestation**.
- Ruminant animals such as **cattle release methane** when digesting grass. Releasing 1 litre of methane has the same effect as releasing 30 litres of carbon dioxide. This is important for Ireland, since we depend on large numbers of cattle in agriculture.
- Global warming will cause **climate change** and a **rise in sea levels** as more glaciers melt. Ireland can expect to see **more violent storms, more coastal flooding and more rain**, Figure 38.3.

▶ Figure 38.3 Global warming will cause more coastal flooding and more violent storms in Ireland.

38.5 What is being done to prevent further global warming?

- At meetings of the United Nations, agreements are being made which oblige countries to reduce their greenhouse gas emissions. Ireland is obliged to reduce its greenhouse gases by 20 per cent of the 2005 levels by the year 2020. If we do not meet this target, we will have to pay large fines to the European Union.
- Our government is reducing greenhouse gas emissions by:
  - **Improving the building standards** of houses so that they use less energy to heat.
  - Giving grant aid to householders to insulate their houses and install more **efficient heating systems and solar panels**.
  - Placing **large taxes on cars that consume a lot of fuel** and release a lot of carbon dioxide. This principle is known as: 'The polluter pays.'
  - Placing a **carbon tax on fuels**. This is just another tax, but it may encourage people to insulate their homes and drive more efficient cars.
  - Encouraging private electricity companies to **supply electricity generated by means of renewable sources of energy** such as wind energy by allowing them to charge higher prices for electricity generated in this way.
  - Introducing the **cycle-to-work scheme**, which subsidises workers to buy a bicycle and cycling equipment that will be used to get to work. This reduces the use of fossil fuels by people who would normally drive to work.
  - Encouraging farmers to **plant more trees** by giving grants to convert the use of land from grassland to forest.

38.6 What has worked so far in the battle against climate change?

- Because of government incentives, there has been a move away from using fossil fuels to generate electricity and towards **renewable sources** such as wind.
- New houses are being built to a much higher **standard of insulation**. This makes them much more energy efficient, as they need less fossil fuel to heat them. All new homes now have solar panels. Grants are provided to encourage people in older homes to improve their insulation.
- When buying or renting a house, you are entitled to see information on its energy efficiency. This is called the house's **building energy rating**. Homes with a better energy rating are more valuable, which encourages homeowners to increase insulation standards and install more energy efficient boilers, stoves and lighting.
- Placing **large taxes on powerful car engines** and **carbon tax** on fuels has encouraged people to buy vehicles with engines that do not cause high levels of pollution. This has encouraged car manufactures to make more efficient engines. There has been a 25 per cent decrease in carbon emissions by cars in the last 10 years.
- The installation of new energy efficient LED streetlighting in cities such as Kilkenny and Cork has halved the electricity use and significantly reduced the carbon footprint in these areas.

▶▶ Science Self-Assessment

Now I am able to:	🟢	🟡	🔴
Describe the stages of the water cycle			
Describe the carbon cycle and link it to global warming and deforestation			
Evaluate the effects of climate change and evaluate the initiatives that attempt to address those effects			
Discuss how human factors influence the Earth's climate			

Coimisiun na Scrudúithe Stáit
State Examinations Commission

Junior Cycle Final Examination
Sample Paper

Science

Common Level

Time: 2 hours

360 marks

Instructions

There are two sections in this examination paper.

Section A   150 marks   10 questions

Section B   210 marks   6 questions

Answer **all** parts of **all** questions.

You may ask the superintendent for a copy of the *Formulae and Tables* booklet. You must return it at the end of the examination. You are not allowed to bring your own copy into the examination.

Not all the questions carry equal marks. The number of marks for each question is stated at the top of the question.

You should spend about 50 minutes on Section A and 70 minutes on Section B.

Write your answers in the spaces provided in this booklet. You may lose marks if you do not do so.

You are not required to use all of the space provided.

This examination booklet will be scanned and your work will be presented to an examiner on screen.

Anything that you write outside of the answer areas may not be seen by the examiner.

You may only use blue or black pen when writing your answers. Do not use pencil.

There is extra space at the end of Section A and at the back of the booklet. Label any extra work clearly with the question number and part.

Section A   150 marks

Question 1   15 marks

All biological organisms are made up of cells.

(a) Name the instrument shown in the picture on the right, which is used to examine cells.

> Microscope

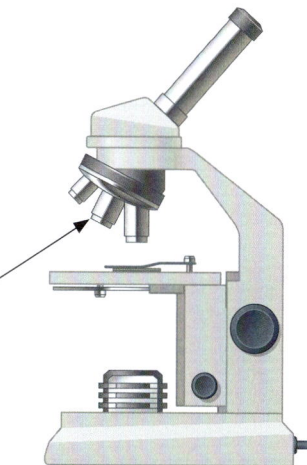

(b) Name the labelled part of the instrument, which makes the cells look bigger.

> Objective lens

(c) The picture below shows cells from an onion, which are typical plant cells.

In the box, write the name of any one part of the cell.

Draw an arrow from the box to the part of the cell you have named.

| Nucleus |
| Cell wall |
| Cytoplasm |

Exam Tip!
Only one part of the cells needs to be labelled.

(d) State the function of the part of the cell you have chosen.

| Nucleus: Contains genes to control the cell |
| Cell wall: To protect the cell |
| Cytoplasm: To carry the organelles (parts of the cell) |

Exam Tip!
Only one of these items is required for the answer.

Question 2 15 marks

Complete the table below for the instruments shown.

In each case, state what physical quantity the instrument measures. Also state the unit used for that measurement.

(Some parts of the table are already completed for you.)

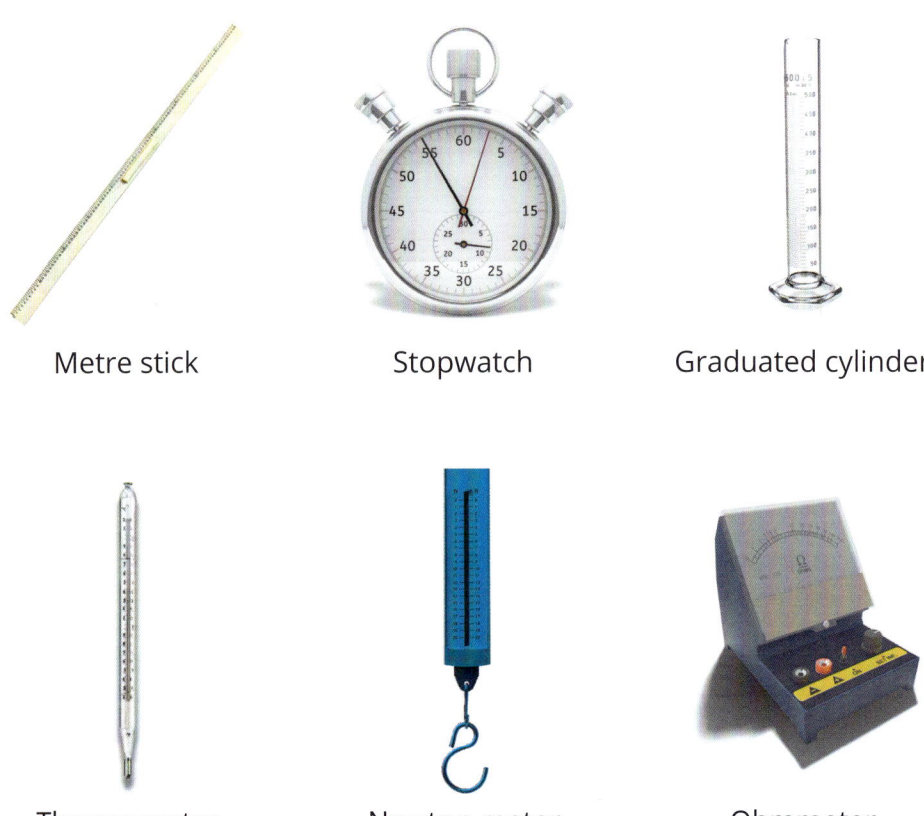

Instrument	Quantity measured	Unit
Metre stick	**Length**	**Metre (m)**
Stopwatch	**Time**	**Second (s)**
Graduated cylinder	**Volume**	**Centimetre cubed (cm³)**
Thermometer	**Temperature**	**Degree Celsius (°C)**
Newton meter	**Force**	Newton (N)
Ohmmeter	Resistance	Ohm (Ω)

Question 3   15 marks

A group of students investigated how solubility in water changes with temperature for solid compounds **1**, **2** and **3**. The graph below shows the results obtained.

(a) Hot water was needed during this investigation.

Name an instrument used to heat water in the laboratory.

> **Hotplate (or Bunsen burner)**

(b) Describe one safety precaution which should be taken when heating water in the laboratory.

> **Wear safety glasses (in case any splashes of boiling water enter your eyes).**
>
> **(Other safety precautions: wear a white coat, wear thick gloves when handling the beaker of hot water.)**

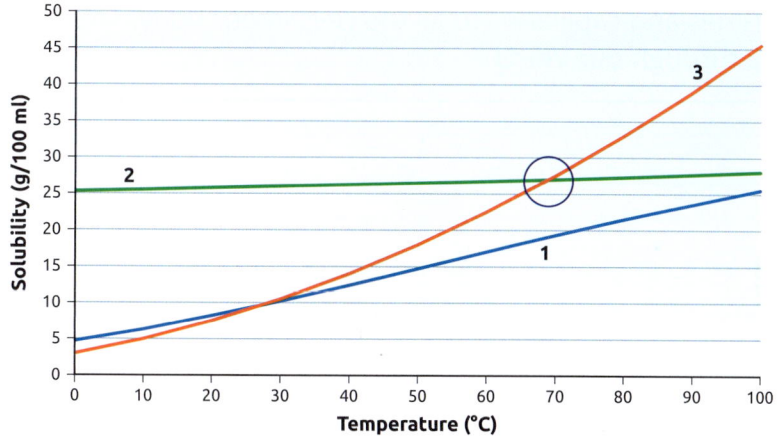

(c) The general trend for solids is that solubility increases with temperature.

Which compound shows the greatest increase in solubility from 0°C to 100°C?

> **Compound 3 shows the greatest increase in solubility.**

(d) On the graph, circle the point where compound **2** has the same solubility as compound **3**.

(e) State one advantage of presenting scientific data using a graph.

> **A graph makes it easier to show and interpret trends or relationships between the variables.**

Question 4   15 marks

The passage below explains how a cell gets the materials it needs for respiration.

The names of five parts of the body are missing from the passage.

Here are the missing body parts:

Heart   Veins   Small intestine   Stomach   Lungs

In the spaces provided, write the names of the missing body parts.

> When we breathe we draw air into our **lungs** where the oxygen in the air is passed into our blood.
>
> After we swallow food it is first stored in our **stomach** for a few hours, where some digestion occurs. Then it travels on to our **small intestine** where further digestion happens and glucose and other nutrients are absorbed into our blood.
>
> Blood is pumped around our body by our **heart**. The blood travels through arteries and capillaries to all the cells in our body. The blood then travels back through our **veins**.

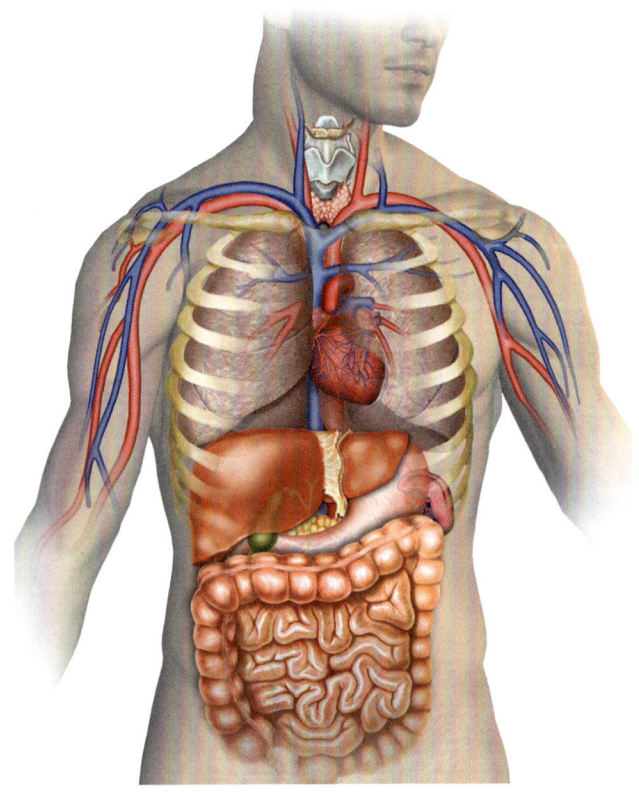

Question 5   15 marks

The diagram below shows some of the processes involved in the carbon cycle.

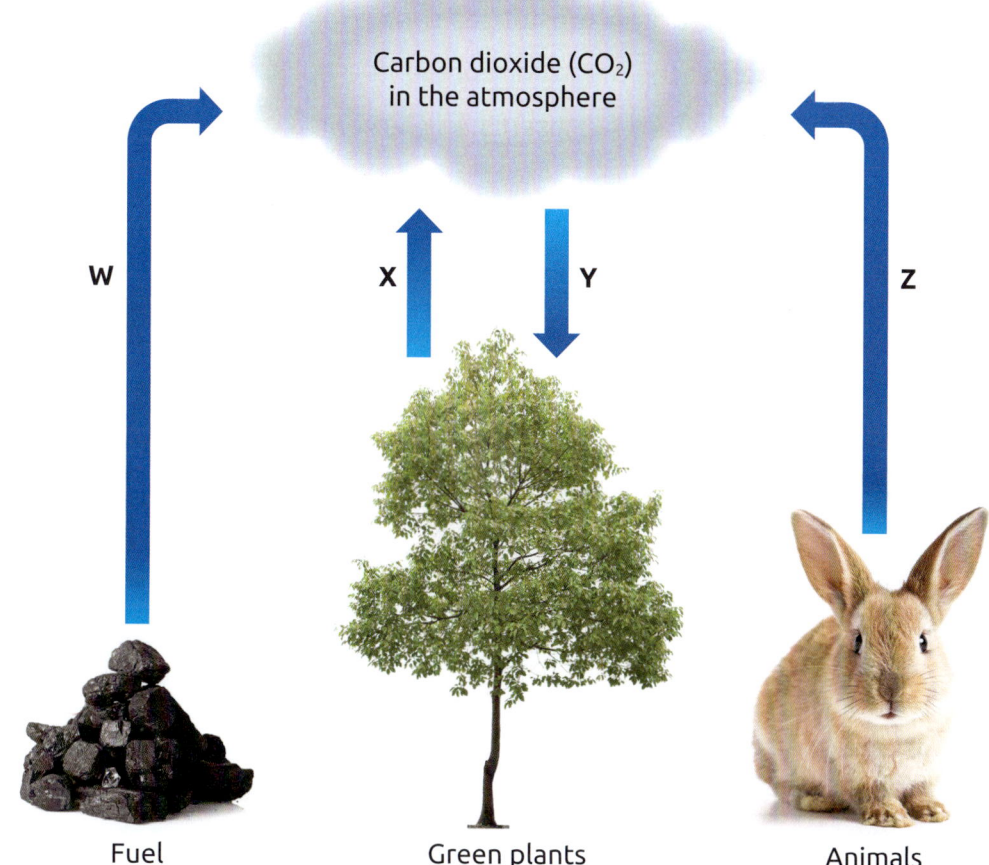

Each of the blue arrows **W**, **X**, **Y** and **Z** represents one of the following three processes:

Respiration   **Photosynthesis**   **Combustion**

In the table below, write the name of each process.
(Note that one process appears twice.)

Process	Name
W	Combustion
X	Respiration
Y	Photosynthesis
Z	Respiration

Question 6 15 marks

In the diagrams below, circles of different colours are used to represent atoms of different elements.

Complete the table below for the substances shown in diagrams **A** to **E**.

In each case, state whether the diagram represents a solid, a liquid or a gas.

Also state whether the diagram represents an element, a compound or a mixture.

(Some parts of the table are already completed for you.)

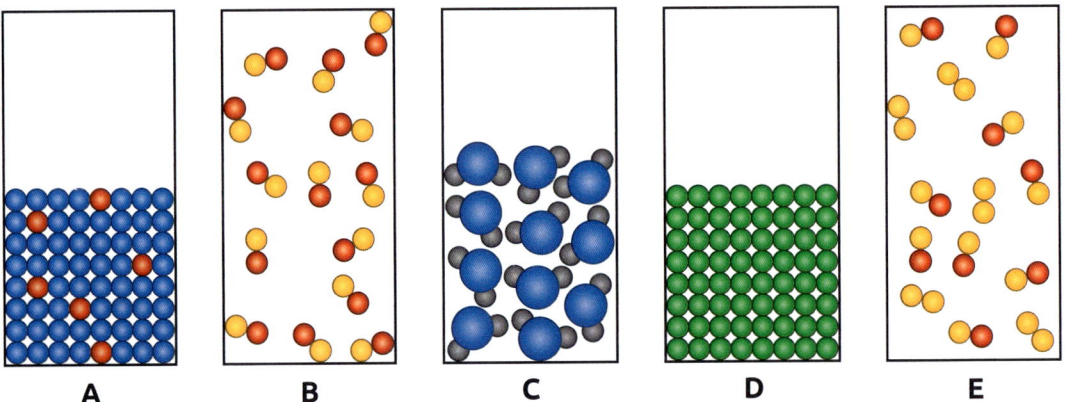

Diagram	Solid, liquid or gas	Element, compound or mixture
A	**Solid**	Mixture
B	**Gas**	**Compound**
C	**Liquid**	**Compound**
D	Solid	**Element**
E	**Gas**	**Mixture**

Exam Tip!

When answering questions of this type, first decide if each diagram represents a solid, liquid or gas. Fill in the middle column of the table first, before attempting the last column.

Question 7   15 marks

The picture below shows a human female sex cell surrounded by human male sex cells.

Answer questions **(a)**, **(b)** and **(c)** by putting a tick (✓) in the correct box.

(a) What is the human female sex cell called?

Sperm ☐
Egg ✓
Vagina ☐
Penis ☐

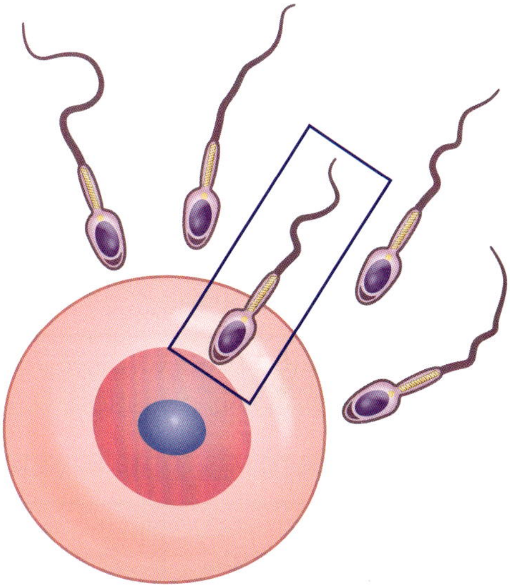

(b) What is the human male sex cell called?

Sperm ✓
Egg ☐
Vagina ☐
Penis ☐

(c) Where in the female reproductive system is the female sex cell produced?

Womb ☐
Testes ☐
Vagina ☐
Ovary ✓

(d) In the diagram, draw a box around the male sex cell that is fertilising the female sex cell.

(e) State one way of reducing the chance that sexual intercourse could result in fertilisation.

> **Use of a condom**
>
> **(Other possible answers: contraceptive pill and diaphragm)**

Question 8
15 marks

(a) Match each of the following sub-atomic particles to their descriptions in the table below.

Electron   Neutron   Proton

Description	Particle
Positively charged	**Proton**
Negatively charged	**Electron**
No charge	**Neutron**

(b) Complete the table below, using the Periodic Table of the elements to predict the ratio of atoms and the chemical formula for each of the compounds listed.

You should refer to page 70 of the *Formulae and Tables* booklet when answering this question.

The first row is completed for you.

Compound	First element	Second element	Ratio	Formula
Water	Hydrogen (H)	Oxygen (O)	2 : 1	H_2O
Magnesium chloride	Magnesium (Mg)	Chlorine (Cl)	**1 : 2**	**$MgCl_2$**
Ammonia	Nitrogen (N)	Hydrogen (H)	**1 : 3**	**NH_3**

Question 9   15 marks

A student investigated the relationship between the potential difference (voltage) across a resistor and the current flowing through it.

The circuit diagram below shows the arrangement of the apparatus used by the student.

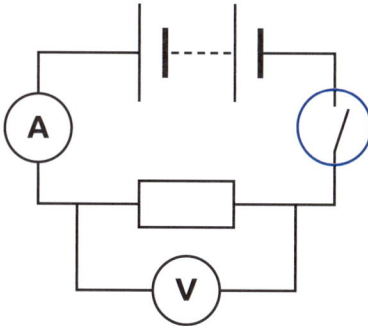

Examine the circuit diagram and answer the questions below.

(a) The instrument labelled **V** measures voltage. Name instrument **V**.

> **Voltmeter**

(b) The instrument labelled **A** measures current. Name instrument **A**.

> **Ammeter**

(c) In the circuit diagram above, draw a circle around the symbol for the switch.

(d) The student found that current is proportional to voltage for this resistor. Using the axes provided, draw a sketch of a graph to show this relationship.

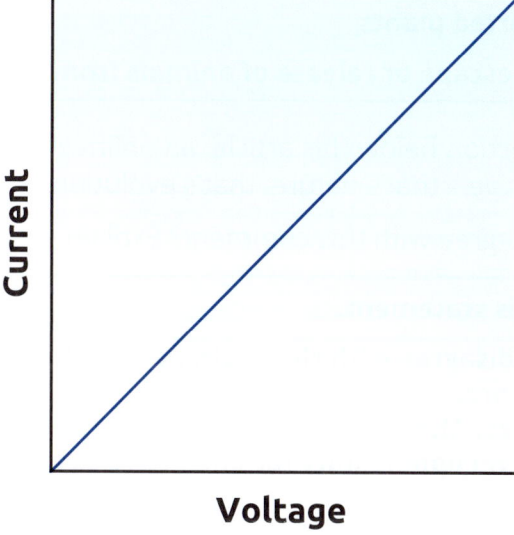

Question 10   15 marks

Read the following article, taken from an online newspaper, and answer the questions that follow.

> **Space invaders: the alien species that are costing us millions**
>
> In 1847 the Japanese knotweed was a medal-winning plant with strong growth and pretty white flowers. Things are very different today, with British house buyers being denied mortgages if this plant is found on the property.
>
>
>
> It has also taken hold in Ireland. Japanese knotweed can grow through the smallest crack and grow up to 2 cm a day, extending 7 m horizontally and 3 m deep. It is one of a number of unwanted and sometimes dangerous invasive species that have taken foothold in Ireland.
>
> Invasive species are often present due to human intervention. Some species have been deliberately released, while others, such as the American mink and the giant rhubarb, have escaped from farms and gardens. Others, such as the New Zealand flatworm, arrived accidentally in the soil of imported plants.
>
> Some invasive plants such as the Japanese knotweed die back during the winter, exposing the soil and leading to erosion.
>
> Irishtimes.com

(a) Name one invasive species found in Ireland.

> **Japanese knotweed**

(b) Describe one way an invasive species could get to Ireland.

> **In the soil of imported plants**
>
> **(Other examples: escape or release of animals from farms)**

(c) In the comments section below this article, an online reader comments that 'all species are invasive – that's nature, that's evolution'.

Do you agree or disagree with this comment? Explain your answer.

> **I disagree with this statement.**
>
> **The reason that I disagree with this statement is that many species are native to their environment. Therefore, it is not correct to say that ALL species are invasive. Also, some species may exist on an isolated island and there may be no opportunity for alien species to invade the island.**

Section B   210 marks

Question 11   30 marks

Citric acid is a chemical found in lemons and some other fruits.

It is a white crystalline solid when pure.

Solid citric acid may be dissolved in water to make a citric acid solution.

(a) Describe how to make up a solution which contains 5 g of citric acid dissolved in 100 ml of water. As part of your description, name each piece of equipment you would use.
(A labelled diagram may help your answer.)

1. Weigh out 5 g of the citric acid crystals on a clock glass, using an electronic balance. A spatula is used to place the citric acid on the clock glass.
2. Add water to a graduated cylinder until the bottom of the meniscus of the water is at the 100 cm³ mark. The bottom of the meniscus is read at eye level.
3. Pour the 100 cm³ of water from the graduated cylinder into a beaker.
4. Add the 5 g of citric acid crystals to the 100 cm³ of water in the beaker.
5. Check that all the crystals on the clock glass have been added to the water. If necessary, use the spatula to scrape off any crystals remaining on the clock glass into the water.
6. Using the stirring rod, stir the solution to help the citric acid crystals dissolve more quickly. Keep stirring until the crystals are fully dissolved.
We now have a solution of 5 g of citric acid dissolved in 100 cm³ of water.

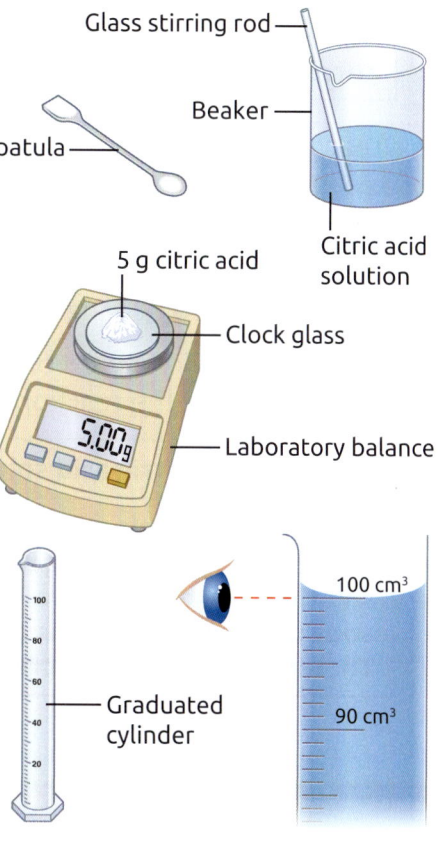

Baking soda is another white solid compound. Its chemical name is sodium hydrogen carbonate.

It is often used in making bread and cakes.

When baking soda is added to a test tube of citric acid solution, fizzing occurs and a gas is produced.

(b) A student holding the test tube notices that it cools down during the reaction.

Is this reaction an example of an endothermic or an exothermic reaction? Explain your answer.

> **Endothermic reaction**
>
> **It is endothermic since the test tube cools down during the reaction. A temperature drop is always observed when an endothermic reaction takes place, i.e. heat is taken in from the surroundings.**

This reaction is also an example of an acid-base reaction.

When baking soda is added to a test tube of citric acid solution, the chemicals react and the pH of the solution changes.

Exam Tip!
To help you remember that this is an endothermic reaction, think of sherbet. Sherbet is a mixture of citric acid and baking soda. When these two chemicals react in your mouth, it feels cold because of the endothermic reaction.

(c) Would you expect the pH of the solution in the test tube to increase or decrease during the reaction? Explain your answer.

> **The pH of the citric acid solution will increase.**
>
> **The pH of the citric acid solution will increase because baking soda is a base. When the baking soda is continually added to the citric acid solution, the baking soda neutralises the acid present. Since baking soda is a base, as more is added, it makes the solution basic (alkaline). Therefore the pH will increase.**

(d) Describe how you could investigate how pH changes during the reaction.

1. Add a small length of universal indicator paper or a few drops of universal indicator solution to the citric acid solution.
2. Note the colour of the universal indicator and compare it with the colour chart that comes with the paper. Note the pH reading.
3. Add the baking soda to the test tube of citric acid solution.
4. Note the colour changes as the reaction takes place. Compare the colours observed to the colour chart on the pH indicator paper. Note the corresponding pH readings.

Alternative method.

1. Place a pH sensor in the test tube of citric acid.
2. Attach the pH sensor to a datalogger and a computer.
3. Add the baking soda to the test tube of citric acid solution.
4. Note the change in pH on the screen of the computer at regular intervals.

Question 12

30 marks

Sankey diagrams are named after H. Riall Sankey, a Tipperary-born engineer, following his 1898 description of the energy efficiency of a steam engine.

Sankey diagrams show the flow of energy to and from a device.

In a Sankey diagram, the width of each arrow represents the energy named.

The Sankey diagrams for a filament lamp and a compact fluorescent lamp (CFL) are shown below.

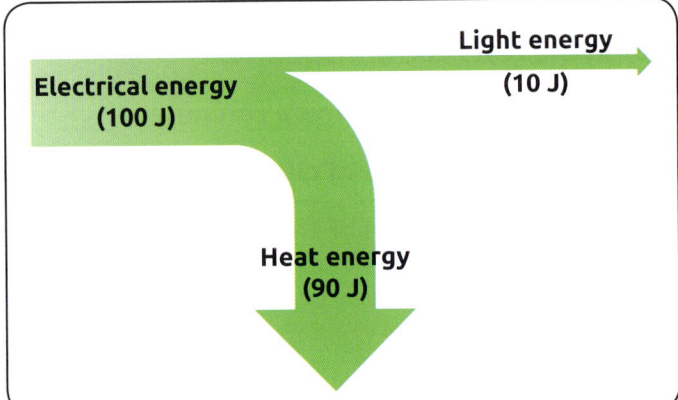

▶ Figure 1 Sankey diagram for a filament lamp

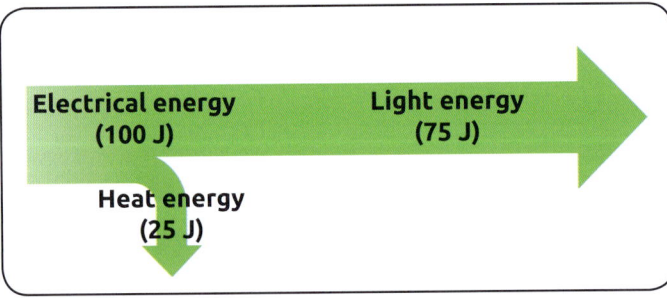

▶ Figure 2 Sankey diagram for a compact fluorescent lamp (CFL)

(a) Examine figures **1** and **2**. Which lamp is more efficient? Justify your answer.

> The CFL lamp (Figure 2) is more efficient than the filament lamp (Figure 1).

> The reason that the CFL lamp is more efficient is because a greater amount (75 J) of the energy supplied (100 J) is converted to light energy. In the case of the filament lamp, only 10 J of energy is converted into light.

> Alternative answer: in the CFL lamp, only 25 J of energy is wasted as heat. However, in the filament lamp, 90 J of energy is wasted as heat.

(b) Why is it important to improve the energy efficiency of household devices, such as lamps?

> The more energy efficient a device is, the less energy is wasted. Therefore, it costs less to run an energy efficient device since less electricity is used.
>
> The energy needed to run many household devices comes from electricity. Most of the energy used to generate electricity comes from burning fossil fuels. This burning produces carbon dioxide which causes global warming. It is important to conserve fossil fuels as they are non-renewable and will eventually run out. Energy efficient appliances use less electricity and help conserve fossil fuels.

(c) A student is asked to investigate and compare the heat energy produced by filament lamps and CFLs.

Apart from lamps themselves, name a piece of equipment that could be used during this investigation. Explain how this piece of equipment could be used during the investigation.

> We could use a black can fitted with a thermometer as the equipment used in this experiment.
>
> 1. Place a fixed quantity of water in two identical black cans.
> 2. Ensure that the temperature of the water is the same in both cans.
> 3. Place a thermometer in each can.
> 4. Place the CFL lamp at a fixed distance from one of the cans.
> 5. Place the filament lamp at the same distance from the second can.
> 6. Switch on both lamps at the same time.
> 7. Note the rise in temperature of the water in both cans after a fixed time.

(d) The energy conversions that happen in a CFL are described in the table below.

Complete the table for another device which transforms energy from one form to another and which you designed as part of your studies in science.

Name of the device	Function of the device	Main useful energy conversion	Main loss of energy
Compact fluorescent lamp (CFL)	To provide artificial light	Electrical to light	Electrical to heat
Solar panel	**To generate electricity**	**Light to electrical**	**Heat**

(e) Sketch a Sankey diagram for the device you described in part **(d)**. Label each part of the diagram.

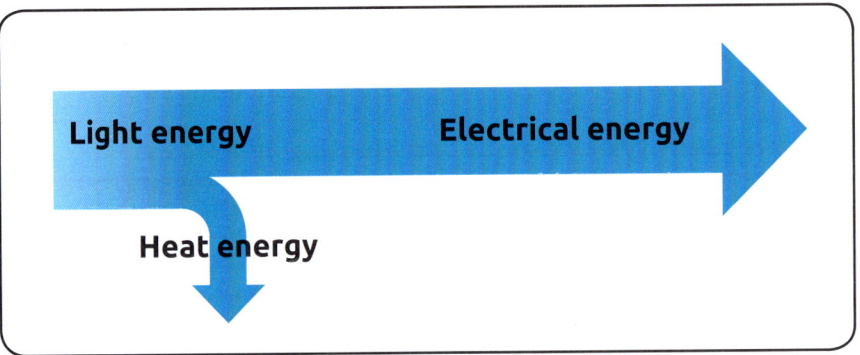

Question 13   30 marks

Solar eclipses can happen a few times each year.

(a) The diagram below shows a simple model of a solar eclipse (an eclipse of the Sun). In the diagram, write the letter **X** for Earth, **Y** for Moon and **Z** for Sun.

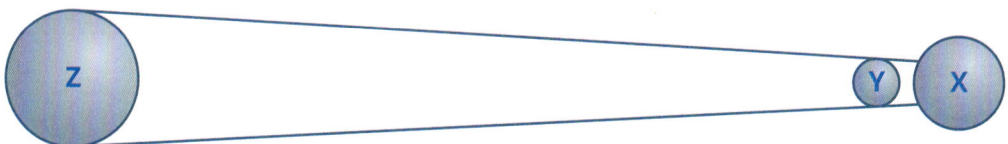

(b) Two weeks before or after a solar eclipse, sometimes there is a lunar eclipse (an eclipse of the Moon). Draw a labelled diagram to show a model of a lunar eclipse.

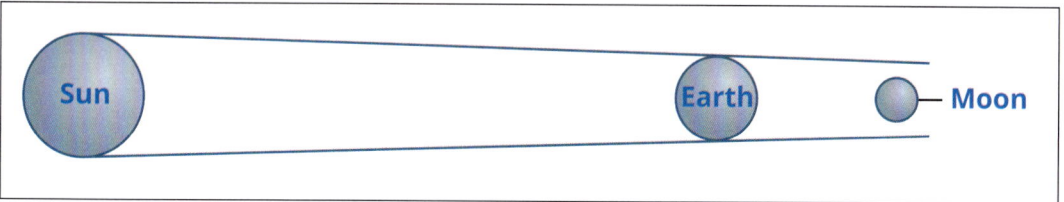

A solar eclipse in March 2015 affected the solar electrical power produced in the German electricity grid.

The graph below shows the solar electrical power produced from Monday to Friday during the week of the solar eclipse.

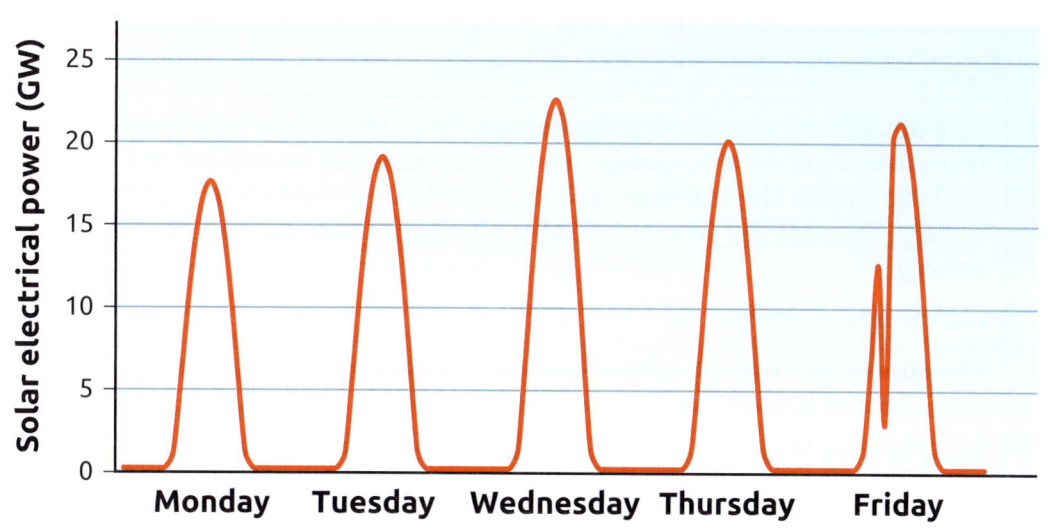

(c) On which day of the week did the solar eclipse occur? Justify your answer.

> The solar eclipse occurred on Friday.
>
> The graph shows that there was a sudden drop in solar electrical power generated for a period during Friday. This is likely to have been caused by a sudden drop in the intensity of sunlight falling on the Earth.

(d) Which was the brightest day of the week? Justify your answer.

> The brightest day of the week was Wednesday.
>
> The graph shows that the maximum solar electrical power was generated on Wednesday, as the peak is the highest on this day. Since light is needed to generate solar electrical energy, Wednesday was likely to have been the brightest day of the week.

(e)

The Sun can also provide power for modern spacecraft. The Juno mission to Jupiter uses solar energy to produce electricity.

Previous long-distance space missions used nuclear power to produce electricity.

State one advantage of using solar energy rather than nuclear energy during space exploration.

> One advantage of solar energy compared with nuclear energy is that the astronauts on the spacecraft are not exposed to radioactive radiation from the nuclear reactor. This nuclear radiation could cause cancer. This risk is removed if solar energy is used instead of nuclear energy.
>
> (Other advantages:
>
> The spacecraft will be lighter and more energy efficient when launched into space if it does not have to carry a nuclear reactor.
>
> Solar energy is cheaper to provide compared with nuclear energy, as nuclear reactors can be expensive to manufacture.)

(e) JunoCam, a camera on the Juno probe, is powered by Juno's solar panels.

Calculate the electrical power (P) generated by JunoCam when it uses a current of 0.5 A flowing across a potential difference (voltage) of 12 V.

Calculation
Power = Voltage × Current
P = V × I
= 12 × 0.5
= 6 W
Answer: Power is 6 watt

Question 14   30 marks

A group of students carried out a habitat study.

(a) Use some of the words in the list to name the pieces of equipment shown below, which can be used in a habitat study.

Beating tray   **Pooter**   **Net**   **Pitfall trap**

Picture	Name
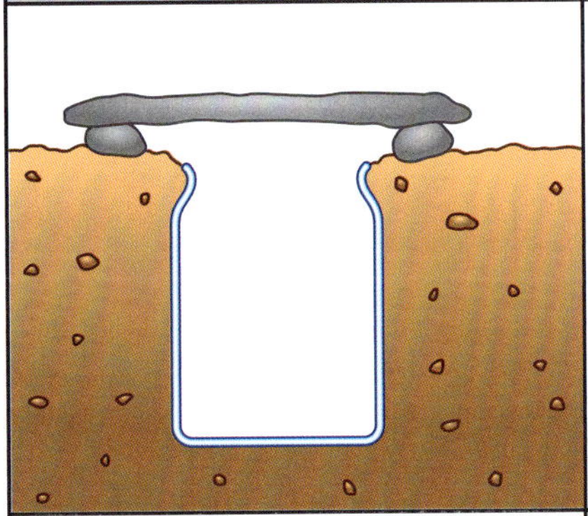	Pitfall trap
	Pooter

(b) The students also used a quadrat during their habitat study.

What shape is a quadrat? Describe how the students might have used the quadrat.

A quadrat is square-shaped.
1. A pencil was thrown over the shoulder.
2. The quadrat was placed where the pencil landed.
3. Using a table of results, the organism of interest was marked as present or absent.
4. Steps 1–3 were repeated nine more times.
5. The number of throws of the quadrat in which the organism was found was counted and recorded.

In one part of the habitat, the students used the quadrat 30 times and found that a certain species was present on 18 occasions. Calculate the percentage frequency of that species.

$$\text{Percentage frequency} = \frac{\text{Number of quadrats in which the species is present}}{\text{Number of quadrats thrown}} \times 100$$

$$= \frac{18 \times 100}{30} = 60\%$$

The students were given permission to remove some green plants from the habitat to take back to their school laboratory. They did this in order to investigate factors that affect photosynthesis.

(c) Imagine that you are one of the students. You have been asked to carry out an experiment to investigate how any one factor affects photosynthesis.

Name one factor which could affect photosynthesis and which you might investigate.

> **The one factor that I will investigate is light.**

List two factors which you would keep constant (fixed) during the experiment to ensure that it is a fair test.

> **The two factors that I will keep constant are temperature and type of plant studied.**

(d) Write a suitable hypothesis for this experiment.

> **I predict that if leaves are exposed to light, photosynthesis will take place in the leaves. I also predict that if I keep some leaves in the dark, no photosynthesis will take place in these leaves.**

(e) Draw a labelled diagram of the setup of your experiment.

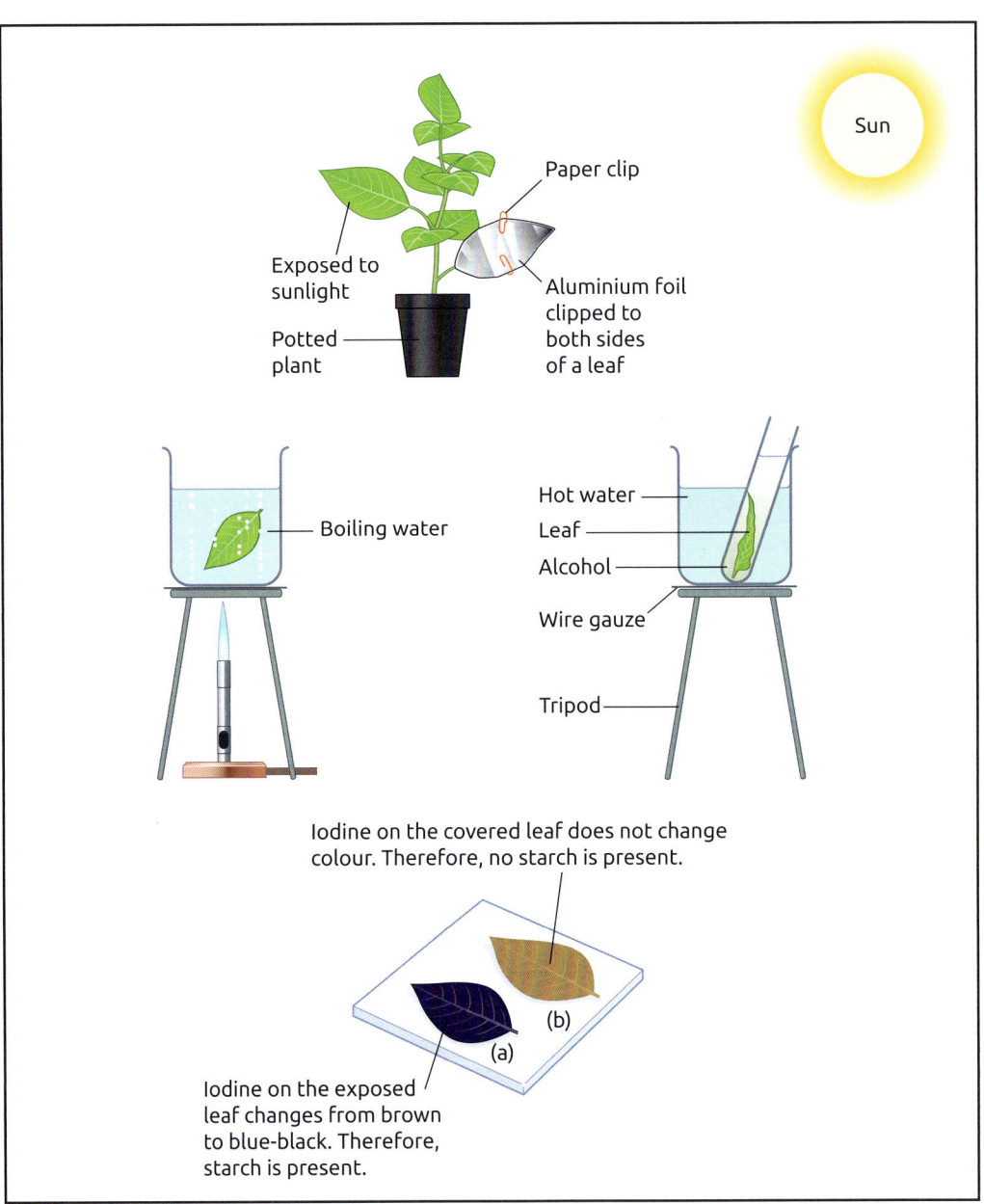

Question 15

45 marks

Some chemical reactions proceed quickly while some proceed at a slower rate.

During your studies, you investigated the effect of a number of variables on the rate of production of a common gas.

(a) Name a common gas that could be produced in the laboratory.

> Hydrogen

(b) Draw a labelled diagram of how this gas could be produced.

Include labels for any equipment and chemicals used.

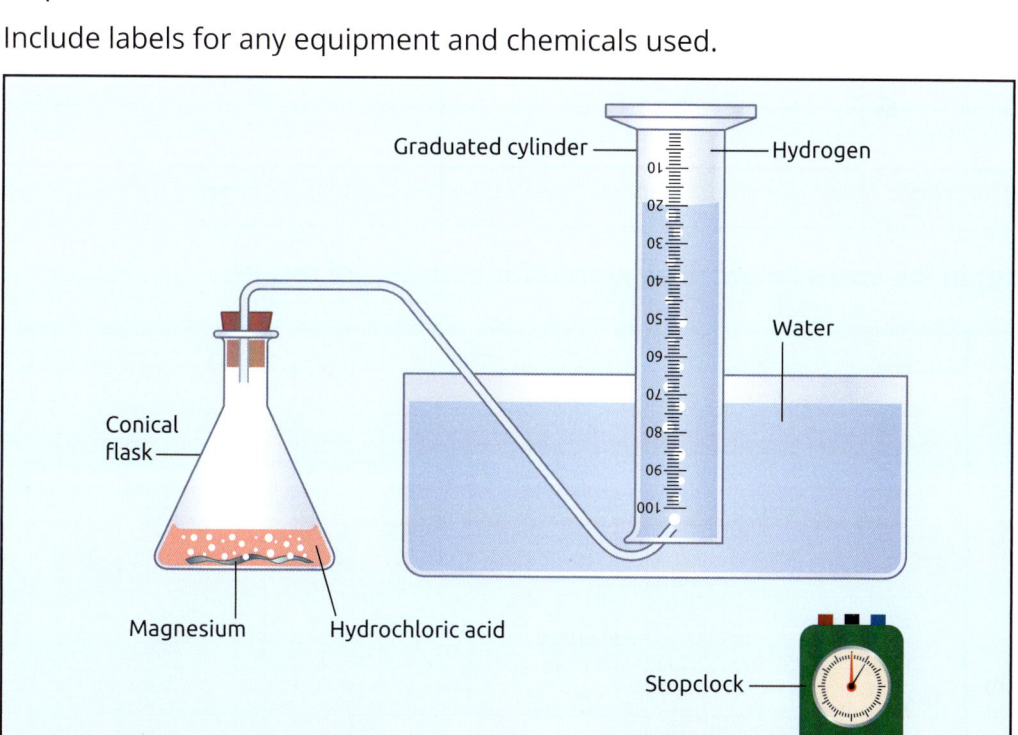

(c) Explain how you tested this gas to confirm its identity.

Include the result of the test.

> A lighted taper is brought near the mouth of a test tube of hydrogen gas.
>
> The hydrogen burns with a pop as hydrogen forms an explosive mixture with air.

A student carried out an experiment to investigate the effect of temperature on the rate of production of a certain gas. The first reaction happened at 20 °C and the second one at 30 °C.

In both cases the gas produced was passed through water as it was collected. This was to ensure that the gas was always at room temperature (a constant) when its volume was measured.

The student recorded the following results:

Time(s)	Volume of gas (cm³) for reaction at 20 °C	Volume of gas (cm³) for reaction at 30 °C
0	0	0
30	7	10
60	13	16
90	17	19
120	19	20
150	20	20

(d) In the space below, draw graphs for both sets of results.

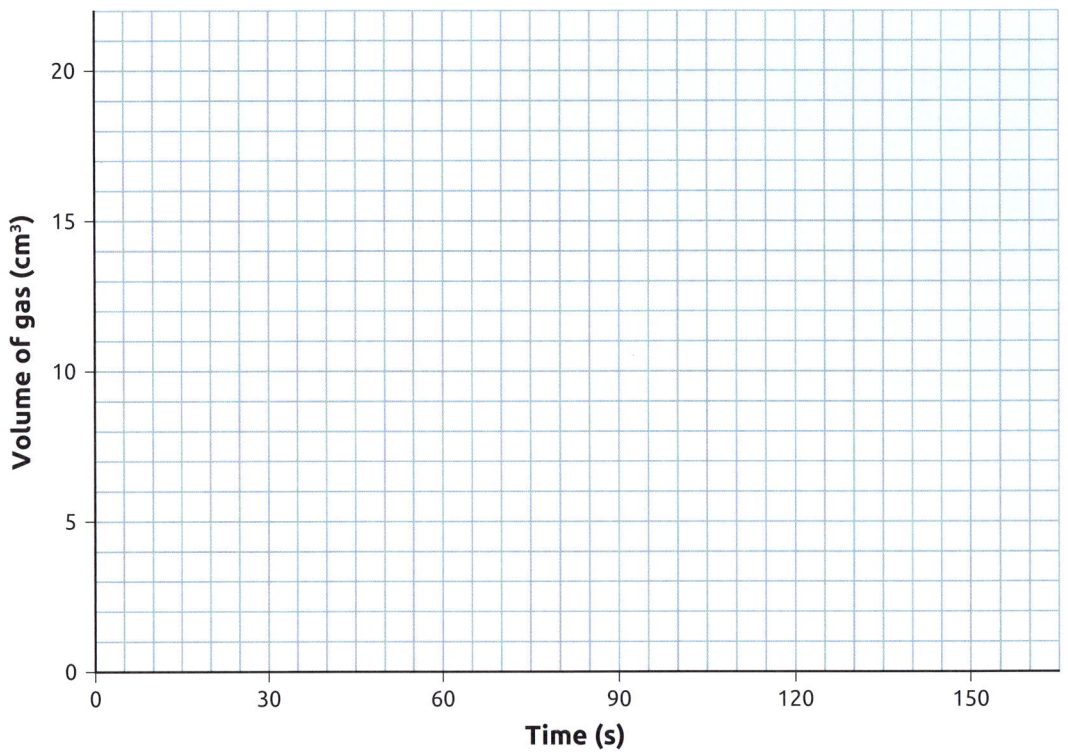

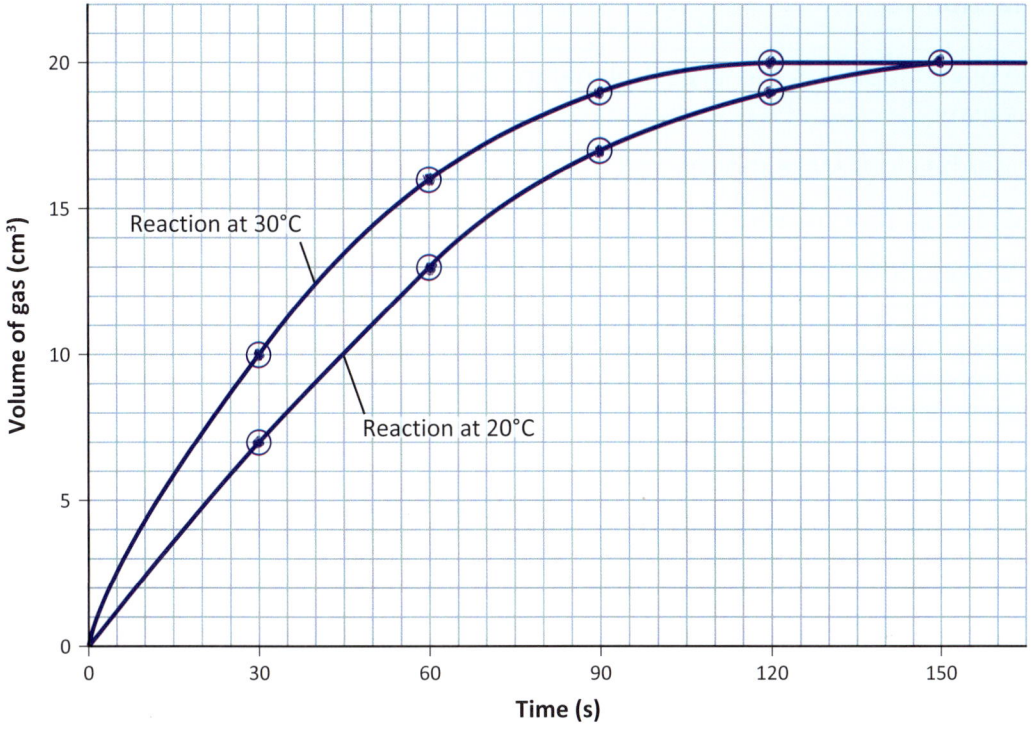

(e) State two conclusions the student could have drawn from the results.

Conclusions:

1. The reaction takes place more quickly at 30 °C than at 20 °C. We see this from the fact that, at the beginning of the experiment, the graph for the reaction at 30 °C is steeper than the graph for the reaction at 20 °C. We conclude that the higher the temperature, the faster the rate.

2. The same final volume of gas was given off in both cases.

Question 16   45 marks

The planet Jupiter is the largest planet in our solar system and is described as a 'gas giant'.

Jupiter has four large moons and many smaller ones.

These large moons were discovered in 1610 by Italian scientist Galileo Galilei.

Data about the size and density of the four large moons of Jupiter are given in the table below.

Moon of Jupiter	Diameter (km)	Density (g/cm³)
Io	3640	3.53
Europa	3120	3.01
Ganymede	5270	1.94
Callisto	4820	1.83

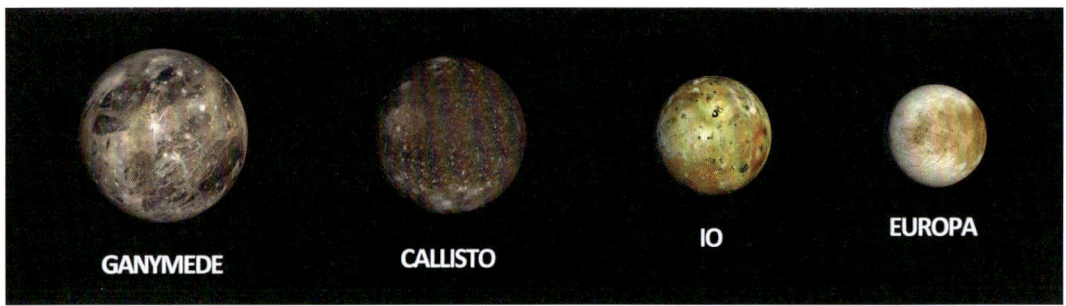

Data about the size and density of some other objects in our solar system are given in the table below.

Object	Diameter (km)	Density (g/cm³)
Mercury	4880	5.43
Earth	12700	5.51
Earth's Moon	3470	3.34
Mars	6780	3.93
Jupiter	140000	1.33
The Sun	139000000	1.41

258

The densities of four materials commonly found in planets and moons are given in the table on the right.

Material	Density (g/cm³)
Water	1.0
Granite	2.8
Basalt	3.0
Iron	8.0

(a) A solid of mass 12 g has a volume of 1.5 cm³.

Calculate the density of the material.
Hence identify the material as either water, granite, basalt or iron.

> Calculation
>
> Density = $\dfrac{\text{Mass}}{\text{Volume}}$
>
> = $\dfrac{12 \text{ g}}{1.5 \text{ cm}^3}$
>
> = 8 g/cm³
>
> **Material: Iron**

(b) Granite and basalt are found in the Earth's crust. Use the data given in the tables to state whether or not it is likely that all of the Earth is made of these rocks. Justify your answer.

> It is not likely that all of the Earth is made up of granite and basalt.
>
> The reason for this is because the density of the Earth is 5.51 g/cm³, the density of granite is 2.8 g/cm³ and the density of basalt is 3 g/cm³. Since the Earth has a much greater density than either of these rocks, it must be made up mainly of substances that have a greater density than either granite or basalt.

(c) Use the data given for Jupiter and Earth to explain why Jupiter is described as a 'gas giant'.

> Jupiter is described as a 'gas' because it has a low density of 1.33 g/cm³ compared with the density of the Earth, which is 5.51 g/cm³. Since gases usually have lower densities than solids, Jupiter is likely to be made up of gas.
>
> Jupiter is described as a 'giant' because it has a very large diameter compared with the planets Mercury, Earth and Mars.

(d) Callisto is a moon and Mercury, of similar size, is a planet.

What is the difference between a moon and a planet?

> A moon is a natural satellite of a planet.
>
> A planet is a celestial body that is in orbit around a star.

(e) Galileo's discovery of the moons of Jupiter changed our understanding of Earth and space. Describe another example of how our scientific understanding changed over time.

> John Dalton proposed that atoms were small, solid objects like billiard balls. Other scientists discovered that atoms were made up of protons, neutrons and electrons. Niels Bohr discovered that electrons were in orbit around the nucleus.
>
> (Other examples are:
>
> - Watson and Crick discovered the structure of DNA. This helped us to understand for the first time how genes are copied and are passed on from parents to offspring.
>
> - Alexander Fleming discovered penicillin, the first antibiotic. Before this time, it was not known how to cure many diseases in the body.
>
> - Another example is the discovery by William Harvey that blood circulates in our bodies. Before this time, scientists did not understand how blood moved around our bodies.)

(f) Scientists estimate that our solar system began to form about 4.6 billion years ago. Scientists also estimate that our universe formed 13.8 billion years ago.

Describe two things that scientists believe happened during the early formation of the universe – before the formation of solar systems.

> During the early formation of the universe, all the mass and energy of the universe existed in a tiny bubble less than the size of a pinhead. This was extremely hot and dense and suddenly exploded. This explosion is called the Big Bang.
>
> Over a period of time, protons, neutrons and electrons were made. Eventually, these combined to form atoms. After a billion years, these giant clouds of atoms were pulled together by gravity to make the first stars.

Notes

Notes

Dedicated to working together

At Folens everything we do is about helping teachers to help students achieve the best possible learning outcomes.

Folens is a leading publisher of educational books for primary and post-primary schools in Ireland.

But that's only where it begins; we also produce a wealth of digital resources including high-quality digital content and innovative interactive resources, for use both in the classroom and at home.

For over sixty years we have been busy listening, adapting and working together with schools, teachers and pupils to constantly produce the highest quality content that matches the curriculum.

That's how we've stood the test of time and to this day remain the first choice for thousands of schools across the country.

Dedicated to better learning

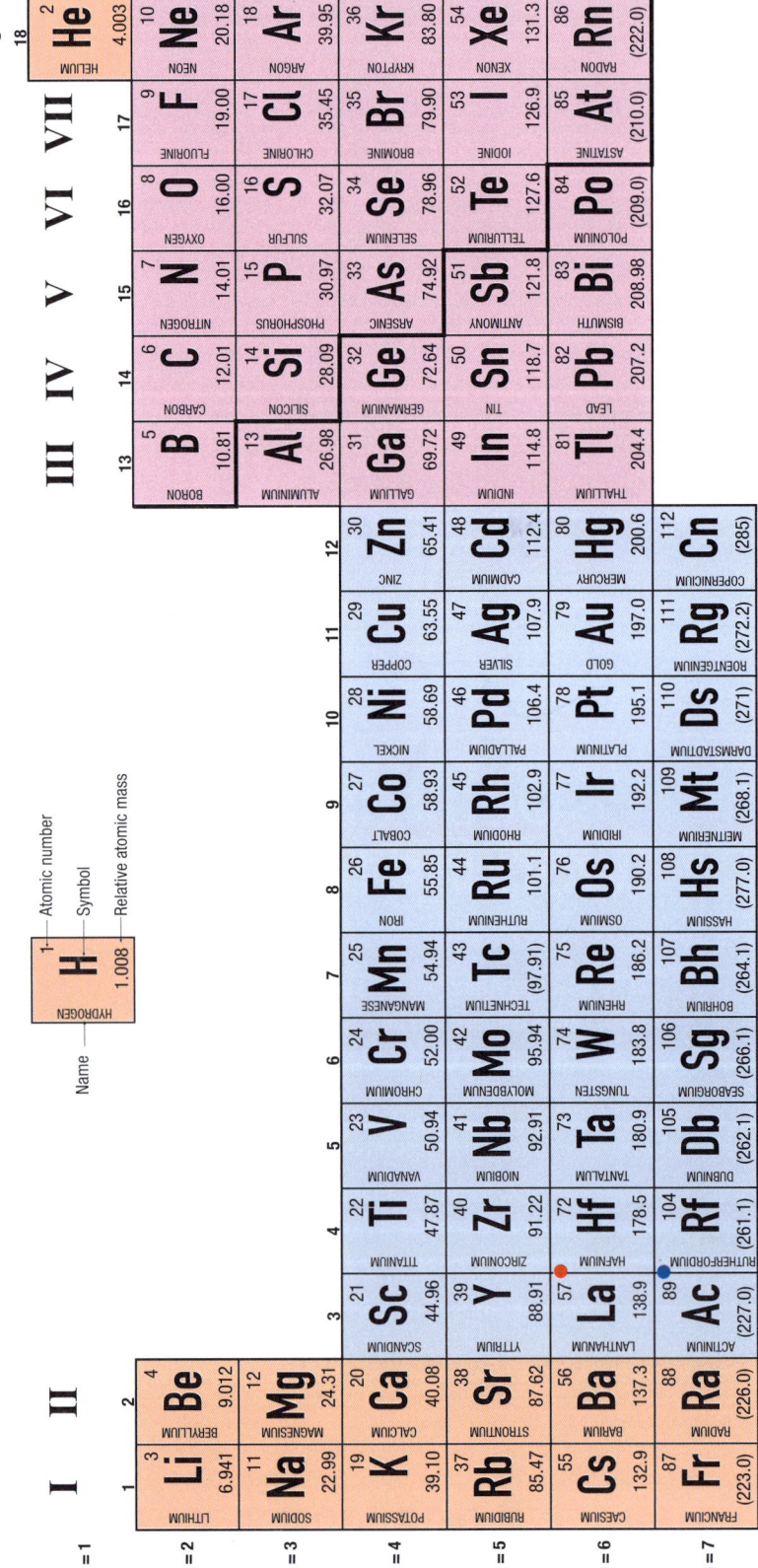